BRITISH INDUSTRY AND ECONOMIC POLICY

BRITISH INDUSTRY AND ECONOMIC POLICY

G. C. Allen
Emeritus Professor of Political Economy, University of London

First published 1979 by
THE MACMILLAN PRESS LTD
London and Basingstoke
Associated companies in Delhi
Dublin Hong Kong Johannesburg Lagos
Melbourne New York Singapore Tokyo

Typeset, printed and bound
in Great Britain by
REDWOOD BURN LIMITED
Trowbridge & Esher

British Library Cataloguing in Publication Data

Allen, George Cyril
    British industry and economic policy
    1. Great Britain – Industries – History – 20th
    century 2. Great Britain – Economic policy –
    1918–1945 3. Great Britain – Economic policy –
    1945–
    I. Title
    338.941   HC256

    ISBN 0–333–25972–6

In memoriam
Eleanorae
conjugis amantissimae

Contents

Preface

The papers collected and presented in this book were written over a period of 55 years; the earliest of them was first published in 1923, and two of the latest in 1975. The majority deal with some aspect of the structure and organisation of British industry or with economic policy as it has affected industrial efficiency. I have followed the principle of presenting the papers with their original content and form unchanged, except where verbal changes, or even the recasting of sentences, seemed necessary in the interests of clarity or style. There are, however, two exceptions. The arguments and proposals contained in a few paragraphs of the paper that now appears as Chapter 4 have been overtaken by events, and there was no point in republishing them in full. The other exception is provided by Chapter 13 which is the result of conflating two papers, one read at a conference in 1970 and the other at a seminar in 1973. I have tried, in an Introduction, to indicate in summary form the burden of the several papers and, at the same time, to bring out whatever themes they have in common.

I express my thanks to the following for permission to republish the articles and addresses of which the book is composed: the Editors of *Economica*, the *Sociological Review*, the *New Statesman* (for an article in the *Nation and Athenaeum*), the *Economic History Review* (for two articles in *Economic History*); the Cambridge University Press (for three articles in the *Economic Journal*); the National Westminster Bank Ltd (for two articles in the Westminster Bank Review); the Editorial Committee of the *Three Banks Review*; John Murray (Publishers) Ltd (for an article in the *Quarterly Review*); the Confederation of British Industry (for an article in *British Industry*); University College London (for my Inaugural Lecture); the Society of Business Economists (for a paper delivered at a Conference); the Institute of Economic Affairs (for a paper read at a Seminar); and the Schweizerisches Institut für Auslandsforschung (for an address subsequently published in a volume entitled *Der Streit um die Gesellschaftsordnung*). Acknowledgements in detail are given in the references to the individual papers.

I wish to thank Mr Ralph Harris and Mr Arthur Seldon of the Institute of Economic Affairs for their help and encouragement to me in the preparation of this book.

May 1978   *G. C. Allen*

1 Introduction

A theme common to most of the papers in this collection is industrial change, the forces that bring it about and the response of societies, or groups within society, to technical and commercial innovation. The present volume pursues this theme in the context of British industry, and particular attention is directed towards the economic policies of government as they affect industrial change. For the second volume, the field of inquiry is Japan's economic progress, and in several of the papers in the present volume I have sought to interpret the recent course of economic development in Britain by pointing to the contrasts between her experience and Japan's during the last half century. When in the early 1920s I began to write on economic affairs, Britain was still the leading industrial power after the United States. Japan was still pre-dominantly a peasant country with a well-developed infra-structure but scarcely more than a fringe of modern, large-scale industry. In the period since the first of these papers was written Japan has stepped into Britain's place as a manufacturing country, while Britain's industrial achievements, in spite of a substantial absolute advance in production and national income, have been far surpassed by those of several Western countries as well as by Japan herself. This reversal of positions, like every change in a nation's history, is to be ascribed to the convergence of many causes. Some of these lie too far beyond the range of an economist's competence to call for more than an acknowledgment of their potency, but it would be unrealistic to ignore them, and I have tried to give them their due.

For the last forty years the majority of applied economists have been preoccupied with macroeconomic problems, especially since the influence of Keynes became paramount. Their attention has been focused on the management of aggregate demand and on policies by which economic progress can be promoted, or fluctuations in employment and income avoided, by the use of the fiscal and monetary instruments available to the government. Few economists today dispute the necessity and high practical importance of such inquiries. Unfortunately this concentration of

1

attention on macroeconomics led, for two decades after the Second World War, to a comparative neglect of microeconomics, with the result that policies have at times been based on an understanding of the *modus operandi* of the modern economic system that has been one-sided and partial. Some of Britain's economic misfortunes since the war may well be attributed to an excessive reliance on demand management. There has been a presumption that the economy would flourish if only the authorities were competent in the application of the 'right' fiscal, monetary and investment policies.

The notion that errors in the management of demand were the chief source of Britain's undistinguished economic performance since the war was challenged in the report on the British economy issued by the Brookings Institution in 1968.[1] According to the American economists who conducted the investigation, the chief causes of Britain's troubles were to be found in the 'general inefficiencies pervading the economy'. In the words of Professor R. E. Caves, who led the team: . . . 'the potential gains in real growth from changes in demand management have been over-estimated and the extent to which attainable growth has been constrained by inefficiency underestimated'.[2] Two years later a group of British economists conferred with the Americans responsible for the report, and their deliberations also threw doubt on the proposition that errors in demand management lay at the heart of Britain's malaise. Indeed, they found the causes of the 'British disease' obscure. Some of them reached the conclusion that a solution could not be found entirely within the chambers of reference where economic inquiries are usually conducted. They made much of institutional factors and social attitudes as the source of Britain's economic shortcomings: ' . . . the long-run relationships that should form the basis of growth policy seem to rest on social and political values at least as heavily as on economic variables'.[3]

These views are in accord with the facts and arguments set out in the papers in this collection. A general conclusion that emerges from them is that an essential quality of a progressive economy is its capacity both to initiate changes in the structure and organisation of industry, and also to accommodate itself to the social consequences that attend the changes. It is not, of course, asserted that other factors have no part in economic success; indeed, as already emphasised, only when several favourable factors converge is a country likely to enjoy a high rate of growth. Nevertheless, without the qualities of resilience and high enterprise, other factors may be powerless.

The proposition that relates economic progress to adaptability in structure and organisation gives rise to a number of questions. What are the determinants of a country's attitude to change? What part is played by institutions, themselves the product of past conditions, in the response of individuals and groups to the challenge of innovation? Can a 'national purpose' normally be identified in this context, and what importance is to be ascribed to it in explaining disparate rates of growth between countries? Why should men's attitude to the conditions that make rapid progress possible differ so profoundly from time to time and from place to place? These are sociological and political as well as economic questions, and the importance that I attach to these non-economic aspects is apparent in several chapters of this and the companion volume. In my view it is unfortunate that institutional factors, which often exert a decisive influence, have received scant attention from economists in recent times, even from those who have addressed themselves to problems of growth. The papers in this collection do not pretend to analyse the social and political factors in economic progress, but an awareness of their importance and of the necessary partial character of purely economic explanations is present in most of them. Alfred Marshall, like many economists in the past, had no inhibitions against admitting these 'extraneous' considerations into his analysis of economic affairs. He noted (his words are quoted in Chapter 11) that great outbursts of practical energy often sprang from regions beyond the realm of economic calculation.

Recent experience seems to confirm this opinion. It is difficult to explain the contrasts in the performance of various countries since the Second World War without reference to differences in national purpose, institutional arrangements and social relationships. Sometimes a 'national purpose' may be imposed on a nation by external events that limit its range of choice. Thus, Germany and Japan after 1945 were left with their former political ambitions in ruins and with no alternative but to concentrate their energies on economic rehabilitation and growth. The rich rewards of this concentration are now apparent: 'Every man profiteth in that he most intendeth'. Britain, left with greater freedom of action, wasted her strength in the pursuit of inconsistent aims. She was not compelled as were her late enemies to make a realistic appraisal of her changed position in the world. She still remembered her imperialist past with pleasure and her policy was affected by her nostalgia. Her people were eager to enjoy the security and comforts of the Welfare State and her politicians, in obedience to popular doctrine, to extend the boundaries of public control. Lip-service was paid to industrial efficiency, but in fact economically progressive policies received conventional deference rather than the assent of conviction. Efficiency came low in the nation's scale of preferences and the result has been what one might have expected. Yet it would be misleading to suggest that Britain after 1945 suffered a sudden change of purpose or became without warning entangled in a labyrinth of indecision. These papers should demonstrate that the genesis of her postwar problems can be found in earlier times. Some of the papers, it is hoped, also throw light on the real difficulties of choice with which the nation and its government have long been confronted.

The book begins with a story of industrial success, the success of a particular region of Great Britain in adapting itself to changes in markets and technique and in pioneering new branches of industry. The theme of Chapter 2 is the course of change in the West Midlands between the 1860s and the 1920s. During that period the industrial structure of the region was transformed. The old industries to which it had owed its prosperity during the first three-quarters of the nineteenth century declined and some of them virtually ceased to exist. Nevertheless the industrial growth of the region did not falter, for new industries took the place of the old, often as a result of the transference of the resources of existing firms to new types of products. By the middle 1920s the West Midlands owed most of its industrial eminence to manufactures of which there were few or no examples in 1860. Chapter 3 examines the same region in detail, chiefly from the standpoint of the distinctive forms of organisation that emerged in the course of transition from the small-scale, domestic, or 'putting-out', system, once characteristic of most of the trades, to a modern type of factory system. Here again industrialists and merchants showed their resilience and ingenuity in adapting their methods of organisation and management to the introduction of power machinery and new technical devices and to changes in the nature of the labour supply and the market.

During the period with which these two chapters are concerned the response of the British economy as a whole to exogenous events was less eager than in the first three-quarters of the nineteenth century, and industrialists were slower in taking advantage of fresh opportunities and in prompting innovations. Their deficiencies in these respects were disguised during the decade before the First World War by the massive growth in the foreign demand for the products of the old staple industries, especially coal, cotton fabrics and ships. But the weakness was exposed when misfortune struck those industries in the 1920s, and in the interwar years Britain lagged behind her foreign competitors in the newer branches of manufacture. In contrast, the West Midlands throughout that period continued to present a conspicuous example of industrial resilience. Consequently, its prosperity, which became increasingly associated with its pioneering role in new branches of manufacture, stood out in high relief against the failures of several other great industrial regions to find new paths of enterprise as their former activities decayed. While South Wales, East Lancashire, the North-East Coast and Clydeside suffered from heavy chronic unemployment, that caused them to be classed as depressed areas, the West Midlands enjoyed something like full employment.

Chapter 4 points to one of several possible explanations for these interregional contrasts. It is argued that the industrial composition of the various regions at the time when they are called upon to face a fundamental change in circumstances has a bearing on their success in adaptation. Regions with a diversified industrial life, regions that make contact with the nation's economic activities at many different points, may find it easier to redeploy their resources than those specialised to a narrow range of trades. The proposition rests on historical evidence which shows that new industries usually emerge from those already established. The general line of argument in this chapter is in accord with the views of Professor S. R. Dennison who, in his explanation of the disparate experience of areas in attracting new trades to replace those in decay, called attention to the importance of the 'initial position' during a period of structural change.[4] Areas which, at the beginning of such a period, were already possessed of firms in the industries about to expand, or of productive capacity that could be easily adapted to serve new demands, were better placed to become the home of the growing industries than areas without those links. One must not, of course, press the argument too far. Specialisation has played a conspicuous part in economic progress, and some specialised areas (the Potteries, for example) have been eminently successful in adapting themselves to new demands and new technical conditions. Another cause of the contrasts in prosperity between the several areas during the interwar years is analysed in Chapter 7.

During the period under discussion Britain still possessed an unplanned, market economy. The reallocation of resources occurred in response to the impact of depression on some lines of business and the beckoning opportunities of new ventures. In those days firms in difficulties could not call on the government to support them, and their decisions to tread new paths were unbiased by subsidies or investment grants. Where the industrialists and workers were well equipped to respond constructively to market pressures, the prosperity of the regions in which they were located was enhanced. But, as already shown, the response in Britain was not uniform and, in some parts of British industry, enterprise seems to have flagged during the later years of the nineteenth century. This fault could not then be laid at the door of government because of its excessive interference in business decisions, for at that time its participation was small. Indeed, some of the deficiencies in industrial management could be attributed to the State's sins of omission; for example, its lamentable failure to provide a system of technical education equivalent to that instituted in several Continental countries.

The main charge against British industry in those years was that of complacency among its leaders, a refusal to acknowledge that by this time efficient management called for men professionally trained for the work they had to do. Whereas large companies in Germany were directed by experts who had received an advanced education in science, technology and commercial affairs, in Britain those in the seats of authority too often owed their position to nepotism or to promotion from the shop floor. A historian of the European chemical industry has explained Britain's loss of leadership in that branch of manufacture to the fact that, while in Germany and Switzerland well-qualified scientists and technologists were members of the directorate, in Britain such experts were usually employed only in a subordinate capacity.[5] Another historian has suggested that Britain lost ground to other countries in the new steel industry after 1870 in part because both managers and men were badly educated. The arrival of the joint-stock company in that industry made matters worse, for it often led to the replacement of the practical men in higher management by men who had neither the appropriate experience nor the appropriate education. [6] Many explanations of Britain's industrial insufficiency in these respects have been offered. Some critics have found the chief cause in her social and educational systems. Business had ceased to enjoy the high prestige of the professions, the civil service or politics, and the older British universities, unlike those of several other countries, showed little interest in training men for industrial life. So British industry was starved of men of first-rate quality. [7]

This interpretation of Britain's industrial performance has been met with the argument that, while it may be true that she was slow in the introduction of new manufacturing techniques, her factor-endowment was such as to justify the methods which she chose to retain or adopt. This contention must be treated with respect. Foreign example is not always compelling. The organisation, methods and resource-allocation appropriate to one country may not be best suited to another country where factor-prices are different. But the objection ignores the dynamic character of economic life. Material prosperity depends not only on a passive adjustment to exogenous changes in demand and technique. It depends to an even greater extent on a capacity to promote change. Schumpeter made the same point long ago in his great work on economic development. [8] In other words, the true entrepreneur does not merely respond to market and technical changes. He initiates them. At any moment the relative factor-endowments of different countries certainly provide a clue to their industrial structure and forms of organisation; but the analysis is incomplete if it ignores the part of the imaginative entrepreneur in changing the data presented to him. By creating new combinations of resources he may alter the significance of given factor-endowments and so set industry on a new path. To take an example from the Japanese, during the middle 1950s when Japan had ample supplies of labour but an extreme shortage of capital, it seemed to many observers that it would be rational for her to concentrate her energies on the labour-intensive industries (on cotton and wool textiles, small metal goods, cameras, pottery) rather than on motor cars, mass-produced steel and man-made fibres. In fact, she chose the science-based, high technology industries and, as commonly happens when imaginative entrepreneurs are at the helm, capital resources came to their hand. A virtuous circle was created by the entrepreneurial drive—the new investment raised productivity and brought rising incomes which provided the means for savings and investment on an ever-growing scale, and this in turn produced still higher production and incomes. Britain at the turn of the century (and afterwards) was not short of capital. She was better supplied than the Continental countries that were ahead of her in introducing new capital-intensive techniques. What her industry lacked were entrepreneurs of high quality and professionally trained managers.

A shift in social priorities alters the way in which institutions work and this change leads to modifications in the industrial system. In Britain a shift of this kind, which began tentatively before the First World War and gathered momentum in the inter-war period, was accompanied by increasing scepticism about the verdicts of the free market. The way was prepared for the Welfare State, the extension of the public sector and uninhibited intervention by government in private enterprise. These new policies as they affected industry are the subject of several chapters. The changes that became manifest as the country began to emerge from the World Depression of 1929–31 are sketched in Chapter 5, which is the text of my Inaugural Lecture delivered at the University of Liverpool in 1934. Here I called attention to the 'recent introduction of a whole group of official measures aimed at modifying the existing structure and organisation of industry, at the regulation of prices and output, and the maintenance of a particular allocation of productive resources', . . . in a word, 'the drastic modification of the system of free enterprise'. Subsequent events suggest that my insistence on the significance of these changes was not misplaced. I pointed to the social and political reasons for the new attitude of government and to the conflict between economic rationality (as judged in the light of the then orthodox economics) and the objectives that the State sought to realise. Traditional liberal economic policies had ceased to be socially acceptable in a period of chronic depression in the staple trades and massive unemployment. Liberal economists might argue that the misfortunes had come about because governments had failed to discharge their prime duty of providing, through appropriate monetary and commercial policies, an environmental congenial to private enterprise. But this argument was rejected by those who considered that the economic discipline necessary for the efficient functioning of the system of private enterprise was no longer to be tolerated. I speculate in this chapter about where the clash of doctrine was likely to lead the country. Schumpeter, in his *tour-de-force, Capitalism,*

Socialism and Democracy, presented much the same argument with brilliance and authority.[9]

In Chapter 6 the same theme is pursued with reference to particular instances of government intervention in industry during the 1930s. By the time this paper was first published (October, 1937), the scope of the policy had been extended and its implications had become clear. Competition as a means of determining the allocation of resources was being discarded over much of industry, and cartelisation, or combination, was being encouraged (or even enforced) by government as a means of alleviating the condition of the depressed industries. The official strategy was almost wholly defensive, and what was being defended was the established producer. In this paper I considered the confusions that arose in the application of the policy, because the authorities failed to distinguish between sociopolitical and economic criteria. I found no objection *in principle* to the government's intervention in industry when, under free enterprise, adjustments of structure and organisation to changes in demand and technique appeared to be tardy. But I was sceptical of the capacity of politicians and civil servants to intervene successfully in practice. Bureaucrats could not be expected to know enough about industry to take prudent decisions, and the advice they received from those who did know was seldom disinterested. I stressed, also, the danger of basing decisions on the opinions of an established majority in any industry, for it is frequently the 'outsider', the non-conformist, who is responsible for innovation and progress.

I had the experiences of the 1930s in mind when I wrote, in 1945, the paper that appears as Chapter 7. I offered an explanation of why some industries found greater difficulty than others in adjusting their organisation to a contraction in the volume of their business. The former were especially liable to resort to cartels as a financial safeguard, and I explored the means by which the government might assist reorganisation designed to maintain or to improve efficiency and at the same time might counter the disposition of industrialists to seek remedies for their troubles in restrictive practices. It was unrealistic to suppose (so I argued) that the problem of contraction in certain trades would not reappear just because the government had committed itself to maintaining full employment in the country as a whole. Whether the remedy I proposed was practicable is open to question.

The wide extension of public control over the economy during the Second World War left a permanent mark. In spite of the repeal of many war-time regulations after the coming of peace, the scope of the State's intervention remained far wider than in 1939, and a return to a liberal economy seemed increasingly unlikely as time went on. So the relations between government and industry moved into the forefront of discussions on economic policy. Could the efficient operation of private enterprise be reconciled with the ambitious claims of the Welfare State, the increased power of organised labour that the social security measures had buttressed, and the insistent demand for the extension of public control over an ever-widening range of processes and transactions? Some aspects of this large subject were considered in my Inaugural Lecture delivered at University College London in March, 1948; this forms Chapter 8. I reviewed, in historical perspective, the forces and motives behind the enlargement of the State's economic functions, and I examined the conflicts to which the then fashionable 'economic planning' was giving rise. Fresh from my wartime experience as a temporary civil servant, I stressed again the dangers to progress presented by the government's increasing reliance on advice from 'representative' bodies in industry.

Even a half-planned system, such as came into being after the Second World War, is liable to obstruct the movements that result from the multitudinous decisions of the free market. No system of planning, however searching the inquiries that precede the formulation of the plans, can predict with any confidence the future course of demand and of technical change. Dependent as they are on extrapolation from past trends, planners cannot be aware of the innovations in sources of supply or technical methods that lie beyond the horizon of present conjecture. I ask (expecting the answer 'No'): in an attempt to attain objectives of which men in their political capacity may approve, can the State's plans afford adequate opportunities in the industrial sphere for entrepreneurial initiative, for the 'free and miscellaneous movements of the mind and will', on which progress has hitherto largely depended?

The papers that appear as Chapters 9 and 10 were both addressed to the problem of the efficiency of British industry in the early postwar years. The first of them examined the criteria of economic efficiency and assessed the performance of British industry by reference to them. The forms of industrial organisation were surveyed and the appropriateness of foreign example to British conditions assessed. It was questioned whether government in

Britain was equipped to play more than an auxiliary rôle in promoting technical and commercial efficiency.

In Chapter 10 the changing structure of British industry is discussed in relation to the competitive position of the country's exports in world markets, as viewed in the perspective of the early postwar years. It was concluded that Britain's economic future would depend closely on the presence of industrial leaders with the imagination and force needed to direct her energies into new forms of enterprise and on whether the government succeeded in fostering an economic and social environment that gave their ambitions scope. To read these papers today can only aggravate dismay at opportunities lost and constructive energies dissipated in futile undertakings.

These problems are examined in a wider context in Chapter 11, which contains the substance of my address to the Economics and Statistics Section of the British Association in September, 1950. This paper may be regarded as central to the book and epitomises many of the propositions presented in earlier chapters. Here I directed my attention to the causes of economic progress and I emphasised the crucial importance of the innovator. The springs of constructive action are to be found in the will and resourcefulness of leaders nourished in the hospitality that congenial social and political institutions extend to their enterprises. It is argued that periods of sustained economic expansion can seldom be explained in purely economic terms, and several examples are quoted in support of this thesis. I also suggested that the priority usually ascribed to high investment as an engine of growth was illusory. High investment is as much the result as the cause of rapid growth. 'Enterprise generates its own savings out of the higher incomes which it makes possible.'

The argument has a bearing on the familiar concept of the aggregate productive function which relates the growth of output to increases in inputs of labour and capital. The theory comes into sharp collision with the facts of development, since the relationship clearly varies widely from country to country and from time to time. These differences are commonly explained by reference to 'the residual', which may cover technical and institutional innovations, changes in the quality of goods, or even the appearance of a 'mood of national exaltation' which, it is said, made a powerful contribution to the economic successes of Germany after the 1870s.[10] In practice it is often the 'residual' that exerts the decisive influence on what is achieved. To borrow a phrase that Schumpeter used in a different context, the 'residual' may often be as much more effective than the other causes 'as a bombardment is in comparison with forcing a door'.[11]

The discussion brings up the question of the extent to which monopoly and restrictive practices may hamper economic growth by thwarting the enterprising for the benefit of the routineer. Chapter 12, which traces the rise of a combination in the copper-mining industry towards the end of the eighteenth century, gives an early example of the disposition of industrialists to resort to restrictive practices when their interests are threatened. The combination took place at a time when several British industries were crossing the threshold of a new technology. The men who organised the Cornish Metal Company equalled their modern counterparts in ingenuity in contriving the means for suppressing competition, and their constructions bore a close resemblance to those of the present day. Consequently, although this chapter deals with distant times, it is relevant to contemporary affairs. Chapter 13, which sets out some of my conclusions after twelve years of experience as a member of the Monopolies (and Restrictive Practices) Commission, calls attention to problems that arose in carrying out Britain's monopoly policy during the 1950s and 1960s. It suggests that bodies charged with the task of administering policy in regard to monopolies of scale (close combines) are in danger of seeing their work reduced to futility unless the government can supply them with a clear principle of action or judgment. But the government is, understandably, reluctant to commit itself unambiguously to any such course. A footnote to this chapter argues that the threat offered by monopoly to welfare differs widely from one type of society to another.

Chapter 14 reviews briefly the confusions of Britain's economic policy during the early and middle 1960s. It shows how the government's preoccupation with 'indicative' planning and with measures of demand management led it into actions detrimental to the enhancement of industrial efficiency. The subject of Chapter 15 is a critical appraisal of the views of J. K. Galbraith on the dominant trends in modern, advanced economies. The final chapter deals with an episode that throws light on the quality of the advice, tendered by economists and experts on business affairs, about remedies for the troubles that afflicted Britain at the time of the World Depression of 1929–31.

In conclusion, I must address myself to two possible sources of misunderstanding of the stance taken in this book. First, the arguments in the papers that treat of economic policy are all based on the assumption that economic growth is desirable. This does not mean that growth, or a high rate of growth, is considered to be the chief end of a civilised community or that increasing efficiency, an essential condition of growth, does not sometimes collide with improvements in the quality of life. In other words, the argument in this book is conducted within a particular chamber of reference. But the assumption is justifiable if merely because the desire to become richer is common to most individuals and nations. Mill's 'Stationary State' now finds few adherents. Even those who deplore the thirst, among the inhabitants of advanced countries, for an ever-growing supply of the trivia of modern commerce, call for a constantly rising provision of collective benefits and the services associated with the Welfare State. Unless industry is run efficiently, neither of these demands can be satisfied. If we refuse to pay the price of industrial efficiency, if we are resigned to a mediocrity of economic performance, then we must be content with squalor.

In the second place, it is evident from several of the papers that I consider that the intrusion of the State into *industrial* affairs has, in general, had a deleterious effect on Britain's economic performance during the last forty years. Many critics of this trend have contended that the chief mischief has been caused by the burden of taxation on enterprise and incentive. Others have found their target in the failure of the government to discharge one of the State's most elementary functions, namely the maintenance of reasonable stability in the standard of value. *My* concern has been with the government's involvement in decision-making in industry, and with the influence it has exerted both over the allocation of resources in general and also over the organisation of particular industries. It is true that enterprise in British industry was flagging long before the State had assumed its present rôle; its intervention served mainly to confirm and strengthen the worst faults of the system. It must be emphasised, however, that this unfavourable verdict applies to Britain; it must not be elevated into a general proposition. Indeed, in several countries the State has played a constructive part in industrial development. The contrast of experience between those countries and Britain has been determined, in my view, not by any differences in the competence of public administration in the several countries, but by the presiding motives of economic policy.

In Britain, as already contended, for many decades efficiency and economic growth have occupied a lowly place in the government's scale of preferences. The protection of vested interests, the maintenance of the status quo, the alleviation of local unemployment, the correction of inequalities in the distribution of the national income, the enlargement of social security, support for the bargaining strength of groups well disposed to the political party in power—all these objectives, some of them very praiseworthy, have been the main considerations behind the acts of intervention. This system of priorities has had a disastrous effect on the relations between government and the men in charge of private industry. Indeed, the hostility extends even to the public sector, for those entrusted with the management of the nationalised industries have frequently been on bad terms with the sponsoring Ministries. The countries in which the State has participated to good effect in industrial affairs have been those where government and industry have found themselves able to pursue the same ends in harmony. For example, in Japan, from the end of the Second World War, the stimulation of economic growth through increased efficiency has been the main purpose of government policy, an objective approved not merely by industrialists but by the mass of the people. Civil servants and politicians have cooperated unreservedly with private industry in raising productivity and in the development of new lines of manufacture. Thus the disastrous British experience must not be taken as proving that State intervention in industrial policy is necessarily incompatible with efficiency and rapid economic growth. Golden rules are best avoided in statements about economic policy.

Britain's economic experience during the present century in comparison with that of other countries prompts another suggestion about the reasons for her unsatisfactory industrial performance. It is generally recognised that massive technological developments, such as have occurred in all Western countries in the present century, are liable to affect social and political relationships in a way that may be damaging to future economic progress unless they are accompanied by appropriate changes in institutions. Considerable institutional changes have, of course, taken place in Britain in recent times, and these seem momentous to many of her people. But Britain's social institutions had further to travel on the road to the twentieth century than those of most other Western countries, and to foreign observers she appears to have been reluctant to modify them—her class system, her methods of recruiting her élite, and her educational system—so as to fit them for their rôle in the modern world. For a country once a pioneer in social and political reform, she has been singularly unimaginative during the last few decades in devising new institutions with a constructive purpose. An example of a particularly calamitous failure is to be seen in her industrial relations. Again, a comparison may be made with Japan. Her people, heavily indebted to others as they have been since the war for technical innovations, have themselves been fertile in contriving new social and political institutions. After the Second World War, they devised a system of industrial relations which did much to promote harmony between workers and management, and at the same time removed from the trade unions any temptation to oppose technical change. Britain, in contrast, has remained stubbornly committed to 'confrontation' in its industrial relations. Organised labour itself has been characterised by bitter inter-union rivalry and jealousy inseparable from sectionally structured unionism and, in consequence, the industrial climate has been inimical to improvements in productivity. The preference of the British for conflict rather than cooperation in industrial relations has had the result, in some important trades, of frustrating technical innovation, impeding or misdirecting investment and discouraging enterprise.

2 Structural Changes in the 1920s[1]

Recently there has been debate about the significance of the changes which have been taking place since the 1914–18 War in the structure of British industry, and which have affected both the relative importance of the various trades and their regional distribution. It is claimed that the old staple industries are in some measure giving place to a number of newer manufactures, and that there is a marked tendency for this country to become concerned mainly with finishing processes rather than as in the nineteenth century with all the stages of manufacture, particularly in the metal group. It may not be out of place, therefore, to look back into the immediate past to see if, in the light of this theory, the origins of any such transformation can be discerned; for it is necessary at the outset to satisfy oneself that the depression in the staple industries, accompanied as it is by great activity in others, is not merely the result of the disproportionate increase in the productive capacity of the former which occurred during the War. The question is, in fact, whether there are grounds for supposing that the present period is really one of transformation and not merely of readjustment. A fruitful method of inquiry into this problem is to examine the recent trend of events in particular industrial areas, and the history of the West Midland District, which may be regarded as including not only Birmingham and the manufacturing towns of Warwickshire, but also the whole of the Black Country, provides some very valuable indications of the existence of new industrial tendencies.

It is probable that when the economic historians of the future survey the history of the last seventy or eighty years they will seize upon two periods as being of special significance. They will first point to the great depression, which lasted from the middle 1870s, broken only by a brief period of prosperity, till 1885, as providing the industrial watershed between the age of Britain's industrial supremacy and a time when the progress of her manufactures faltered under the assaults of foreign competitors, and they will then

16

go on to show that the Great War confirmed the direction of the new stream of forces, and thus had a part in the 'new industrial revolution' comparable with that played by the Napoleonic Wars in the first industrial revolution. The Birmingham District will appear to have been during both 'revolutions' peculiarly sensitive to the forces of change. It is a district which attained a high degree of industrial development comparatively early in the modern era; its rise coincided with the growth in the relative importance of the metal trades; and it seems that the new industrial tendencies, which were scarcely apparent elsewhere until stimulated by the War, affected this area much sooner than they did the northern centres of industry.

In the 1860s and early 1870s the forces which had created the industrial greatness of the Birmingham District reached their most triumphant expression. South Staffordshire was still the most important centre of the iron industry, especially of malleable iron production, upon which the British supremacy in the metal trades had until then rested. And while the production of coal, iron and heavy iron goods was the main concern of the Black Country, Birmingham itself and a number of neighbouring towns and villages were chiefly engaged in the manufacture of a wide variety of small metal wares. The most important of these were guns, jewellery, pens, buttons, bedsteads, brassfoundry, and a thousand small products of the foundry, stamp and press. At that time highly composite articles were few. Then, between 1874 and 1885, the decade of the depression, the activities of the area entered upon a period of transformation. The coming of mass-produced steel crippled the great iron industry, while many of the foreign markets of the hardware trades were closed by the growth of native industries. The future of the district seemed far from bright. Its deposits of coal and of iron were approaching exhaustion; and owing to the heavy transport charges to and from the coast it could not hope to compete in the production of steel with districts more favoured by situation. During the early 1880s there began, in consequence, that migration of the heavy trades to the coast which has gone on ever since. Of all the great metallurgical centres the West Midlands have enjoyed, since then, the fewest benefits in respect of transport charges and proximity to raw materials; and so the area has to a large extent anticipated the change which has only recently affected British producers in situations of greater economic advantage. Yet even though some of its most characteristic trades never recovered from the effects of the depression, the development of the district after 1886 continued. During the next twenty-five years it attracted to itself a multitude of new industries which were then appearing. It became a home of the electrical trades, the motor and cycle industries, and the weldless tube trade, and an important centre of light engineering, the chemical industry, and food and drink manufacture. By 1914, Birmingham had ceased to be exclusively, or even chiefly, a hardware town, just as the Black Country was no longer predominantly a centre of iron production. The district was turning increasingly to a new group of industries, and was tending to become a centre for the production of highly composite articles and of the semi-finished materials necessary for their manufacture.

The 1914–18 War gave a stimulus to these tendencies. If the most marked result of the great depression has been to bring down the iron industry, the effect of the War was to cripple the hardware trades. The old staples, with a few important exceptions, have fallen from their prewar position. The pin, needle, button, jewellery, gun, hollowware, pen, saddlery and harness trades have all declined, and the local producers who before 1914 supplied them with their components and semi-finished materials are now engaged largely in satisfying the demands of the newer industries. The rolling mills and the tube mills in the non-ferrous trade have found markets in the motor and motor accessories industries. The weldless steel tube trade, which in prewar days was mainly concerned with boiler tubes for the shipbuilders, now looks to the cycle trade as its chief market. Many foundries which previously specialised on hollowware now use their capacity for the production of castings for the electrical and light engineering trades. The tanners and curriers of Walsall, who in the past sold almost exclusively to the local saddlers and harness makers, now produce leather for the coachbuilders; while their former customers, having lost their foreign markets, have changed over to the manufacture of fancy leather goods. Meanwhile, the food and drink trades have risen to greater prosperity, and in some of the old centres of the iron trade, such as Wolverhampton and Dudley, industries of a type quite new to the area, such as the artificial silk and readymade clothing industries, have been established. The old brassfoundry trade has maintained itself largely because it supplies the sheltered industries, such as the building and the furniture trades, though even this trade has responded to the increasing demand for motor accessories. The structural changes as a whole owe more to the rapid development of the motor and electrical industries than to any other cause; for the products of these industries are of so complex a nature and make demands on such a variety of materials that opportunity has been presented to most of the multitudinous trades in the district to benefit by their expansion.

Thus the area which fifty years ago was mainly concerned with the production of iron and of hardware has now become associated with manufactures of a very different kind. As a centre for raw materials and semi-products it has now become of small importance. The famous thick-seam coal of the Black Country is practically exhausted and fuel is brought from Cannock and elsewhere. The foundry iron used in the district comes from Derbyshire and Northamptonshire; and steel is brought from South Wales, Sheffield, or, in the case of certain industries, largely from Belgium. At the same time, the small metal trades have been gravely injured by changes of habits and by the loss of foreign markets. Yet the prosperity of the area has been maintained by the rise of industries engaged in producing motors, cycles, rubber, artificial silk, electrical equipment, machine tools, wireless apparatus, fancy leather goods, food, and drink. Many of these products require large plants for their manufacture, and the small unit, once characteristic of the Birmingham District, has become less conspicuous as the hardware trades have declined.

The radical change that has occurred in the economic structure of the West Midlands has been achieved with less economic friction than might have been expected. If, as it is claimed, the same modifying forces are now making themselves generally felt in this country, it may be hoped that British industry as a whole will prove as sensitive to the new tendencies as the section of it which has here been considered. If industrialists are to weather the period of transition without great loss, however, it is of first importance that they should become conscious of the necessity for adaptation and should realise that it is not an essential condition of prosperity for the future structure of British industry to be identical with its past.

3 Industrial Organisation in the West Midlands, 1860–1927[1]

The West Midland area has received undeservedly fickle treatment from economic historians. Their attention has been repeatedly directed towards the industrial development of the district during the eighteenth century, to its early iron trade, to its brass and copper trades, and to its great pioneers in the sphere of engineering; but its history during the nineteenth century has been neglected. This is unfortunate, because the changes which have occurred in the economic structure of the area during the last sixty or seventy years have not only been of great intrinsic interest, but they reflect in a clear and unmistakable fashion the forces which have been modifying the industrial character of the whole country. It is with one aspect of these changes that I wish to deal. In an analysis of the rise of the factory system and, indeed, the totality of those changes which we describe by the term 'the industrial revolution', there is a well-recognised danger in generalising from a few staple industries. We cannot, in fact, get a true and balanced picture of the movement unless we also take into account the multitude of minor trades, which together have employed a large proportion of the population. For this purpose no area can be of greater interest than the West Midlands, where a remarkable variety of industries have flourished and which may be considered representative of all the unspecialised industrial areas of the country. Many of these Midland trades remained, until well into the last quarter of the nineteenth century, independent of the tendency towards large-scale organisation, which by 1850 had carried the staple industries into the factories, and it is with the causes of this conservatism and with the forces which ultimately led to a transformation that I wish to deal. There is also another problem upon which I propose to touch. Up to the present there have been few attempts to study the stages of growth in the evolution of the factory, especially from the point of view of its administration and control, and, since the West Midlands has

20

an important contribution to make to this neglected subject, certain aspects of it will also be considered. I must explain that I have taken the year 1860 as a starting-point, because the decade which followed corresponded roughly to the period when a stage of industrial growth, which had begun about a century previously, reached its culminating point, and when just ahead lay an era of far-reaching change.

In the first place, some idea must be given of the type of manufacture carried on in the 1860s; and, for this purpose, the area may be divided into two sections, one consisting of Birmingham itself and the immediate neighbourhood, and the other that part of South Staffordshire and Worcestershire which is known as the Black Country. Both divisions of the area were then, as now, renowned for the multiplicity of their trades; but whereas the former was engaged in the manufacture of highly finished articles expressed in many different materials, the Black Country was the home of the heavier and the cruder manufactures and was concerned mainly with iron. In Birmingham itself the four leading manufactures consisted of the gun, jewellery, button and brass trades. The pen, bedstead, screw and wire trades were of substantial, if secondary, importance, and the town shared with the Black Country such industries as the flint glass, saddlery and harness, edge tool, tinplate and japanned ware and rolling stock manufactures. In the Black Country the largest amount of employment was afforded by the heavy industries, such as coal and ironstone mining, pig-iron and wrought-iron production, and the manufacture of railway material and constructional engineering work. Scarcely less important than this group was the wrought-nail trade, which, employing some 18,000 persons, was the leading small metal manufacture of the area. In addition, there were the highly localised industries, lockmaking at Willenhall and Wolverhampton, chainmaking at Cradley, needle-making at Redditch, flint-glass manufacture at Stourbridge, nut and bolt manufacture at Darlaston, and saddlery and harness production at Walsall, to name only a few.[2]

When we consider the nature of the producing units in these trades we find some pointed contrasts. There were certain industries which required the association of large bodies of men for the manipulation of heavy materials and, from their inception, had been conducted in large establishments. The sheet-glass and rolling stock factories employed upwards of 500 persons each; the constructional engineering works and the iron tube mills were necessarily extensive; and there were one or two light industries, such as the steel pen manufacture, in which, because the productive process involved the co-ordination of the labour of semi-skilled press operatives, the factory had made its appearance.[3] But the large establishment was most typical in iron manufacture. From the time of the application of pit coal to the smelting and puddling processes, this trade had tended to fall into the hands of large concerns, many of which were integrated in character. Thus, while in the 1860s many small 'jackey' pits, as they were called, were being worked on the thick coal measures, which outcropped in South Staffordshire, and while many small ironworks were operating, the greater part of the trade was in the hands of firms which not only obtained coal, iron ore and limestone from their own local mines, but also controlled blast furnaces, forges and mills, and often produced finished products, like edge tools, as well. Some of these concerns are said to have employed as many as 5000 men in the various branches of their business.[4]

When we look at the small metal industries, which together employed the greater share of the local labour force, and more than any other stamped the industrial character of the area, we find the small unit almost everywhere predominant. It is true that from the eighteenth century in almost every trade a few large factories, the creation of some organising genius, had flourished—the businesses of Boulton and of Clay are examples—yet such concerns were in the nature of magnificent exceptions rather than samples of the prevailing industrial pattern. In the finished goods trades the concentration of production in factories was unusual. The great economic expansion of the area during the century preceding 1860 was marked by a large increase in the number of its producing units rather than by a growth in the size of the existing few. At a time when the heavy metallurgical and the textile industries had passed under the sway of machinery, the hardware manufacturers of Birmingham and district still pursued for the most part the older methods of hand production. A French observer in 1856 noted that, in contrast to the position in the northern centres of industry, the manufacturing class of Birmingham had not raised itself socially in any large degree, and that the concentration of capital and the development of large-scale enterprise had not taken place there.[5]

I propose to examine the leading small metal trades with the object of testing this generalisation, and in considering the workplaces of the time I shall distinguish between three classes of producer: first, the 'outworker', 'garret-master', or domestic worker proper, who carried on his trade in a part of his dwelling-house with the assistance of members of his family or of an occasional journeyman; secondly, the workshop-owner, who employed up to forty persons in a converted dwelling-house in which little or no power machinery was used; and finally, the factory employer, who had a larger establishment, often built specially for the purpose of his trade, and who made use of power machinery. The representative concern in the section of West Midland industry which I am now examining fell within one of the first two categories in nearly every case. Thus, the largest of the small metal trades, the nailing industry, was essentially of a domestic character. The nailor commonly drew a bundle of nail rods at the beginning of each week from a factor's warehouse, provided his own fuel and the few simple tools which he required and, with the help of his family, he produced in a forge adjacent to his home a quantity of nails which were 'weighed in' at the warehouse each Saturday.[6] Here and there the factors had erected in the vicinity of their warehouses nail-shops, which they rented to nailors without forges of their own;[7] but this was the extreme limit to which the factory employer had gone in this industry. The chain trade differed from the nail trade in some respects because the manufacture of certain types of chain necessitated the use of a power blast. Yet, although the heavy chain was made in factories, all other kinds were produced by shop-owners or by domestic workers under conditions similar to those in the nail industry.[8] With a few exceptions, the producing units in the Willenhall lock trade were of the same character; the nut and bolt manufacture of Darlaston was conducted in establishments employing from fifteen to twenty workers, or by single-handed outworkers; and much of the edge tool industry and of the other hardware trades of the Black Country was organised in the same way.

The manufactures of Birmingham itself, however, present more interesting and peculiar features. The industries so far described were engaged on comparatively simple products, of the type for which a single workman could undertake all the processes of manufacture; but Birmingham was concerned with a different class of article. The gun, jewellery and brass trades were all engaged on composite products, which called for many distinct processes and a variety of skilled labour. In all of them there was a highly subdivided labour force, yet—and here is a point I must emphasise—

this subdivision was not inconsistent with the prevalence of the small unit. Thus in the gun trade, the master gunmaker in most instances possessed merely a warehouse. He purchased parts in the shape of locks, sights, barrels and stocks from the 'material makers', who were generally independent craftsmen working on a small scale, and these materials he gave out to a long series of 'setters-up', each of whom performed a specific operation in his own workshop.[9] Similarly, in the jewellery trade, where the bulk of the industry was in the hands of shopowners with under twenty employees, the firm producing finished goods relied on outworkers or small firms to perform such operations as stamping, gilding, plating, rolling and stonesetting. In both these industries there was, of necessity, a constant transport of semi-finished goods from one craftsman to another, and this led to the location of each of them within a special quarter of the town, for example, the gun quarter and the jewellery quarter. In the brass trade the small unit was less ubiquitous. Firms engaged in producing tubes, wire, or sheet metal naturally required a power-driven plant and a fair-sized mill; and even in the manufacture of finished brassfoundry several large factories existed. Nevertheless, in this industry the garret-masters and the small shopowners were also numerous; for whereas in the factory the various processes could be conducted in separate departments under one roof, they could also be carried on economically in distinct businesses by specialists. For example, the small manufacturer could have his foundry work 'done out' by a class of master called a Caster for Hire. He could obtain his stampings from a similar type of specialist; while some operations requiring power, such as polishing, could be relegated to outworkers.[10] Indeed, the application of power machinery to certain processes during the first half of the nineteenth century had done little, in the leading trades, to change their system of organisation; for the small master was provided with opportunities of employing power without the necessity of laying down a plant himself. Buildings had been erected which were divided into separate workshops, through each of which shafting, driven by a steam engine, projected. Here manufacturers who required power for certain operations could hire the facilities they needed, and it was common at the time to see the notice 'Power to Let' affixed to mills in the neighbourhood.[11] As a final example of the type of small-scale industry in which the productive process was highly subdivided, the saddlery and harness trade may be considered. A few small factories existed to deal with the demand for standardised goods from the government and from the export markets, but the greater part of the industry, engaged in producing leather and metal parts which local saddlers and harness-makers throughout the country assembled, was carried on by little masters, each of whom specialised on some component, such as stirrups, bits, buckles, saddle-trees or bridles.

The causes of the survival of the small unit in Birmingham and district industries are not difficult to discover. The economies of large-scale factory production are much less substantial in the small metal trades than in the textile or the heavy metallurgical industries which are concerned with homogeneous and standardised commodities. Many of the Midland products were of an ornamental character. They possessed, of necessity, an individuality of design inconsistent with mechanised methods of manufacture. Certain industries, moreover, such as the gun and saddlery trades, were subject to wide fluctuations in demand, which increased the risks of employers with a large factory. Under the existing system, the master gunmaker could throw the burden of depressions on to the shoulders of his outworkers and so escape the weight of heavy overhead charges. Nor must technical factors be ignored. Even the small metal manufactures in which conditions were favourable for large-scale production required machinery that made much greater demands on the engineer than did that employed by the textile trades. So the reorganisation of the Midland industries had to await later developments in engineering and metallurgy.

The most remarkable feature of the industrial organisation of the time was the survival of the small unit in trades in which there was a high degree of division of labour. This phenomenon, it is true, was found in the early woollen industry; but the differentiation of processes had been carried very much further in several local manufactures (the gun trade, for example) than it had been in the early textile industries. It might be thought that the better co-ordination of the various processes, which the factory would have ensured in such industries, would alone have led to the supersession of the little master. Yet it must be remembered that in those days men were restive under the yoke of factory routine, that it was difficult to induce them to forego their 'Saint Mondays' and 'Saint Tuesdays' and their habit of crowding six days' work into the last three days of the week,[12] and that the better co-ordination of different types of labour, which it was one of the objects of the factory to secure, was thus made extremely difficult. Until machinery had become an essential condition of economical production, the entrepreneur could obtain little advantage from the establishment of a factory. In trades, such as gun and saddlery and harness-making, in which the productive process, far from consisting of a series of consecutive operations, took the form of a number of independent efforts by skilled craftsmen, each of whom was concerned with producing a finished component for a composite whole, the economy of assembling the labour force in factories was negligible.

At this point I should like to consider briefly the figure who occupied a key position in the small-scale industries of the period, that is, the factor or the merchant. In the West Midland area the former term applied to middlemen who catered for the home market, and only those who dealt in the export trade were called merchants. Their main functions were similar to those exercised by their counterparts in all the small-scale industries. They supplied materials to the outworker, they financed the manufacturer by taking his products at weekly intervals, and often by granting him a loan with which he might purchase tools, and finally they marketed his manufactures. But the factor's part varied considerably according to the trade with which he was concerned. Thus, the nailing industry provides an example of the domestic system in its simplest form. There the nailmaster, who had a warehouse in each specialised nailing district, gave out the materials and paid weekly wages to outworkers who laboured, with little or no outside help, at their own forges. In many of the other hardware trades general factors with similar functions existed. When we come to the more complex industries, however, the factor had other duties to perform. Thus, the master gunmaker was not only required to have an intimate technical knowledge of his trade, but, since he had to co-ordinate the activities of a multitude of 'material makers' and 'setters up', he had also to enter into close contact with the manufacturing operations. Similarly, the saddlers' and coachbuilders' ironmonger (the factor in the saddlery and harness trade) was responsible both for bringing together in his warehouse the various components which were produced by the little masters, and also for purchasing the hides and for supplying such of his craftsmen as were leather workers with the particular section of the hide which they required in their craft. In the jewellery trade, on the other hand, the co-ordination of the work of specialists was done mainly by the shopowner and not, as in the gun and saddlery industries, by the factor. Single-handed craftsmen or garret-masters, moreover, who made such articles as wedding rings, found a readily available supply of reliable raw material in the shape of the sovereign, and so even they were independent of the factor in one respect. In this trade, indeed, the factor's functions were largely confined to distributing the products and perhaps to providing the makers with credit. In some of the industries in which factories existed alongside the small units, the duties of the factor were performed by the large employer; in the chain trade the orders for various types were placed with the manufacturer, who then produced the large sizes in his factory and gave out orders and materials for the rest to shopowners or single-handed workers. And there were, in every composite product industry, many out-workers who never came into contact with the factor, because they were engaged on special operations for other manufacturers.

There was, then, a gradation from the factor, who was con-cerned with the distribution of products and with the financing of the little master, to the type who exercised an intimate control over the materials supplied to the workers, and co-ordinated the labours of many specialist craftsmen. The fact that the craftsman in certain trades worked mainly for one master must not be taken to imply that his position was more subservient than that of the worker who was less permanently attached to a particular factor. The degree of the employer's penetration into the productive side of an industry, indeed, had little bearing on the economic strength and wellbeing of the worker. The latter's position was determined mainly by the amount of skill required by his trade and by the ease with which outsiders could enter it. In the highly skilled industries the craftsman was in a position to make a good bargain with his factor, who would be loath to lose a valuable workman to a competitor; but in the less skilled trades, where there was frequently an oversupply of labour, the factors pitted one man against another in attempts to drive down prices. It was in such trades, where the workers' position was weak, that the 'slaughtermen', 'foggers' and 'truck-masters' flourished. The wellbeing of the worker had, in fact, little or nothing to do with the extent to which the factor had assumed control over the industry.

My second theme is the methods of administration which were pursued in the larger units of the time. In the first place, we must consider their origins. We may trace the rise of the factory from two sources. From below, we may watch the outworker, dependent upon the factor for his materials and for the co-ordination of his work with that of others, develop into a shopowner, who employs several workmen and has assumed the task of co-ordinating the work of independent specialists, and then into a factory employer, who can contract with the factor as between equals, and uses the latter merely to distribute his goods. Or, from above, we see the factor advance towards the position of a manufacturer when he builds workshops and rents these, together with the tools required, to his outworkers. He goes a stage further when, finding the demand for a certain class of goods outstripping the capacity of his men, or seeing that a particular line may be produced more profitably by machinery, he erects a factory for manufacturing that line, while he still continues to factor other classes of goods. Finally, as he takes up the factory production of other lines, his functions as a factor become subordinate. Yet, having arrived at the factory, we have not arrived at the modern type of factory. We have arrived at a stage in its organisation which I will call the 'subcontracting sytem.' This I must describe in some detail. The significance of the system, which once prevailed throughout the majority of industries, and still survives in many in some form or other, has received less recognition than might have been expected. But it must be considered in any study of industrial evolution, because it represents a definite stage in the growth of the modern factory.

The idea that the employer should find as a matter of course the plant and materials and should exercise supervision over the details of production did not spring into existence as soon as the men had been drawn within the factory. On the contrary, in the larger establishments of the period arrangements came into being which were obvious survivals of an earlier form of organisation, and represented a transitional stage of development. Just as the typical manufacturer who had grown out of the factor remained at heart in his earlier capacity, and tried to hold himself aloof from the details of the productive process, so the employees brought into the factory the traditions of the domestic workshop. The various compromises which reflected the struggle of the employer and the worker to maintain their ancient relationship in a period of change are of considerable interest. The idea that the former's function was to supply materials, to pay for and to market the completed articles, whereas the worker's part was to provide the workshop and the tools, survived, when a factory was established, in the custom of charging deductions. Even in large concerns it was common for sums to be subtracted from the employee's wages for shop-room gas and power, just as if those things were normally supplied by the worker and not by the employer. In the few factories in the lock trade deductions were made for 'standings and light', which persisted right down to the 1914–18 War. In the brass-foundry trade charges were made to cover the cost of light and power; in the foundries the head caster had to pay for the use of the sandmill which had superseded the pestle and mortar, while a rent for shop-room was often required from the head of a gang.[13] In the flint-glass trade of the period a deduction of twelve shillings was made from the weekly wages of workers in the cutting shops to pay for the power which has been introduced to take the place of the old method of operating the machinery by means of a handle turned by a boy-assistant.[14]

The chief feature of this stage of industrial organisation, was associated with subcontracting. This practice had long existed in all industries in which the large unit was found, from the coal and iron trades to the manufacture of brass goods and cut nails. According to the subcontracting system, an intermediary acted as a buffer between the employer and the workers. Termed 'subcontractors', 'overhands', 'fitters', 'charter-masters', 'butties', or 'piece-masters', according to the industry with which they were connected, they all had much the same general function to perform, namely to contract with the factory-owner to produce a certain quantity of output for a fixed sum, and then to engage, pay and supervise workers for the task. The relation of the overhands to the employer in these larger establishments was similar to that between the shopowners and the factor in the small-scale industries. The details of their duties varied from trade to trade. In some cases they had large numbers of underhands, whom they provided not only with tools but with certain raw materials as well, and they thus relieved the employer of a great deal of responsibility and of capital expenditure. Elsewhere they were little more than skilled men who, though hiring a few assistants, relied on the factory owner for all the tools and materials required.

The practice of subcontracting involved the wage-system in all kinds of complications. After the overhand had made his bargain with the factory-owner, the former alone was concerned with fixing the wages of the subordinate labourers; but he could not claim payment from the employer until the quantity of work contracted for was completed. Yet neither he nor his men could afford to wait several weeks without money in cases when the work was spread over a long period. So, to meet such difficulties, it became customary for the overhand to draw on the employer at each weekend for a sufficient sum to provide a reasonable wage for himself and his underhands. When the work was completed, then the price contracted for was balanced against the weekly drawings, and the remainder was paid over to the subcontractor and represented his profit. In trades where his economic position, relative to both workers and employer, was strong, the subcontractor did well financially; but sometimes the employer was in a position to drive down the subcontractor's prices and, apparently, he occasionally fixed the weekly drawings without consulting the overhand. This system of 'blind piecework', as it was called, often led to the subcontractor's being in debt to his employer at the end of a job.[15] In any case, however, a double wage contract was involved, that between the employer and the overhand, which was for a piecewage, and that between the overhand and his subordinates, who were usually paid day-rates. The functions of the entrepreneur were, in fact, in some measure shared between the two parties.

The advantages of the system to the employer are obvious. If wide functions devolved on the overhand, the manufacturer had no need to concern himself with the supervision of his labour. He required no large administrative staff and no elaborate costing system, and he could keep his overhead charges to a minimum. His position, in fact, approximated to that of the factor. The method of organisation might not be applicable to industries in which the productive process required the co-ordinated activity of large numbers of semi-skilled workers; but few local trades in 1860 were of that type. In those that did exist, such as the pen trade, the subcontracting system was absent.[16]

That there were serious disadvantages attending the system cannot be denied. It was frequently declared that the overhand sweated his men and made disproportionately high gains himself. For such exploitation the employer was often responsible; for he had every inducement to drive a hard bargain with the subcontractor, since the odium of low wages which necessarily resulted would be directed against the subcontractor rather than against the employer. The fact that the employer was a more remote figure in the wage contract than he is to-day, is of great significance. In a comparatively small factory, the public opinion of the workers has a more powerful influence on business policy than is generally realised. As to the overhand's high earnings, it must be remembered that he discharged wider functions and suffered greater risks than the modern foreman.

From the standpoint of business efficiency the system had many faults. Since the whole process of producing a finished article usually had to be performed by the subcontractor and his gang, it was impossible to set up separate departments within the factory for performing each operation, or to take advantage of the economies of dividing the processes among specialist workers. Each subcontractor might have certain machines allotted to his use, and while he and his underhands were performing other operations, these might be idle. Much time was lost while the subcontractor was obtaining materials for his work; and, as was pointed out by a trade union secretary, 'if a workman has to supervise a large shop, he is supposed to look out his work, look up patterns, and do a great deal which would be done for him by a general man' in a modern type of establishment.[17] Finally, the overhands, who were almost invariably sceptical of new methods, were generally opposed to change, and the employer, fearing to arouse the hostility of his key men, could exercise in many industries little control over them. Thus the system was disadvantageous inasmuch as the principle of the division of labour could not be extensively applied, an uneconomical use was made of the plant, and reforms in productive methods were difficult to effect. Yet, in the early days of the factory, when no costing system, no trained office and works staff, and little experience of centralised management existed, it is hard to see how the subcontractor could have been dispensed with. Once established, the system was difficult to change; for any attempt by the employer to relegate his overhands to the position of the modern foremen aroused their bitter opposition. The existence of a subcontracting class, however, provided a stepping-stone by which the workman might rise to the position of an independent employer, and many of the new businesses during the latter part of the nineteenth century were founded in this way.

From this account of the administration of such factories as existed during the 1860s, I must return to a consideration of the small-scale industries and to their subsequent history. This I can treat only in outline. At once it may be said that not until the later 1880s did any fundamental changes occur in the organisation of the small metal trades. During the twenty-five years following 1860 the only industry that was transformed was the manufacture of the

military rifle. This product, by 1872, had definitely left the workshops of the old gun trade and had come to be produced in great
factories—a change which had been made possible by the introduction of the 'interchangeable rifle', that is, an arm produced by
the assembly of standardised, machine-made parts.[18] With this
exception, however, the organisation of the small metal trades
remained unaffected. The persistence of the old forms can be
ascribed mainly to the type of products. As they were individual in
character, they could not be economically produced by machinery,
and so the large unit had no marked advantage over the association
of independent little masters. But there was another cause which
I must emphasise. Up to the 1880s, when cheap mild steel first
became available, the staple raw material of the trades of the area
had been wrought iron. This did not lend itself readily to manipulation by machine tools and presses. So, even where the nature of the
products imposed no obstacle to mechanised production, there
were serious technical difficulties to be overcome. To give one
instance, a power press had been introduced into the tinplate ware
trade from the United States in 1870; but it could not be used
extensively until that industry had given up wrought iron in favour
of steel sheets.[19] The coming of cheap mild steel, then, removed a
hindrance to the advance of mechanical methods during the 1890s,
and these began to be extensively employed for the first time in a
variety of local trades. The introduction of this new material was,
indeed, of the utmost significance; for it resulted in carrying the
factory system to a group of industries which had remained
unaffected during the earlier phases of the industrial revolution.
At the same time, a change began to occur in the type of article
required for domestic fittings, for which so many Midland trades
catered. Elaborate and massive products began to give place to
light and cheap articles. This tendency was particularly noticeable
in the brass trade, especially when electric lighting began to spread;
for the result was to create a demand for small machined parts
instead of for cast ornamental gas fittings. An opportunity was thus
given to the manufacturer to produce by presses and machine tools
what had previously been made in the foundry and finished by
hand.

Other forces were also at work. The great depression which lay on
British industry during the ten years following 1875, with only a
short prosperous interval from 1880 to 1882, dealt hardly with the
West Midlands. During that period, not only was the old iron

trade overwhelmed, but many of the most ancient finished man-
factures began to suffer for the first time from foreign competition.
The button, gun, wrought nail and glass trades, to name only a few,
declined in magnitude,[20] and all had to struggle for their existence.
The age of unchallenged British supremacy had given place to an
era of international competition. The effect on the organisation of
the West Midland industries was twofold. In the first place, manufacturers were stimulated into seeking cheaper methods of production, which they found in machinery, and, secondly, the older
and more conservative small metal industries began to lose their
predominant position among the district's trades. By the end of the
century the loss of foreign markets and changes of fashion had
carried this movement still further by injuring such manufactures
as tinplate wares, saddlery and harness and metal bedsteads. In
place of these industries, a number of new trades had appeared,
among them the cycle, electrical engineering, machine tool, and
the food and drink manufactures. Early in the twentieth century
the motor and the artificial silk industries became important local
industries. They were for the most part conducted in large establishments. Being new, they cared little for the traditions of domestic
industry, and they were ready to adopt new methods of administration and control as well as the latest mechanical devices. The
advance of the new engineering trades, moreover, had an important
influence on the hardware producers. A large demand arose for
engineering components which the small metal industries, now that
the demand for their former products had fallen, attempted to
meet. These components were of a more standardised character
than were the older hardware products, and the employment of
machinery was thereby facilitated. The shifting of emphasis from
hardware to engineering components may be noted in nearly all
the older industries; but the change from the production of domestic
brassfoundry to that of motor accessories may be offered as a
typical illustration.

By 1914, the small unit was no longer typical of the West Midland
area, nor even of the majority of its small metal trades, although it
was still common in many of them. The change had been caused
not only by the increase in the size of the representative businesses
in the older industries, but also by a change in the relative importance of the different manufactures. New industries, conducted in
large establishments, had come to the front; while the nail, gun and
saddlery and harness trades, to mention the typical small-scale

manufactures of the 1860s, had shrunk to small proportions. The only large industries in which the outworker and shopowner maintained their ground were those, like the chain trade, which continued to use wrought-iron as a raw material, or the ornamental trades, like jewellery. Even in jewellery, however, small factories began to encroach on the sphere of the workshop during the decade preceding the 1914–18 War.

The transition from the workshop to the factory was facilitated during the last two decades of the nineteenth century by the introduction of the gas engine, which played a part in the history of the small metal trades analogous to that of the steam engine in the development of the staple industries of the country. When, as in the 1860s, the steam engine had been the only form of prime mover available, except in districts where water power was still used, then the small manufacturer had been reduced to the necessity of hiring power when he required it; for the running cost of the steam engine was too great for him to bear. The gas engine, however, gave him just the type of power he needed in a convenient form, and by the late 1880s, according to a factory inspector, the system of hiring power was rapidly dying in the West Midlands, and manufacturers in many industries had introduced gas engines.[21] Not only did the new type of engine permit manufacturers with a comparatively small capital to employ machine tools, but it also had a marked effect on the organisation of all trades in which the productive process was complex and had previously been split up among a multitude of independent specialists. For the adoption of the gas engine meant that power was now available in many work-places for the performance of a whole series of operations. So, gradually, there occurred an integration of the various processes of manufacture and a consequent rise in the scale of production of the representative firm.

These tendencies would not have been so apparent if there had not occurred, in this district as elsewhere towards the end of the last century, a notable improvement in urban transport. Before the era of the tramcar and bicycle, manufacturing establishments were necessarily confined to the heart of the Midland towns; for unless they were in close proximity to populous districts, they had great difficulty in recruiting their labour. But the centres of the old industrial towns were congested; the existing workplaces were old-fashioned in layout and ill-suited to modern productive conditions, and sites were not available for extensions. The acceleration of urban transport, however, enabled the manufacturer, who wished to modernise his plant and to increase his scale of production, to establish himself in industrial suburbs, where cheap land could be had, and to undertake for himself operations previously left of necessity to specialists.

By the 1890s these changes had considerably modified the functions of the factor and the merchant. When the typical manufacturer had been a man without much capital, the factor had controlled industry because the producer had been financially dependent on him. The factor had then been looked to for the provision of materials and, sometimes, of tools. He had bridged the whole period between production and sale by taking the goods at weekly intervals. It was he who normally provided the considerable working capital required in the manufacture of articles that were complex in character and passed through the hands of numerous small masters in the course of production. But, as the producing units grew in size, the representative manufacturer became a person with enough capital to purchase his own raw materials, to assume the task of co-ordinating the different productive operations, and even to keep stocks of finished goods; he was, also, of sufficient standing to treat directly with the banks when he needed credit. What is more, the producers began to trespass on the factor's functions even in the sphere of marketing. Though they might still deal through factors, they began to attempt to influence their customers by the appointment of their own agents and travellers. By the end of the century the factor had lost his dominating position in most of the local trades and was rapidly being reduced to the position of a mere wholesale merchant. In industries in which the small units survived alongside the large firms and the factor had still a part to play, his functions often came to be exercised by the larger manufacturers, who, as we have seen, had frequently developed from factors.

The 1914–18 War gave an immense stimulus to the forces that were transforming the character of West Midland industry. Many of the older hardware trades, in which machinery was only just beginning to play an important part in 1914, were forced to adapt themselves to the quantity production of munitions, and the mechanical equipment of the area was much increased. Since 1918, certain of the new industries, including the motor, cycle, electrical engineering, tyre, artificial silk, and the food and drink trades, have advanced rapidly, and there are several factories in the area which now employ from 5000 to 12,000 men each. The rise of the motor trade has not only resulted in the appearance of a number of large concerns for the production of cars and cycles, but it has led also to the manufacture in quantity of parts and accessories by a multitude of firms which previously confined their activities to hardware. There is scarcely any local trade in which the units have not changed their methods and their scope of production to meet the needs of the new industries. The effect of the appearance of the mass-produced car on the local foundries, for instance, may be seen in the wide extension of die-casting and machine moulding— processes entirely dependent on a quantity demand. An illustration of how several of the older trades, previously conducted on a small scale, have been influenced, is provided by the laminated spring industry. Until recently this trade was carried on entirely in small factories and workshops, and little use was made of machinery. The demand for large quantities of standardised springs by the motor manufacturers, however, has resulted in the rise of factories equipped with plants for turning out springs on mass-production lines. While the new large-scale industries were advancing, the 1914–18 War and the postwar depression have seen a positive decline in several of the older trades, including some of those which had remained progressive up to 1914. Among these are such manu- factures as jewellery and chains, which are still the home of the small master.

Thus, just as the Great Depression marked the end of the wrought-iron age and of the Birmingham area's unchallenged supremacy as a centre of the small metal trades, so it saw the beginning of a new stage in the development of industrial organisa- tion. From then onwards handicraft, which formerly played such a large part in the finished manufactures, began to give way to the machine; the process of production, hitherto subdivided among a host of specialists, began to be conducted under one roof; and the small unit lost ground to the factory. These associated movements I have attributed to a conjunction of causes, for instance, the introduction of cheap mild steel and the gas engine, the change of fashion in domestic fittings, the improvement in urban transport, the stimulus of foreign competition, and finally the change in the type of industry conducted in the area.

In a generalised historical account such as this, there is a danger of overemphasising the extent of the transformation and of giving the impression that a form of organisation which has become typical is universal. It should be made clear, therefore, that in several industries the representative factory is still the small factory, and that opportunities for the shopowner, or even for the out-worker, are still afforded by certain sections of trades in which the large factory is the rule. Many of the more ancient industries, moreover, have never been completely transformed by machinery. The small unit is still very common in the manufacture of jewellery, chains and leather goods. The old sporting gun trade has changed its methods of production but little in the course of a century. But these once staple manufactures no longer occupy a primary place, and their organisation cannot, therefore, be counted typical of the present industrial life of the district.

In conclusion, I must revert to the system of administration within the factories. Here the changes were very gradual; yet, in most of the industries, we can follow the slow emergence of modern methods. With the rise of machine production and with the greater division of labour, the skilled craftsman began to give place to the semi-skilled operative, and there grew up of necessity a more centralised system of control. As the scale of production became larger, and as the difficulties of co-ordination were thereby in-creased, so more and more functions devolved upon the manage-ment. As power machinery became a usual feature of the work-place, and as the traditions of the domestic system died, the practice of charging deductions for shoproom and power ceased. With the application of metallurgical science to manufacture, functions previously carried out by the overhand according to empirical methods passed to the works laboratory. From about 1890, in fact, the subcontracting system in most industries began to decline, and the authority once vested in the overhand began to be assumed by the central management and the technical staff. Yet, if the system was slowly dying, the local trades could still furnish many instances of it in 1914. Some employers clung to the system because it relieved them of responsibility and reduced the duties of manage-ment; while the subcontractors opposed their relegation to the position of the modern foreman. Where subcontracting survived, however, it was generally in a modified form. Even when the over-hand was left with important functions, the practice arose of paying all the men through the office and, in some instances, the wages of underhands came to be regulated by trade union agreements or by pressure from the masters.

The 1914–18 War dealt a heavy blow at this decaying system of organisation. The new methods of production which the needs of the nation enforced, and the change in the personnel of the factories, ended many anachronisms. Where the system survived the War, the general reduction in the working day in 1919 and 1920, which involved for many trades a reorganisation of the manufacturing process and a speeding up of production, brought the subcontracting system to an end in the majority of the small metal industries.

4 Labour Mobility and Unemployment[1]

The postwar unemployment problem has been complicated by the tendency of the newer industries to become localised in the south of England; for this has impeded the mobility of labour and has led to the concentration of unemployment in those areas in which the older trades are situated. It seems probable that while this movement may be partly attributed to temporary and artificial advantages attaching to southern sites, it represents a fundamental tendency in industry, and that during a time of rapidly changing technique such as the present, the traditional centres of industry are unlikely, for various reasons, to attract new trades or fresh units in old ones. If this is so, and as changes in location producing serious economic and social losses have been, and are likely to be, recurrent, it is useful to inquire whether this tendency can be beneficially counteracted by some form of conscious and corporate control. The experience of one of the older districts may throw some light on the problem. The area in question is the West Midlands which (as the preceding chapters have shown) has presented an outstanding example of industrial resilience. The structural transformation, which had been in train ever since the 1870s, has continued during the 1920s. Although the 1914–18 War completed the destruction of several of the older industries, long in decay, their place has been taken by the growth of many new manufactures. So, in contrast with the chronic depression and heavy unemployment suffered by many other great industrial centres, the progress of the West Midlands has continued unchecked and its rate of unemployment has remained low.

Since its success has been bound up with its ability to attract the new industries, it may be asked to what this ability may be attributed. No doubt several influences have been at work; but the main influence is probably to be found in the fact that Birmingham and District throughout its history has been a centre with a highly diversified industrial life, and has possessed, in consequence, a wide variety of commercial, managerial and technical skill. The

39

multiplicity of its interests brings the district into contact with the industrial activities of the nation at many points, and thus places it in a position of advantage for attracting or developing any new trade which may arise. This advantage is particularly evident at the present time, when the advancing trades are concerned with highly finished or highly composite goods; for each of these manufactures requires a supply of many different kinds of skill and technical and commercial knowledge. Further, manufacturers who are operating in a district with a varied industrial life, where one trade or another is always changing its methods or its markets, may well be more flexible and adaptable, and less inclined to regard their present activities as settled by laws of nature, than those persons who live in an area dominated by one trade. I should infer, then, that an area with a highly diversified economic life is capable of weathering periods of transition with greater ease than a more specialised centre.

It is not suggested that, when new trades arise in a diversified area, the problem of the maldistribution of labour does not arise, but only that its seriousness is minimised. While industries have been rising and falling in the West Midlands, it has been possible for brass-workers to find employment in the cycle factories, for gunmakers and woodworkers to secure remunerative employment in the engineering trades, for jewellers to take up gauge-making, and for penmakers to turn to the production of fine stampings. But a wholesale transference of adult labour from decaying to advancing trades can never take place without some unemployment and lowering of living standards during a period of change. A skilled Coventry watchmaker, for example, could not count on securing equally remunerative employment in the cycle and motor factories. But where the diversified area with its capacity of attracting new industries presents advantages over specialist centres lies in the fact that the former offers more ample opportunities to fresh entrants into industry. It has been shown that changes of considerable magnitude can be made in the distribution of the labour force in a short space of time merely by the failure of decaying trades to replace their wastage by recruitment. An area with a multiplicity of manufactures soon finds that those which are unable to support a high wage level quickly decay, since young people are attracted to occupations that offer better prospects. In a word, the industrial activities of such an area respond rapidly to any change in economic forces. Both its workers and its employers are likely to be alert to seize new opportunities as they arise, and there is no question of the life of an industry being prolonged merely by means of a progressive fall in wages. Trades which are threatened with extinction must either reorganise or go, and the stimulus to do this comes sooner and more strongly in diversified areas than in specialist centres, where other measures may be taken to meet an alteration in economic circumstances, and where employers are loath to acknowledge the signs of permanent change. In districts of the latter type, such as some of the coal-mining areas, which have failed to attract the new trades, the industrial life is involved in a vicious circle of cause and effect. Because there are no alternative employments in the neighbourhood, the recruitment of young workers by the advancing trades is impeded and they are forced into the decaying industries. The consequent underemployment and low wages, both of them and of the adult members of their families, produce a deterioration in the quality of the labour force which, if protracted, will ultimately render the areas unsuitable for the establishment of new trades.

The adaptability shown by the West Midlands has not been equally shared by all sections of the area. If we compare, not the whole district with others, but particular towns within the same area with one another, we find additional evidence in support of these conclusions. While Birmingham and Wolverhampton have been distinguished by the multiplicity of their trades, several other places in the neighbourhood, though separated by a very few miles, have been specialist in character and have been much less adaptable. Consequently, when the flint-glass trade began to decay during the 1870s, the labour force engaged in that industry diminished much more rapidly in Birmingham than in Stourbridge, where glassmaking was the chief industry. The reason for this was that in Birmingham there was much competition among the multitude of industries for clever youths, so that the decaying trades failed to attract them; whereas in Stourbridge the lack of alternative occupations of the same class kept large numbers attached to glassmaking in spite of chronic underemployment. In the same way, on the decay of the saddlery and harness trade, the Birmingham firms soon closed their factories or turned to the production of other classes of leather goods, and the workers became absorbed in fresh employments. But in Walsall, where saddlery and harness was the staple manufacture, the decline in the size of the labour force was much less rapid. Another instance is provided by the hand-wrought nail trade, which fought a long struggle against the competition of the cut-nail and wire-nail industries. The workers in this unfortunate industry suffered severely from underemployment and falling wages. Yet, although the trade was driven out of the centres with a diversified life, the total number of workers declined at a very slow rate during the second half of the nineteenth century. Again, the explanation is that much of the manufacture was conducted in towns and villages that afforded few other openings to boys and girls in search of employment; at that time immobility could not be attributed to restrictions imposed by trade unions on entry into other trades. During the postwar period the economically weak industries have been unable to maintain themselves by resorting to wage reductions to the same extent as formerly, with the result that the specialist areas have suffered from a much higher percentage of unemployment than the diversified areas.

The experience of the West Midlands shows that a distance of only a few miles is sufficient to separate the centres of high unemployment and low wages from those that are better off in these respects. This intraregional immobility has been a feature of the area's history for some time past. Even today, it is evident that the mobility of the workers (including the new entrants into industry) may be frustrated by what appears to be an insignificant barrier of distance. The cost of travelling between home and the place of employment, or the expense of moving residence, is not the only factor responsible. A population bred in a single-trade environment may be less alert to seize fresh opportunities than people who are exposed to the bracing climate of a varied industrial life. Recent investigations into the cotton trade seem to support this proposition. In that industry, conducted as it is to a large extent in towns specialised to particular classes of yarn and fabrics, no considerable movement has occurred from the depressed towns in the American section to the more prosperous. Even in the depressed areas themselves, the large towns have suffered less severely from unemployment during the postwar period than the smaller places. This contrast has sometimes been explained on the grounds that in the cities a high proportion of the occupied population finds work in the 'sheltered' industries. One may doubt whether this explanation is sufficient to account for the wide disparities that exist. It is at least possible that, since the larger towns usually have a more varied industrial structure than the smaller places, the former display exceptional alertness and capacity for adjustment to changed conditions.

One may conclude, then (at least provisionally), that a country whose industries were carried on in highly diversified centres would find the recurrent problem of transference less difficult to face than a country where the industrial areas were of a specialist character. The former would tend to breed an alert and easily adaptable population, and new manufactures would be likely to take root in existing industrial districts, at any rate the manufactures of the type called 'footloose'. A change in the direction of economic development might be effected in such a country without causing a prolonged period of maldistributed labour. One must not ignore, of course, the advantages that local specialisation sometimes confers. For some trades geographical concentration is no doubt inevitable; but it is arguable that the economies derived from such specialisation have been exaggerated by those who disregard the ever-changing character of the economic structure and the heavy social losses caused by periodical industrial migrations.

It may be objected that the location of industry is determined by economic forces and that these cannot be controlled by policy without detriment to progress. This proposition may be questioned. It is true that broad changes in location occur in response to market forces and that allocative efficiency might be endangered by measures introduced by the government to thwart them. But, in the past, the selection of the actual site for an industrial establishment has often been determined by chance. Specious reasons have been put forward to explain how trades have become located in the places where we now find them, but if one tries to relate these general explanations to the history of the pioneer-firms, one is often left with a feeling of scepticism. The chances of a birthplace, or the temporary advantages attached to a particular site, have often been decisive. This argument should not be pushed too far. In recent times large firms have usually taken their locational decisions after a careful assessment of the merits of alternative sites. For example, one of the first artificial silk factories in Britain was located near a coal-mining area where it could recruit female workers from the miners' families, workers who had previously found few opportunities for employment. Again, some firms may be tied to particular localities because of their dependence on raw material supplies, or on proximity to component-manufacturers. For the 'footloose' industries, however, some prompting by the government over the choice of sites for new ventures may be justified because it could make allowance for social costs ignored by the private entrepreneur. In other words, where the prospective advantages of alternative sites to the manufacturer do not differ substantially, it would be reasonable for the government to tilt the balance so as to favour the creation of diversified areas by diverting new industries to places at present highly specialised. A national policy of industrial location would thus have as its purpose both the alleviation of heavy localised unemployment and also the shaping of industrial centres which would be less vulnerable in times of change than the old specialised regions have shown themselves to be during the last decade.

5 Economic Thought and Contemporary Economic Policy[1]

It is sometimes said that economists show an unworthy preference for the safe side of prophecy—for writing and speaking after the event. But I shall not be too rash, I hope, if I suggest that one of the main differences between the economic data with which Sir Edward Gonner and Professor J. R. Bellerby, my distinguished predecessors, had to deal during their tenure of this Chair and the economic data which will concern economists for the next two or three decades will be found in the violent change in governmental economic policy that has taken place during the last few years. I am speaking now not merely of the reversion of this country to a protective system, for that is just a symptom of a deeper world change. I refer to the whole group of official measures which have been aimed at modifying the existing structure and organisation of industry, at the regulation of prices and output and at the maintenance of a particular distribution of productive resources. We have seen, in fact, the drastic modification, in some countries the final overthrow, of that system of free enterprise which spread from Great Britain over a large part of the world in the nineteenth century. The attitude of the economists to these changes has been on the whole hostile; almost to a man, in this and in many other countries, they have condemned the chief manifestations of this policy,[2] even though some may have approved of it in principle. This disagreement between the economists and the politicians has caused some bewilderment among those who are in neither group. I thought, therefore, that this might be an appropriate occasion on which to discuss the divergence between theory and practice, and, at the same time, to reply to certain criticisms that are levelled against professional economists. The chief of the criticisms, to deal with these first, is the reproach of ineffectiveness. Why, it is asked, have the economists allowed the world to get into its present confusion? How is it that they are unable to produce some agreed solution for our troubles, instead of quarrelling among themselves about theories which the layman has not begun to understand, or indulging in purely destructive criticisms of the efforts of the politicians? The economists are compared very unfavourably with the physical scientists. The physical scientists too may be at sixes and sevens, doubtful about the validity of principles of which they were once sure. But they can at any rate give us results. Indeed, some people think that they are too successful in assisting us in our efforts to control natural forces. If the physical scientists, so it is argued, for all their theoretical differences, can solve our technical problems, why cannot the economists solve our social and economic problems? What are economists for, if not for this? Surely, in economics as in other sciences, knowledge is desired chiefly as an instrument of control? Yet, say the critics, the economists spend their time in formulating more and more precise statements of formal relations between quantities, in working out an articulated system of equations, highly abstract and incomprehensible to the ordinary man. They may get some aesthetic pleasure out of this exercise, but are their conclusions relevant at the present time? Does the abstract world they contemplate bear any relation to reality? It seems not; for when they are asked for guidance on practical questions, their advice differs from economist to economist.

The reply which such a challenge elicits from the economist runs like this. First, in justifying his abstractions, he says that since controlled experiments are impossible to workers in the social sciences, he must employ some other method for isolating the forces which he desires to examine. The abstract deductive method enables him to do this. It may have its defects; but these arise out of the nature of the subject-matter and the economist is not to blame for them.

To the complaint that the present condition of the world testifies to the ineffectiveness of economists, the answer is simply that since economists are not in control of affairs, they cannot be held responsible for the mistakes of those who are. Economists have been consulted by governments on many occasions since 1918; but their advice has nearly always been ignored. The criticisms levelled by expert opinion against the economic provisions of the Treaty of Versailles have now been proved to be justified; but they were not accepted by governments at a time when such an acceptance might have led to the avoidance of disaster. The folly of many of the official valorisation schemes introduced to maintain prices at an artificial level was exposed by economists long before the collapse of those schemes and the intense depression that followed in agricultural countries made it apparent to all. The disastrous consequences of economic nationalism and of universal restrictions on the free movement of goods and persons have been emphasised repeatedly by economists; and politicians, at at least two great international economic conferences, have accepted these views; but the acceptance of this diagnosis as sound has had no effect whatever on political action. It seems that politicians, and indeed the public, look to the economist to provide not impartial advice and unbiased criticism but, rather, a theoretical justification for whatever policy is at the moment being pressed forward.

There is finally the complaint that economists have been far from unanimous in their advice on practical affairs, and in this complaint there is some justification. Yet differences among economists have been exaggerated. On many of the fundamental issues, such as those I have already mentioned, there has been a large measure of agreement among them. But certainly there have been, and are, important conflicts of opinion. Yet here, I suggest, many of the main differences have been in connection with matters on which unanimity is not to be expected at the present time among any body of men. When an economist is asked for advice on most questions of policy, his reply involves not merely economic analysis but also a judgment of what is politically practicable and politically desirable. And economists, like other men, may differ in these political judgments while agreeing in their economic analysis. For example, the conflict of opinion among economists over Great Britain's return to the gold standard in 1925 depended largely on whether or not it was considered possible, or desirable, for the country to implement the cost-deflation implied by that policy— a political judgment. Yet if the economist should set out all the political and ethical assumptions underlying his answer to every practical question, he would be called pedantic.

Nor is it to be expected that the economists should spend much of their time in discussing the fallacious explanations of our troubles which are so popular at the present time. The argument that the trade depression is due to the increased efficiency of the productive machine and that we should become richer if we produced less; the argument that all would be well if our governments made available unlimited supplies of currency; the view that a favourable balance of trade is more important than the total volume of trade; the argument of Mr Walter Elliott that agriculture is superior to industry because in agriculture nature works with man;[3] his more novel contention that, owing to technical improvements, international trade is unnecessary because things can now be produced equally well anywhere, and the remarkable conclusion to which he comes, namely, that it is necessary for the government to impose drastic restrictions to prevent people from buying imports which, according to his argument, they would have no advantage in buying anyhow; arguments of this kind have been disposed of by many economists in the course of the last century and a half, and the modern economist is perhaps unduly reluctant to repeat the refutations that he finds in the works of his predecessors.

Now these answers to the criticisms levelled against the economists are, I think, incontrovertible. But they raise another question. Much of what I have said was true of economists in the early nineteenth century, when they were able to give answers to practical questions with some degree of unanimity and, what is more, when their advice was accepted as a guide to policy. How can we explain the contrast between the enormous prestige and influence of economics in the generation following Ricardo and the position to-day? The contrast is indeed surprising, especially as the apparatus of economic enquiry has been greatly improved since that time. Yet from the end of the eighteenth century throughout the classical period the doctrines of the orthodox school were accepted by statesmen and were embodied in legislation. It is easy to find examples of this. In France the liberal measures of the last years of the *ancien régime* gave expression to the views of Turgot and the Physiocrats. The younger Pitt was influenced by Adam Smith's *Wealth of Nations*. The Poor Law of 1834 reflected the doctrines of Malthus. McCulloch supplied arguments which showed the economic advantage of large-scale farming and so weakened the resistance to the agricultural changes then going on. The Bank Charter Act of 1844 clearly revealed the economists' influence, and their arguments in favour of *laissez-faire* helped to destroy the restrictions on private enterprise, the privileges of the landed oligarchy and the protective system. And the influence of economics was not confined to statesmen; through the agency of Miss Martineau's tales it permeated the general public. It was a popular study.

Undoubtedly one important reason for the prestige enjoyed by classical economics was that its doctrines coincided with the interests of the new industrial and commercial class that was just rising to power. This class stood to benefit from a liberal trading policy and from the abolition of restrictions imposed by a government that was administratively inefficient and under the control of a landed aristocracy. The economists provided the theoretical justification for the policy of this new class. The Ricardian analysis of distribution, for example, demonstrated that the interest of the landed proprietors was necessarily antagonistic to that of other classes, and this analysis accorded well with the political cleavage of the times and supplied the arguments directed against the Corn Laws by both working-class and middle-class leaders.

But this was not the only cause of the economists' authority. Economic doctrine was then infused with the spirit of the times. There was no need then for the economist to make explicit the political or psychological assumptions which underlay his science, for the science was part of philosophic radicalism, the creed of the majority of the progressive thinkers. The economist found no difficulty in offering advice on practical questions, nor need he fear that his judgment would be derided by a fellow expert, for the same political bias was common to all the proponents of the science. As part of the dominant political philosophy, economics was strengthened by its contacts with other social studies which derived from the same source. The principle of utility which Bentham expounded formed the psychological foundation of economics, and this principle seemed an appropriate basis for a science since, as it has been said, it appeared to differ from other moral precepts in that it was the expression 'not of a subjective preference of the moralist but of an objective law of human nature'. The atomistic view of the State which these thinkers held was a view implicit in the current economic teaching. The close relationship between the economists and the utilitarians is forcibly demonstrated by a parallel consideration of Bentham's theory of punishment and Smith's theory of value. The 'natural' measure of punishment results, according to Bentham, from a comparison between the amount of physical suffering inflicted by the judge and the amount of physical suffering which follows from the act classed as a crime. The 'natural' measure of value, according to Smith, arises from a comparison between the amount of pain suffered to produce an object and the amount of pleasure which is expected to result from the acquisition of that object.[4] These two thinkers were clearly surveying very different fields of study from the same point of view. In the sphere of juris-

prudence Austin, and in history Buckle, worked within the same
philosophical tradition. Even the theory of evolution was influenced by Darwin's reflections on the Malthusian principle of
population. Thus in the early nineteenth century economics was
part of a large group of studies bound together by the same underlying principles. It was part of philosophic radicalism and as such it
accepted the political ends of that school. It accepted the thesis of
the natural identity of individual and social interests[5]; it based
itself on an atomistic view of the State and a hedonistic psychology.
The policy it advocated was at bottom a policy of *laissez-faire*,
freedom of individual contract and the abolition of restrictions
on the movement of goods and persons. And this policy was in
accordance with the interests of a powerful class and with the
prevailing tendency in other social studies.[6] Little wonder, then,
that the classical economists were able to influence policy. Publicists, or perhaps I should say prophets, like Carlyle and Ruskin,
novelists like Dickens and Disraeli, satirists like Peacock, might
scorn the utilitarians and the economists. Yet they could do little
to stem the tide when the only alternative seemed to be a maintenance of the authoritarian and mercantilist State.

Today the situation is widely different. No powerful party or
social class believes that its interests are to be fostered by a pursuance of the policy of the philosophic radicals. The social evils
that accompanied the rise of modern industrialism have discredited
laissez-faire in the minds of 'progressive' thinkers. The psychologists
have abandoned hedonism, and a new conception of the State
has replaced that of the utilitarians. In economic policy, with our
tariffs and trade restrictions, with our concern for that odd and
ancient fetish the balance of trade, with our talk of self-sufficient
empires, we are back in the seventeenth century. For the moment,
indeed, the world seems to have abandoned even its belief in
individual liberty as it was understood in the nineteenth century,
and to be drawing its inspiration from policies which have no basis
in reason at all, although doubtless the leaders of the dominant
movements would defend themselves by saying, like Mr Mystic in
Peacock's *Melincourt*, that they do not expect anyone but themselves to see the connection of their ideas, as they arrange their
thoughts on an entirely new principle.

Now these changes in allied studies and in the world of fact have
naturally affected economics. And a glance at some of these effects
will reveal a source of weakness in the subject. One result has been

to rob the economist of a working psychology. The classical economists who accepted the current 'pleasure and pain' psychology developed a theory of real cost. The end of production could be regarded as the pleasures or satisfactions received from goods; while labour (together with the so-called 'abstinence' of the capitalist) represented the 'pain' of this process, and this 'pain' was equivalent to the *real cost* of production. Pleasures and pains, it was argued, formed the ultimate quantities in economics. But this analysis was necessarily modified when the inadequacy of hedonistic psychology was demonstrated, with the result that the idea of 'real cost' has tended to disappear from economics. Among many modern economists the real cost of production of any article means merely the value of other goods which might have been produced instead of it by the capital and labour employed. It is a conception of displaced alternatives; as one economist has said, the real cost of obtaining anything is what must be surrendered in order to get it.[7] This is a different conception from the old idea of real cost; for according to Smith 'the real price of every thing, what every thing really costs to the man who wants to acquire it, is the toil and trouble of acquiring it'.[8] Similarly, in dealing with demand, a large body of modern economists no longer base their analysis on utility, but confine their attention to the objective facts of consumer preferences as revealed in the market.

The changed point of view is very clearly brought out in the writings of one of the younger English theorists who declares that economics is not concerned with ends at all, but only with the means by which the ends set for itself by society may be most economically realised. He says further that modern economics is based on the objective phenomena of the market—not on any assumption about the nature of man.[9] This interpretation implies that economics should cut itself off from a psychological background and should abandon its normative doctrines. By a development of this kind the economist can make his science more objective, more abstract and more universal than it was formerly. But it may be doubted whether this change really represents an advance. It has certainly helped to rob the economist of his popular influence and has rendered him less able than his predecessors to give a guide to policy. To this the answer is sometimes given that economics is not concerned with giving a guide to policy; it ought to be classed rather with the physical sciences. With this view I disagree. There is a fundamental difference between the physical and the social sciences. When the physical scientist formulates a hypothesis or discovers a law governing the relationship between things, he does not thereby alter that relationship. The course of the stars is not, so far as we know, changed in any way by the theories that astronomers have held about their movements. But when the economist formulates a theory, he is liable to alter the data on which he is working. Let me give one or two examples. There can be little doubt that the attempt by some of the early economists to destroy the dualism established by tradition between the public and the private interest, their theory that the best means of promoting the social wellbeing was to allow self-interest free play, greatly strengthened the operation of the self-regarding instinct by making it respectable and so helped to establish the reign of a market economy. To take another example, whether we agree or not with Marx's view of the part played by class struggles in social evolution, there is no doubt that his theory had helped to intensify class consciousness since his time, and so has affected the subsequent social and political history of the world. Thus, economics must necessarily be more than a scientific enquiry into the relations between certain quantities; the economist cannot leave ends out of account when he is theorising, for (whether he likes it nor not) his work may help to determine what those ends shall be.

So far, then, from regarding the divorce of economics from political theory and psychology as an advance I think that this divorce accounts for some of the ineffectiveness of modern economics. Undoubtedly the modern science is far superior to classical economics in its analysis of the major theoretical problems; it is a more powerful instrument for analysing the conditions of a given situation; it is admirable as a weapon of destructive criticism—for bringing to light inconsistencies in the different parts of national economic policy, and for showing the inconsistency between the policy aimed at and the means by which governments attempt to carry out the policy. But it is weaker than the classical school on the constructive side, because it is not based, as the older economics was based, on a widely accepted social and political philosophy, and because it has no coherent and explicit theory of how people act. That economists feel this lack is shown by the fact that when they leave the realm of pure theory and pass on to deal with applied problems they are forced to make political and psychological assumptions. These assumptions tend to be the assumptions of the classical school—an atomistic State, a hedonistic psychology and a cosmopolitan world. The economist comes trailing his clouds of philosophic radicalism into a world that is drifting farther and farther from belief in that doctrine. So, that part of his teaching which is independent of these philosophical obsessions[10] and which demonstrates the inconsistency of modern economic policy and the unforeseen consequences attendant on particular action is unheeded, because the standpoint as a whole is discredited.

I should like to illustrate this point by referring to the formal analysis of value. It is the fashion among an important school of economists to base their analysis of value on the objective facts of demand, rather than on utility. In other words, consumer preferences as expressed in the amount of money offered for various goods are regarded as the basic quantities with which the economist must deal. Now in pure theory there is no need to associate consumer preferences with the satisfaction received for an outlay of money— the latter is a matter of psychological speculation, the former is a fact which can be observed in the market. But when the economist passes on to deal with questions of social policy and with the distribution of resources in the real world, he necessarily introduces the idea of satisfaction resulting from these economic processes. He is bound to do so, since in dealing with social policy we are supposed to be dealing with an 'ought to be' as well as with an 'is'. Many economists argue (when they reach this point) that when consumer preferences are free, then, on the whole and with some qualifications, resources will be distributed in the most economical and desirable fashion, and that any interference with this free choice, except in certain specified conditions, will reduce the total satisfactions enjoyed by the individuals who make up society. It follows then that State planning, as it is called, will reduce these satisfactions, since planning implies an arbitrary decision concerning the allocation of resources. The presumption remains then in favour of the free market. But this antithesis between production according to arbitrarily judged needs and production according to the actual wants of individuals as determined by their free offers of money for goods is not really so sharp as it appears. The State must necessarily exercise an arbitrary influence on the nature of production whether it wishes to or not. Consumer preferences, the sort of things that people buy, would be different from what they are at present if the distribution of wealth were different, and the distribution of wealth is largely determined by institutional factors, such as the laws of property and inheritance. Furthermore, consumer preferences depend in some measure on the nature of the persuasive influences that are brought to bear on the public. If the State had not taught us all to read since 1870, consumer preferences would be very different from what they are now, since the influence of advertisement and the Press in canalising the demand for goods would be less than it is, and the demand for those goods and services which lend themselves to written advertisement would not have increased so fast as it has done. New wants are cultivated by a process of education, and clearly wants will be different if we leave this educative process in the hands of salesmen, advertisers, press lords and cinema magnates from what they would be if the educative process were in the hands of some other agency. The absolute character of consumer preferences, of the consumers' freedom of choice, disappears the moment we introduce these considerations, and the impossibility of ruling out ethical and psychological considerations from any analysis of an applied problem is at once apparent. As one of the most stimulating of the American writers has implied,[11] we may very well drift towards social and biological disaster if we are left with this so-called freedom to acquire what salesmen and advertisers make us think we want. If so, where are the satisfactions which consumer preferences are supposed to represent?

The reply of a fashionable school of economists to arguments of this kind is that they are not concerned with these larger social and psychological problems. All they attempt to do is to state the conditions of equilibrium given a certain scale of consumer preferences. To this I would say that economics must be more than a series of equations, and that if it is to provide any guide to policy, as I think it should, it cannot leave psychological and social considerations out of account. In practice, economists of all schools admit this implicity whenever they attempt to deal with current problems. I hope I have made clear what the dilemma of the modern economist is. It is that if he clings to the older traditional treatment of these problems, his enquiry is partly vitiated by the weakness of his psychology and the lack of any guiding political principle. If he contents himself with a statement of the conditions of equilibrium given a certain scale of consumer preferences, if he cuts adrift from his hedonistic psychology, then, as an acute critic of modern economics has said, he becomes incapable of passing any judgment on the distribution of resources in the actual world.[12]

Another change which has occurred since the days of Ricardo, a change which has, as yet, insufficiently influenced the corpus of economic theory, has been the alteration in the underlying social situation. Economic science was built up when industrial society was only just beginning to assume its modern form. At a time when the country was emerging from the age-long poverty of the agricultural state it was clearly desirable, in the interests of the maximisation of the national income, that labour should be drawn into those employments where its productivity was greatest. Such restrictions on labour mobility as were due to ignorance, habit or legislation seemed clearly mischievous and demanded abolition. Further, the weakness of trade unions and the labour movement as a whole, the undemocratic nature of the government and the inarticulateness of the masses, meant that labour's own resistance to the pressure of economic forces was weak. When changes in technique or demand required a redistribution of labour among other employments, then economic forces could be left to bring this about. Workers were driven out of industries in which they were no longer needed, by starvation wages and unemployment as well as by a desire to better themselves in the new higher-wage occupations. The social consequences of these changes to particular groups might be regarded as regrettable; but they were considered inevitable, and in the long run, salutary. This was the normal method by which the price system secured a more effective distribution of labour, the normal method of providing for an increase in the national income. Resistances of workers, or employers, to movements of this kind could be treated as 'frictions'—as temporary interferences with the working of economic laws, and they would, it was thought, tend to disappear as men became better informed, more rational and able to follow the dictates of enlightened self-interest. But today, as we know, these 'frictions' have developed into rigidities. Social resistances to these economic changes can no longer be ignored. They are part and parcel of the situation which the economist has to examine.[13]

Some economists. however, are unwilling to admit this. They say: 'Our job is merely to describe the economic conditions inherent in a particular situation. We are not concerned with social policy. For example, if a particular country loses some of its advantages as a producer, then its labour and capital can only be fully employed if incomes are reduced. If this reduction is resisted a chronic depression is inevitable'. This type of argument was common during the last decade—before the onset of the world

56 *British Industry and Economic Policy*

depression. It was said that the main cause of the chronic unemployment experienced by Great Britain during the postwar period was due to the fact that wages were too high. A reduction of wages—and of other rigid incomes too—was the proper method of restoring employment. This wage-adjustment and the redistribution of labour that was necessary were being hindered by unemployment insurance and the strength of the trade unions. So, it was argued, the proper policy to be pursued was to modify the provisions of the Unemployment Insurance and the Trade Union Acts, and then wage rigidity would disappear. Now I will suggest that, even if this diagnosis were correct, the solution here set out was totally unreal. Unemployment insurance and the present status of the trade unions are the product of a particular stage of social and economic development. They are properly to be regarded as institutional facts which may be modified by legislation, but of which account must be taken in analysing the situation and in formulating remedies for it. In the early nineteenth century the situation was such that in practical questions of this kind it was possible to isolate economic from social and political phenomena. Subsequent developments have made this an unreal treatment of a concrete situation such as the one I have mentioned.

As another example of the argument I am advancing, let us consider the American agricultural situation. Long before the present slump set in, many groups among the American agriculturists were suffering severely from the competition of lower-cost producers, and this in a world in which the demand for many types of raw materials is very inelastic. The orthodox remedy for a situation of this kind is to rely on bankruptcy and lowered incomes to drive the high-cost producers from the industry until its size has been reduced to that required by the new situation. But this process is bound to be slow among farmers and small highly-specialised raw-material producers, since it is difficult for them to transfer their activities elsewhere and to find new uses for their land. Further, in a democratic country, the distressed producers can exert a much stronger pressure on the government than could the English peasant or handloom weaver a century ago. So the government was forced by political pressure to respond to this situation by instituting valorisation schemes for the purpose of raising the price of the commodity to a level which would satisfy the farmer and so relieve him at the expense of the public. Such schemes, of course, provided no remedy. In fact, they made matters worse in the long run, for higher prices at once induced consumers to buy less and producers to produce more, as Mr Elliott has since found in this country. The result in America was an accumulation of unsold stocks and, ultimately, a collapse of prices, with disastrous consequences to all the members of the artificially swollen industries. Now the economist had no difficulty in showing the absurdity of remedies of this kind. He has attributed to this type of governmental interference with economic processes responsibility for the intensity and duration of the present depression. But the traditional remedy of the liberal economist—to allow economic forces to work themselves out in the way I have described—was not one that the social and political situation of the time permitted.

Again, let us consider the American Recovery Programme. Many parts of this, though not all of course, seem to depend on a number of economic fallacies. Yet the economist has difficulty in discovering a practical alternative. The view of one important group of economists, that economic forces should have been left to produce the liquidation which would create the conditions for recovery, is a view that takes no account of the temper of the American people last spring. Many of the things that President Roosevelt is doing may retard recovery and may even damage the American economic system. But to have done nothing, to have pursued a *laissez-faire* policy, might very well have produced a social upheaval in the United States which would have left no economic system worth having.

Professor Gregory, having in mind certain criticisms of this kind, has replied to them in the following passage. He says:

Why has the depression which set in in the autumn of 1929 lasted so much longer than the depressions of the nineteenth century? I answer unhesitatingly, because the precedent boom was allowed to go on unchecked to a much greater extent, and because, again, in the name of 'stabilization', the necessary corrective measures have not been applied. Instead of insisting upon the vital necessity of greater flexibility, an increasing degree of *inflexibility* in all directions has characterized the last four years.

It is no answer to say that the measures which would have cured the depression, had they been applied, were impossible of application because 'public opinion would not have tolerated them'. No doubt patients very often refuse to follow the advice given them by their doctors, but, if they subsequently die, their

death is not usually regarded as evidence of the inherent
wickedness of the advice given.[14]

Now the analogy of the doctor and the patient might be true
enough if society represented a single interest, if there were no
conflict of interest among different social classes, if the losses
occasioned by economic readjustment and liquidation of the type
he has in mind fell equally on all members of society, or at any rate
on the shoulders of those responsible for the mistakes, *so that no
sense of injustice was aroused in the process.* In fact, of course, the
sufferings occasioned by the orthodox remedy would necessarily be
partial in their incidence. The structure of industry being as it is,
members of over-expanded industries would be condemned to
desperately low incomes and huge capital losses for a very long
period—until the necessary readjustments had been secured. And
this fate the members of these industries consider unjust—they
think that their burdens should be shared by society as a whole,
since the over-expansion in the first place may have been due to the
pursuance of a particular monetary policy by the State for which
they were not responsible. So far as this attitude is common (and
given the present distribution of political power) I should say, then,
that Professor Gregory's analogy is misleading, and that the orthodox measures which he favours are rather of the nature of the
operation which is certain to cure the specific disease, but is likely
to kill the patient with the shock to his constitution.

In this connection the degree of flexibility which it is reasonable
to expect from a modern society is a most important question, but
one that has scarcely been discussed. The economist has rightly
emphasised the absurdity of the common expectation that society
can enjoy both stability (or security) and at the same time rapid
economic progress. If we are determined to press on with technical
change and so to enjoy the benefits of greater cheapness, and if we
expect to be able to indulge freely a capricious demand for ever-
changing classes of goods, then we must be prepared for violent and
frequent fluctuations in the fortunes of different groups of producers, for frequent redistributions of labour and capital among
different employments, for great changes in the relative economic
importance of different localities and different countries—in a
word, for extreme flexibility in our social and economic life. The
troubles that have overwhelmed us in the last few years are due
largely to the fact that society has been unwilling or unable to

display the flexibility which is a necessary accompaniment of rapid economic change. In this diagnosis there is no doubt but that the orthodox economist is correct. The vested interests of particular groups of capitalists or wage-earners cannot be regarded as sacred in a society that demands this progress and this freedom. But the question that arises immediately is how far is society willing, or able, to sacrifice its social and political ideals (for flexibility implies this sacrifice) in order to enjoy greater wealth and greater freedom in its choice of goods. Is rapid economic progress compatible with the type of social organisation that we possess at present? Is it possible to reconcile the present economic system and the present social and political policy? Can we realise the benefits of one without abandoning the ideals implicit in the other? Here is a conflict that was not apparent in the days of the classical school. A modern economist with his eye on the economic dislocation caused by the failure of governments and peoples to accept the conditions inherent in a progressive economy of the modern type may conclude that the abolition of the 'rigidities' is the only solution. Yet these 'rigidities' are largely an expression of deepseated political loyalties and conceptions of social justice, which are just as real as the economic forces with which they often come into conflict. To borrow a parable from D. H. Robertson—one which he employs in talking of some of the remedies that have been proposed for dealing with the trade cycle: 'When I am killed by a motor car in the streets of London, my slayer may maintain that the accident happened because of my "rigidity", because I was too slow in getting out of the way; but my indignant relatives will probably remain of the opinion that it happened because the motor car came so fast that, given my limited powers of rapid movement, I had no possible chance of escaping'.[15]

The inconsistency between the principles underlying our economic system and those governing our social and political policy is partly due, no doubt, to the fact that the full consequences of economic actions are never clearly before us at the point when decisions are made. As a result, technical progress, in itself desirable, leads to social developments which are entirely unforeseen and undesired. In a world in which the majority of people, even if all our present productive resources were fully employed, would have insufficient wealth to enable them to enjoy a civilised existence, we naturally approve of the technical progress which makes us wealthier and gives us more complicated and therefore more interesting lives; but we disapprove most heartily of many of the social changes which our new technique provokes. For example, we are anxious to be able to buy our basic foodstuffs more cheaply, and so we applaud the increasing efficiency of agriculture; but we are inclined to look with disfavour on the rural depopulation and the decay of agriculture in the parts of the world least favourable for the application of advanced techniques, although those are the inevitable consequences of the improvements. Under the present economic system man is always getting changes which he did not foresee or desire in company with (and necessarily so) changes of which he approves. Now within the price system there exists no method of balancing the advantages and disadvantages of any change so that they are clearly before the individual (or the collection of individuals) whose actions determine the change. For the benefits of the change come as measurable financial gains to individuals as consumers or as wage-earners or profit-earners. And it is individuals—individual consumers seeking by their purchases in the market to satisfy their wants more effectively and cheaply, and individual wage-earners and profit-earners seeking to improve the returns to their efforts—who determine what the change shall be. But the losses—the unforeseen and undesired results of the change—are of necessity left out of account in the calculations of these individuals, for the losses accrue to the social system as a whole, or to particular groups within it; and as these losses are often not measurable financial losses, they cannot be evaluated in the same terms as the gains. When the losses or the burdens due to the change become intolerable—usually long after the change has taken place—society, or the part of it adversely affected, takes defensive action through its political machinery. And the corrective measures which it adopts often destroy many of the advantages accompanying the technical change and produce the sort of chaos which we have at present. According to a distinguished American economist, J. M. Clark, the way out of the difficulty lies in the institution of public control at the point where decisions are made in the economic process itself.[16] Government interference has been so clumsy and harmful during the past decade because it has proceeded on the principle of leaving those decisions to be made in the market and then of attempting to remedy unforeseen or undesired consequences by palliative measures long afterwards. Just how the public control is to be instituted, whether (governments being as they are) it would be effectively and wisely exercised are debatable questions—and questions that lie far beyond the horizon of this paper. Even if it is true that J. M. Clark's proposition (which, of course, states the socialist solution) represents a *logical* method of avoiding the disastrous consequences of the conflict between the principles underlying our economic system and our social and political ideals, it does not follow that the practical results of its application to policy would be beneficial. Nevertheless, it indicates the line of action that governments and most advanced industrial societies are likely to favour in the future. Whether they do so or not, however, a solution of the problem will continue to elude us until we have a clearer conception of the ends we wish to promote than we have at present, and until we have abandoned the fatuous pursuit of economic, political and social purposes that are inconsistent with one another.

6 State Intervention in Industry[1]

The problem of the State's part in economic life has been frequently debated since the day when John Stuart Mill devoted the last section of his 'Principles of Political Economy' to this subject. But the problem is not hackneyed, because, with changes in economic circumstances and in the political outlook, it takes on a new form from decade to decade and needs continual restatement. It does not lend itself easily to scientific discussion, for it involves both political and economic considerations; and in controversy these two aspects are often confused, so that a judgment which has really been determined by political opinion is made to appear as though it were a conclusion derived from a process of economic reasoning. Now no-one will contend that economic doctrine itself enables us to decide whether this or that action by the State in the economic field is justifiable or not. A judgment of that nature must depend upon many factors outside the province of economics. For example, those who hold the views of the early radicals, who believed that the State's functions should be limited to providing a sound currency, enforcing contracts, and defining property rights, naturally deal with any question of intervention not upon economic grounds but in the light of their own philosophy. On the other hand, those who regard the profit motive as unworthy or the wage-contract as incompatible with the dignity of man, are likely—again for non-economic reasons—to be in favour of a wide extension of public control. Persons with strong political convictions such as these are often indifferent to the economic aspect of problems. Their judgments do not emerge from an economic analysis of the issue under discussion, but are in fact predetermined. Even those persons who take full account of the economic aspect may regard that aspect as of secondary importance, and if they do so the economist has no quarrel with them provided that the true grounds for the judgment are clearly indicated. But the fact that economic considerations are generally not decisive in questions of this kind does not mean that economics has nothing to offer to the discussion of them. Frequently a pseudo-economic argument is put forward to justify a policy which really derives its driving-force from quite other motives, and so the economist has the task of defining the issues involved and of showing how far the decision may be justified on purely economic grounds.

It is, of course, not possible here to deal with the whole vast question of the State's part in economic life. This article will be concerned merely with certain aspects of intervention that have been prominent in recent years, chiefly with the efforts of the government to determine the structure and organisation of industry. This is not a new field of State activity. For instance, for years past in most countries governments have had a definite attitude towards industrial combinations, an attitude which has been expressed in their legislation. In prewar Germany the law and public opinion were favourably disposed towards cartels and combinations in restraint of trade; while in prewar America the government made determined efforts to break up large combinations and to preserve competitive conditions. Our own government took a midway course; but, on the whole, public opinion regarded them with hostility. Within recent years the question has assumed prominence in this country, as elsewhere, because the State has abandoned its traditional policy and has been actively encouraging particular forms of organisation within the staple trades. In transport, in several branches of agriculture, in the coal, iron and steel, and cotton industries, and in fishing it has intervened with the deliberate purpose of calling into existence a form of organisation different from that worked out by businessmen engaged in those industries. The new form usually involves the concentration of control and often the establishment of a complete monopoly.

To explain this change in policy one can point to the depression which has threatened the existence of a great part of several leading industries. Many of them are among those considered to be especially important from a political standpoint or those in which decay has created serious social problems. Government attention has been attracted to coalmining largely because its plight has led to heavy localised unemployment. Support has been given to shipping and agriculture because those industries are associated with national prestige and defence, and with a way of life and a type of skill that are believed to be particularly valuable to the community's social and political experience. Thus intervention has not arisen out of a general desire to raise the level of economic efficiency; its direction has not been determined by the fact that the organisation of some trades has failed to satisfy a criterion of effectiveness, but by political and social reasons. The State has wished for such reasons to maintain some industries at a certain size or to keep the incomes of wage-earners or profit-earners in other industries above the level warranted by the economic conditions of those industries. The State has several means for achieving these ends. It may grant a subsidy to a decaying industry; it may increase that industry's competitive strength in the home market by imposing a duty on imports; it may help to create a monopolistic organisation which enables those concerned in the trade to get higher incomes, or sometimes facilitates the spreading of employment. Finally, it may rationalise the industry, i.e. it may promote a form of industrial combination which will permit costs to be reduced. It is over the last two methods that confusion is likely to arise. For both of them involve the concentration of control in the industry; and to the outsider the form of organisation appropriate to one purpose may be indistinguishable from the form appropriate to the other, and quite different, purpose. Moreover, the combine which the State may have promoted with the object of securing reductions in costs may use its power over the market, once it has been created, to exact higher prices and may neglect to introduce the economies which the new organisation is supposed to make possible.

Intervention which creates monopoly and leads to higher prices cannot be condemned as immoral. The poet tells us that when Divine Justice left the earth her last steps were among the farmers. Economists cannot claim that the State is mistaken when it acts in such a way as to raise the price of bacon and so to increase the incomes of pig-breeders, whose qualities are presumably so much more attractive to the Divinity than those of chocolate manufacturers or accountants. That is a question of values and is outside the province of economics. But the economist can attempt to measure the cost of the action to the community as a whole. He can also demand that the motives leading to the intervention shall be clearly expressed and that the issue shall not be obscured by appeals to pseudo-economic arguments in justification for the action. The quaint assumption of many of the Agricultural Marketing Boards that a rise in price will leave the quantity of demand unchanged may rightly be exposed by him. Again, it is sometimes said, perhaps with justice, that a country with a population divided equally among agriculture, manufacturing industry, and commerce has a better-balanced and more varied *social* life than a country which is more highly specialised. But this argument is often illegitimately carried over into economics, and there it emerges as the proposition that the first type of country possesses a more stable *economic* system than the other type, because the markets of agriculture and manufactures are reciprocal. This, however, is true of any groups of industries. The income that accrues to those engaged in the cotton industry is available for the purchase of coal, metal goods, and so on, just as is that of agriculturalists; while the income of persons in the coal trade is used for buying manufactured goods no less than for buying agricultural products.

Still, while economic reasoning may be employed to refute pseudo-economic arguments that have been advanced in favour of particular schemes or organisation, and to expose the true nature of the schemes, it cannot challenge the social and political motives and arguments which are usually behind them. Often people wonder why governments have persistently followed economic policies which expert economic opinion has condemned. No satisfactory reply has been given to the expert criticisms, and yet political action has remained unaffected by them. The explanation is that economists and politicians have conducted their disputations on different planes of thought. The economists have directed their criticism against the feeble economic arguments that have been put forward to justify certain acts of intervention of the kind here under discussion; but they have failed to see that those arguments are merely a cloak for the real reasons, which are political and social in character. Their criticism, therefore, seems irrelevant to the politicians. It may be asked why a cloak has been considered necessary. The answer is that in the past economic policy has usually been discussed in terms of costs and proceeds. So, even today, when economic considerations are no longer held to be paramount, politicians cast their arguments in an economic form, The result is to confuse the real issues and divert expert criticisms to aspects of the problem that seem to the government relatively unimportant.

So far the argument has gone to show that the *direction* of State intervention is determined by political and social reasons, and not by economic reasons, and that often the form of organisation that is created by the State is due to those reasons also. But in imposing a new form of organisation on an industry, the government has frequently declared that, besides improving the incomes of the members of those industries, the scheme will bring about a reduction of costs and so benefit the community. In other words, the schemes have usually been defended on economic grounds. It is true that up to the present their success from this point of view has not been striking; but are we to conclude that State action cannot effect any improvement in an industry's organisation? Are the planners, who think that costs might be reduced if the structure of every industry were rationalised, hopelessly engaged? This is a question that can be examined in isolation—without the intrusion of politics.

There are in every branch of trade at a particular time a certain scale of operations and a certain form of organisation that are appropriate for that trade. The scale and form for one trade are likely to be unsatisfactory for another, as they are determined by many factors which differ from industry to industry—the size of the market and the nature of demand, the technique of production and marketing, the nature of the raw material supplies and the labour supply, and the kind of management that is required, to mention the most obvious. Under competition the organisation appropriate to the peculiar conditions in each industry will be worked out by the businessmen concerned with it. Although the ideally best organisation may not be attained in any trade, yet businessmen who are least successful in their efforts to approach it will fail to sustain themselves in competition with the others. So the most efficient scale and form of organisation are not matters to be determined arbitrarily or derived from general principles—they have to be arrived at by people actually engaged in each industry by reference to changing conditions of demand and technique. Almost every trade has some peculiarities which force it to develop a type of organisation in some respects different from that of the rest. Further, as conditions are always altering, the most appropriate form of organisation in any trade changes from time to time.

It may sometimes happen that industries fail to adjust their organisation to a change in conditions or that the process of adjustment is too slow for the maintenance of the previous standard of efficiency. For example, some contend that the preservation of independent organisations on the manufacturing and marketing sides of the Lancashire cotton industry has made it very difficult to bring about the reduction of costs necessary to meet postwar conditions. The merchants, it is said, try to maintain themselves against the growing fierceness of competition by ordering fabrics with slight differences of weave and design. This practice has an unfortunate effect on weaving and finishing costs, because it is impossible to obtain long runs when there are innumerable varieties of product. The total business of the cotton industry is less than it would otherwise be on account of the trade's unsatisfactory structure. It is curious that this defect is usually attributed to excessive competition, when it actually arises because competitive forces are acting imperfectly in the trade; that is to say, it is due to the intrusion of monopolistic elements. In other industries, also, in which demand has been reduced and a contraction has occurred, costs are kept up, so it is claimed, by the 'goodwill' of the several firms which delays the concentration of output on the technically most efficient. In such cases there appear to be grounds for State intervention for the purpose of hastening the adjustment of industry to meet the new conditions. To this principle there can be few objections.

It is, however, in the application of the principle to particular cases that difficulties arise. If the government is to plan the organisation of an industry, how is it to obtain the knowledge that may enable it to determine the content of the plan? The substitution of planning for the free market will be to no advantage if the planned form is less efficient than the old one. The appropriate form cannot be deduced from general principles, since it differs in each industry according to technical and other conditions peculiar to that industry. It is highly unlikely that persons outside the industry can discover a form more efficient than that worked out by men who have spent their lives in running it. It has been suggested that the general trend of industrial organisation at home and abroad may provide some guide to administrators. Yet there seems little reason for supposing that because some industries have been successfully conducted by large combinations, other industries, which have not hitherto moved in that direction, may benefit by being forced to do so. The refusal of the latter to adopt a trustified form may be completely justified by technical and marketing conditions. It has also been suggested that the judgment of industrial leaders should be regarded as a sanction for reorganisation schemes. If the chief manufacturers in any industry are in favour of a particular scheme, cannot the State conclude that it might with advantage be enforced over all of them? Many planners would agree; others would prefer to put the point in a rather different way and affirm that the State is justified in enforcing on an industry the form of organisation that the majority of its members want. At first sight this answer seems reasonable; but it may be challenged from several points of view.

The proposed change in organisation, since it is designed to meet the troubles of a whole industry, usually involves the concentration of control—the establishment of an authority possessed of some degree of monopolistic power, such as the Marketing Boards in agriculture or the price associations affiliated to the British Iron and Steel Federation. In other words, a scheme, in practice, never involves merely the adjustment of organisation to enable the industry to increase its efficiency within the framework of existing market conditions; the scheme leads also to a change in these market conditions themselves—the substitution of monopoly for competition in many instances. Thus, businessmen, when giving their approval to a proposed rationalisation scheme, are not much concerned with it as a method by which costs can be reduced. They fully recognise the fact that the new organisation may enable them to take advantage of the more favourable market conditions that the institution of monopoly will create for them. For some years before 1932 the government, which was apparently convinced of the economies to be derived from rationalisation, had been pressing the members of the iron and steel industry to form large combinations; but little movement in this direction took place until the imposition of heavy import duties in 1932 freed the industry from foreign competition in the home market and so provided manufacturers with greater opportunities for monopolistic exploitation.

There is another objection to the view that the opinions of the leaders or of the majority in an industry should be decisive. In every trade there are firms working at different levels of efficiency, and usually the more efficient are in process of absorbing the business of the others. A scheme for rationing output in agreed proportions (usually determined by past experience) may commend itself to the majority because it will help them in their competition with rivals of outstanding efficiency. If majority rule is allowed to decide, such a scheme may be imposed on the industry against the wishes of the few; but this decision will clearly be to the disadvantage of the community, because it will impede the transference of demand to the more efficient (i.e. the lower-cost) sources of supply. If, on the other hand, the leaders are allowed to exert the greatest influence, other difficulties may arise. The leaders in a trade are those in control of the largest and most prominent firms. But these firms are not always the most progressive. So their directors' interests may lie in checking the development of new and enterprising firms, and they will be likely to support a scheme which helps them to do this.

The difficulty of defining an industry is another source of confusion. Firms that are generally considered to form part of the same industry are often engaged in very different processes or types of manufactures. The organisation suitable to one branch of the trade may be inappropriate to another, because of the different technical and marketing conditions under which they operate. It is significant that the opposition to the iron and steel scheme came mainly from firms with special types of products. Thus, of the six members of the executive committee who opposed the scheme put forward by the iron and steel trade in 1933, three were producers of foundry iron and one was a wrought-iron manufacturer, who were all faced with very different problems from those with which the great concerns producing steel-making iron and ingot steel had to deal. It might seem easy to exclude firms of this kind from a general scheme; but as one branch of a trade shades into another, it is always very difficult to decide where the line of exclusion is to be drawn. A firm may demand to be allowed to stand outside a scheme not so much because its technical and marketing problems are really different from those of the rest of the industry (though that will be the ostensible reason), but because it hopes to take advantage of the higher prices that are anticipated from the operation of the scheme and at the same time to be free to extend its output without the restrictions to which the others will be subjected. An outsider can seldom say whether the objections to inclusion in a scheme are legitimate or not.

So far the discussion has been confined to cases in which the business leaders or the majority of the manufacturers are in favour of a State-enforced scheme. What is to be thought of State intervention when it takes the form of imposing on an industry a form of organisation of which the vast majority of the members disapprove? This has happened in the coal industry. Is such action always to be condemned on economic grounds? Where strong opposition of this kind exists, the government obviously ought to act with caution;

but the scheme is not necessarily to be condemned for such a reason. Businessmen act from a variety of motives. Manufacturers in industries in which there is a strong individualistic tradition may sometimes object to a scheme merely because it involves compulsion by the government or what they consider to be an unjustifiable interference with property rights. The opposition in the coal trade to the proposals of the Coal Mines Reorganisation Commission seems to be based on a dislike of the compulsion with which they are associated rather than on a disbelief in the advantages of large combined concerns. Sometimes businessmen may approve of a particular scheme that is put up to them by the government, but may fear that it is the forerunner of legislation which will deprive them ultimately of the control of their industry, and they may oppose the scheme for that reason. Again, in large companies, management is often in the hands of men who have no substantial investments in those companies, and the expressed attitude of the firms to a rationalisation scheme may be influenced by other considerations than economy or financial success. Those in control of some firms may favour a scheme not because it will be for the benefit of the trade as a whole but because it may help them to extend their administrative range and so satisfy their ambitions. On the other hand, others may oppose a scheme, even if it is likely to benefit their shareholders or the public, because they fear that they might lose their jobs if a consolidation of firms were effected.

If a decision cannot be left wholly to the businessmen themselves, cannot the government take the advice of an impartial tribunal or commission which hears evidence from all parties? The efficiency of this method may be doubted. The analogy of the law courts is misleading, owing to the absence of any objective standards which can be applied to test the efficiency of different kinds of organisation. So long as the competitive market exists, of course, there is a rough-and-ready test of the relative efficiency of each firm. But when competitive conditions are drastically modified or abolished (as happens under a rationalisation scheme), then the objective test disappears. In a law court the judge has to apply a definite body of principles to the cases brought before him. Even on a tribunal like a Trade Board the task of the chairman and the other appointed members is fairly straightforward, for they are guided, in judging whether wage-rates in a particular trade should be altered, by such objective tests as movements in the cost-of-living index and by what is happening to wages in other industries. Further, the Trade

Board adjudicator takes the wage system and the relations between the wages of different grades of workers in each industry as he finds them. He is not called upon to alter the whole structure of the wage system. But the adjudicator in a dispute about rival types of industrial organisation has no such aids or tests, but only the weak presumptions already discussed. The most important evidence with which he has to deal consists of the opinions of experts engaged in the trade. But these expert witnesses are all interested parties, for their livelihood depends on the way the decision goes, and it cannot be expected that in giving their views they will be influenced primarily by such considerations as the material wellbeing of the whole community. Yet they alone are competent as a rule to speak on technical matters, and the adjudicator has to remember, before he takes a decision to which most of them are hostile, that it is they who must work whatever scheme is put forward.

During the era of economic liberalism the political authority, while it might set up the institutional and legal framework of the economic system, did not itself venture to take particular decisions about the pricing of goods or the structure of industrial enterprise, except in the case of natural monopolies like public utilities. But now that the State has been compelled to intervene in these matters, those officials or adjudicators who are called upon to make such decisions are naturally inclined, in the absence of other criteria, to apply principles derived from the political sphere to the economic questions which they are expected to answer. Yet a principle which may be satisfactory enough in one sphere of human activity may not be applicable to another. An example may be illuminating. The chairman of a board dealing with a recent scheme that involved State intervention listened to the arguments of the minority group of manufacturers who were hostile to it and admitted that these arguments seemed strong. But as a layman he realised his inability to pit his judgment on a technical question against that of members of the trade. So he gave his decision in favour of the majority's proposal, saying that in a democratic community the majority must decide. This shows an unfortunate confusion between the principles that can be applied in the political and economic spheres. Majority rule is satisfactory in politics because the greater number of those who are consulted, though concerned in the decision as members of a commonwealth, have no intimate and immediate financial interest in the decision as individuals. In other words, majority rule is successful when the issue is of a kind that makes possible disinterested judgments. Moreover, in forming an opinion about a particular question the citizen is guided by the views of the political party of which he is an adherent, for that party has a body of principles in accordance with which every proposal is examined. But when the State is trying to decide whether this or that type of organisation is the more efficient for a certain trade, it is faced with an issue that is different in kind from the ordinary political issue. The deciding factor is usually a technical one, and so it is only the men with an expert knowledge of the industry who can form the constituency to which the issue must be referred. Yet all these men have a direct pecuniary interest in the decision, and there is thus no possibility of obtaining judgments which are both informed and disinterested.

A further difficulty should be mentioned. Sometimes intervention may be decided upon in order to meet the troubles of an industry that are of a temporary character, such as may result from a cyclical depression. It may not be at all easy, however, once the structure of a trade has been altered by legislation so as to enable it to meet an emergency, to return to the original form when the emergency has passed. Indeed, the kind of plan that may be satisfactory for dealing with a temporary difficulty may be positively harmful in the long run. An example will clarify this point. Part I of the Coal Mines Act of 1930 provided for the establishment of a Central Council to fix the total output of coal and quotas for different districts, and also District Councils to allocate the district-allowance among the pits and to fix minimum prices. Now this scheme had much to commend it at the time when it was first applied—in the middle of a deep depression. The demand for coal is very inelastic at such times, especially nowadays when export sales depend not merely upon prices but also upon political agreements and quotas instituted by the importing countries. So a scheme for restricting output, spreading it over the different fields and pits, and maintaining prices, might be regarded as an acceptable method of preventing both a further fall in wages and profits and also the intensification of localised unemployment. Apart from the cyclical depression, however, the coal industry since the 1914–18 War has been suffering from a chronic decline. To deal with this second problem quite a different policy was needed, a policy that would lead to the lowering of costs by the closing of high-cost mines and the concentration of production on the most efficient. This process of concentration was in fact taking place before the Coal Mines Act was passed; but the operation of the Act has apparently checked it and so has actually proved a hindrance to the development of a more efficient organisation. It is true that Part II of the Act set up machinery for dealing with this second problem; but since its provisions were inconsistent with those of Part I, they could not be applied.

As it is so difficult for a tribunal or commission to make use of the evidence of an economic character presented to it, and as it lacks objective tests to apply to alternative forms of organisation, it commonly looks elsewhere for guidance and ends by basing its decision upon grounds that are not economic at all. The decision will usually depend upon the political views or the social philosophy of the members of the commission. The commission may be excused for seeking this way out of its perplexities, since its terms of reference are generally extremely vague. The government commonly appoints it to inquire into the causes of the depression in an industry and to recommend remedies. But the commission is seldom clearly informed whether it is to advise on the methods by which the organisation of the trade is to be rendered more efficient, or whether it is to show how the size of the trade is to be maintained (or wages and profits increased or employment spread), irrespective of considerations of efficiency and the cost to the community. In other words, it is not told whether it is to make an economic or a political decision. Now although social and political considerations may sometimes, quite properly, be given priority over economic ones, the grounds on which the judgment is based ought to be explicit. A decision which is of a political character ought not to be presented as though it were the result of a process of economic analysis. If it is so presented, as has happened in connection with many important acts of State intervention in industry in recent years, then the real issues are hidden behind a façade of irrelevant discussion. A democracy cannot be expected to make wise judgments if issues are not set before it fairly and honestly.

7 The Reorganisation of Contracting Industries[1]

During the interwar years Great Britain was faced with the necessity of scaling down several of her major industries. An adjustment of this sort was not, of course, novel to her experience, nor indeed to the experience of other industrial countries; for alterations in the size and structure of industries must occur from time to time in any economy subject to changes in technical methods and in demand. Yet in this period the effect was to create a new problem in the field of economic policy. The novelty was attributable in part to the fact that the downward adjustments required were on an exceptionally large scale, in part to the character of the industries affected, and in part to the lack of opportunities for expansion in other directions. Although during the twenties the most seriously depressed industries (for instance, coal, cotton, shipbuilding) were not among those in which strong cartels had been formed, competition worked too imperfectly to bring about the necessary contraction of capacity with sufficient speed to alleviate the condition of chronic depression. When at length efforts were made, often with official encouragement, to secure the necessary adjustment by means of organised schemes for the several industries (by rationalisation in other words), the results were by no means satisfactory. Indeed, the measures taken to deal with this condition of excessive capacity must be classed among the noteworthy failures of economic policy of the interwar period. It was not merely that the process of removing excessive capacity under the new policy was very slow in most cases, but also that the effects on the subsequent efficiency of the industries that had undergone the process were seldom favourable. Where the financial position of the industries was improved, this was usually not because production costs were lowered as a result of rationalisation, but because the schemes strengthened the power of the producers over the market and enabled them to raise prices. During the protracted negotiations that preceded the acceptance of the schemes, attention was frequently concentrated not on questions of technical efficiency, but on the financial arrangements for compensating the owners of the plants that were to close. Those arrangements commonly left the surviving firms with an increased burden of prior charges or with higher costs in the form of levy-payments on their plant or turnover. There was some force in the argument that the slow decay of an industry under *laissez-faire* was preferable to government-sponsored rationalisation of this kind, since the former method did not at any rate mean that the public was mulcted in order to maintain the incomes of the owners of redundant capacity.

After the war it is to be hoped that government intervention in economic affairs will take the form of applying stimuli to progress rather than of administering poor relief to industries in distress. If, moreover, the problem of excessive capacity reappears, it may be anticipated that it will do so in circumstances that make its solution easier; for the maintenance of monetary demand at a constant high level (on the large assumption that the government's employment policy succeeds) will provide producers with much stronger inducements and much wider opportunities than were present in the interwar years to transfer their activities quickly from decaying to advancing trades. Yet it would be very rash to conclude that the problem will not recur, at any rate in industries of a type presently to be described. It may well become serious in some of the war-expanded industries, and it may appear in others because of far-reaching technical improvements or because of movements in demand which render a large proportion of an industry's capacity redundant. Some of these changes may be the result of public policies which have a sudden and almost catastrophic effect on particular industries; of this the interwar years provide several examples.

It may be considered that, in view of these possibilities, it would be desirable to formulate a policy for dealing with large trades with a high proportion of redundant capacity that is unlikely to be removed quickly in the absence of a general scheme. This policy will only be beneficial if it succeeds in avoiding the main errors of the prewar schemes. But before proceeding to an examination of the kind of scheme that might, in principle, be acceptable, we must consider rather more closely the conditions which lead to the persistence of an excess of capacity in an industry once that excess has arisen.

While many industries have from time to time been affected by a long-continued decline in the demand for their products, the persistence of a problem of excessive capacity is found only in those industries in which either one or both of the following conditions exist. The first condition is that a large proportion of the labour employed is exceptionally immobile, either because it possesses highly specific skills, or because opportunities for alternative employments in its own neighbourhood are lacking. The second condition is that the capital resources of the industry are embodied in highly specific equipment. Historically, the first condition has been of great importance; examples may be found in the cases of the handloom weavers and the nailers in the nineteenth century. In many depressed industries in the interwar years both these conditions existed together. It seems reasonable to suppose, however, that after the war the first condition will not be nearly as important as in the past. The application of measures to maintain a strong demand for labour, both over the country as a whole and in particular areas, should do much to remove quickly any surplus of labour that arises from the decline of a particular industry, although it would be optimistic to expect that these measures will always and everywhere provide a complete remedy. Further, in two of the major industries (cotton and coal) that before the war suffered from excessive capacity (both equipment and labour), the working force by 1939 had been considerably reduced by the slow attrition of the previous two decades, and this reduction has been carried farther during the war, especially in cotton. It is not at all likely that these two trades will suffer from a surplus of labour immediately after the war; rather is the reverse probable. For these reasons attention will be concentrated in this article on the problem as it arises in industries with highly specific equipment.

At once it should be pointed out that this second condition is found only in a limited range of industries, although some of these are very important ones. The majority of firms in manufacturing industry produce, even over a short period, a fairly wide range of goods; and changes in the demand for any one of their products can be dealt with by a series of relatively small modifications in their organisation, layout and equipment. The process of adaptation is thus not difficult, and new industries have risen from the ruins of old ones without creating a legacy of firms with half-used capacity. The history of the small-metal trades, light engineering and many other industries producing highly finished manufactures will provide ample illustration of this. The steep fall in the demand for lighting brass-foundry did not create a persistent problem of over-capacity among the brass-founders, for they could easily adapt their plants to the manufacture of motor and electrical components. The saddlers and harness-makers, when their markets were destroyed, found it possible to use their workshops and their skill in the production of fancy leather goods. But no such opportunities were available to the shipbuilders, cotton-spinners or the mine-owners in the interwar years.[2] The industries that work with a large quantity of highly specific equipment directed to the production of a narrow range of goods are inevitably in a different position from those that are less specialised. If there is a fall in the demand for *their* products, the adaptation of plant and organisation to the production of entirely new types of goods for which demand is growing does not, and cannot, readily occur. To argue that, even so, excessive capacity could not persist in these industries if the firms that compose them were perfectly competitive does not dispose of the problem; for an approximation to perfect competition, or the establishment of cost conditions equivalent to those under perfect competition, usually requires, in such an industry, a fundamental reorganisation which can only take place quickly if there is a 'scheme' for the whole of the industry. It should be emphasised that the purpose of a satisfactory redundancy scheme is not machine-breaking, but rather the creation for the industry of a structure best adapted in form to the new conditions.[3]

Experience shows, moreover, that under *laissez-faire* firms in industries which have much specific equipment, far from competing with each other more vigorously during periods of persistent depression, will try to distribute the diminished volume of trade among all of them by quota arrangements and to maintain prices by agreement. A resort to restrictive practices is the most natural response of industries with much highly specific capacity to a persistent decline in demand, just as the most natural response of firms whose capacity and organisation can be readily adapted to the manufacture of other products will be to abandon the lines for which demand has fallen and to concentrate on more promising lines, or to take up new products. The creation of an effective cartel, by which the diminished amount of business is spread over all the members of an industry, will raise unit-costs and will delay the transference of trade to low-cost producers and the creation of a structure suited to the new circumstances. A scheme which will bring about quickly what competition, if it had existed, might have been expected to bring about slowly is obviously to be preferred, in the public interest, to such a cartel. The same arguments apply to a situation in which a fundamental change in structure is required, not through a decline in demand, but through the introduction of improved technical methods which may require the substitution of a few large, up-to-date plants for a large number of old-fashioned ones owned by independent firms. In an industry already cartelised, it will be extremely difficult to effect these necessary changes without providing for the compensation of the withdrawing capacity.

The contention may be put forward that the maintenance of a high level of demand, under a full-employment policy, will make special measures for the removal of excessive capacity unnecessary, even in these cartelised industries. This may be doubted. For instance, all cotton mills closed under the concentration policy are to be permitted to reopen from a date to be decided. It is clear that the effect of the reopening in view of the labour supply in prospect, will be to leave most of the mills, even during the period of the restocking boom, running well below their capacity, and therefore inefficiently. The structural changes needed to reach a condition of full running and maximum efficiency in the industry are not likely to take place quickly under *laissez-faire*. During the restocking boom price conditions will be so favourable to manufacturers that they will be under no inducement to introduce structural changes. When, later, prices show signs of weakening, the industry will probably attempt to fix minimum prices by agreement, and will so delay, perhaps for a considerable time, the elimination of the higher-cost producers; the report issued by the industry last year shows that a minimum-price scheme occupies an important place in its reconstruction plans. Indeed, while the problem of excessive capacity may be easier to solve than in the past, it does not seem that the maintenance of a generally buoyant demand will necessarily produce quickly the structural changes that efficiency requires.

It is not always possible for manufacturers to create effective cartels. In some industries, especially those composed of numerous independent units, efforts to do so are sometimes frustrated through the operations of 'weak sellers'. When the cartel breaks down altogether and is not reconstituted, then the decline in business will be accompanied by low prices and a consumption of capital until the surplus capacity has been removed. Nowadays, for a 'specific equipment' industry to operate in circumstances in which no cartel exists, or is completely ineffective, is unusual. Yet since it is here that the case for a 'scheme' is at its weakest, the circumstances deserve examination. It may be argued that the shrinkage of the industry by the process just described is preferable to any 'scheme' by which the surviving firms incur the burden of paying compensation to the retiring firms; for if an industry is too large, then it is reasonable that its capital equipment should be used to the point at which the returns from its operation fail to cover prime costs. Yet if the process of capital reduction is a long one, the technical efficiency of the whole trade may well decline, or fail to keep pace with that of competitors abroad. During such a period even the more efficient firms may be unable, or unwilling, to invest in improved machinery, and so at the end of the period a large proportion of the equipment still required by the industry may be obsolete, and costs may be out of line with those abroad. Further, during an era of prolonged depression in a particular trade, the quality of management and labour is liable to deteriorate, since enterprising people will be reluctant to enter it. For all these reasons, the decline of the industry may well go farther than would have been necessary had the excessive capacity been removed quickly and had a new structure been created by a 'scheme'. There would be no grounds for objection if the virtual extinction of the declining industry were deemed to be inevitable, as may sometimes happen. In that case it would be all to the good that the new capital resources of the country should be invested elsewhere, and that young and enterprising persons should shun the industry. But if what is expected is merely the substantial contraction of a large trade and its subsequent continuance at a lower level that before, then the prolongation of the period of contraction may affect adversely its subsequent efficiency, and may even carry it towards extinction. Thus, even where the industry in unable to cartelise itself effectively, a *laissez-faire* policy in the type of industries now under consideration is unlikely to bring about a substantial reduction of capacity, or to lead to the establishment of a new structure, in a sufficiently short time to avoid serious secondary consequences.

It may be objected that the arguments put forward in the last paragraph are relevant only to circumstances in which there is general unemployment, and in which it is possible for employers in depressed trades to impose worse conditions on their employees

than those in industries that require comparable skill. If there were
a strong general demand for labour, it may be said, the process of
contraction in non-cartelised trades could *not* be prolonged, because
employers in them would be unable to retain labour at lower wages
than those paid elsewhere, and the necessity for maintaining wage-
rates would hasten the process of capital consumption and the
concentration of output. There is force in this argument, and it may
be decisive in a majority of cases. Yet it seems probable that when a
very substantial contraction of capacity and a fundamental
reorganisation are needed, a considerable time might elapse before
they were achieved, even under these relatively favourable conditions. It must not be forgotten, moreover, that among workers in
industries which were chronically depressed before the war, and in
which the average age is high, mobility is likely to be much less than
among workers in general. In spite of the existence of a strong
general demand for labour, therefore, employers in those industries
may find it possible to retain their labour for a long period at
relatively low rates of wages, and so the necessary reorganisation
may be retarded. Thus, even on the assumptions of a buoyant
labour demand and the absence of cartels, the possibility that a
problem of excessive capacity will arise in some important trades
cannot be lightly dismissed. In any event, the objection is relevant
only to a minority of industries, for in the typical case there is resort
to cartelisation when excessive capacity makes its appearance, and
this is likely to be even truer of the postwar than of the prewar
period.

The acceptance of the case for a 'scheme' under any conditions
obviously depends on the assumption that it is possible to make, not
necessarily an accurate, but a broadly correct forecast of the prospects of the trade concerned. It is, of course, by no means easy to
decide, when depression overtakes a particular industry, whether it
is likely to be temporary or prolonged, and, if prolonged, whether
the circumstances are such as to lead to contraction followed by
stability at a reduced level, or to a virtual disappearance of the
industry. An estimate can be made with much greater assurance
for some trades than for others. In some cases public policy may set
the lower limit to the size of the industry, as when national defence
is involved. In other cases, an act of public policy may itself be
responsible for the contraction. Sometimes an important technical
change may leave very little room for doubt that a large amount
of redundant capacity is likely to be created in an industry in which

conditions are unfavourable to its early elimination in the absence
of a scheme. Occasionally, the loss of an important foreign market
as a result (say) of the introduction of a new protective tariff may
indicate broadly the scale of the contraction needed (as when
Lancashire lost the Indian cotton market). It is true that even when
informed opinion agrees that *some* permanent contraction is needed,
there may be differences of view among the manufacturers about
its extent. But this uncertainty may not prove to be a serious
obstacle, since a scheme which provides for a substantial contraction of capacity may yet make possible a variation of output
within fairly wide limits.[4] It must nevertheless be admitted that
quite often a decision on the part of government to support a
scheme on the basis of a forecast can only be defended on the
ground that the sole practicable alternative to the scheme is intervention for the purpose of maintaining incomes by undesirable
methods. This conclusion presupposes that means for organising the
contraction can be found which are superior to those employed in
the interwar years, and we must now consider the principles to
which a satisfactory scheme should conform, and, in outline, the
way in which it might be introduced.

In the first place, it is clear from prewar experience that great
difficulties will be encountered in working out a policy that is
both acceptable to the producers and also advantageous to the
rest of the community. Secondly, the initiative must frequently
come from the government; for, from what we know of prewar
schemes, from the proposals put forward by organised industries
for reconstruction, and from *a priori* reasoning, we can be confident
that schemes evolved by particular industries, in the absence of
official guidance, would be designed primarily to strengthen the
powers of the producers to fix prices and to compensate the
proprietors of the plants to be withdrawn out of some kind of levy
on the running firms. Contraction by slow attrition would probably
be preferable to such a solution; although it is doubtful if this
alternative will be acceptable either to government or to industry
in postwar Britain, at any rate for large, staple trades. If so, then it
is for the State to concern itself with finding a rational solution that
industry will accept.

In any instance, the government would, first of all, have to make
an estimate of the prospects of the industry, an estimate that would
sometimes, though not always, be highly speculative. After taking
the views of the members of the trade, the government would then

reach a decision on the maximum amount of capacity required, which would no doubt have reference to the existing output of the industry modified by long-run prospects of demand, prices and costs. It would next require the members of the industry to work out a scheme for concentrating output on a limited number of plants working at full capacity. Such a scheme would be analogous to the wartime concentration schemes, except that the choice of the survivors and the form of the new organisation would be determined solely by considerations of efficiency, qualified by the requirements of the new Location of Industry policy, and that the closed plants would be scrapped, and not, as under wartime concentration policy, preserved on a care and maintenance arrangement. In judging the scheme presented to it by industry, the government would have to consider how far the proposals would leave the survivors 'running full' by reference to the total assumed output, and also whether the selection of the continuing firms had been governed solely by considerations of efficiency and suitable location. The judgment would tax the powers of the technical experts and accountants employed by the government, for they would have to examine not merely the financial position of the several firms, but also the technical efficiency of the plants and the organisation of the firms. Since accountants perform at present this sort of work for large investors, they could, however, presumably act in the same way for the government.

The greatest obstacle to satisfactory rationalisation in the past has been in connection with the financial arrangements. It is a serious disadvantage of any 'scheme' for removing excessive capacity, as compared with the selective operations of competition, that it involves the provision of compensation in some form or other for the withdrawing firms, and the payment of compensation can only be justified because, in the industries under consideration, the alternative method of reducing capacity and securing the establishment of a new type of structure is, for reasons already discussed, not available. The owners of the surviving firms must therefore be prepared to share the financial benefits arising from the new structure with those of the retiring firms, or of the firms that are absorbed. The form in which the compensation is paid, however, is of great importance to the future of the industry.

The arrangement which both sets of shareholders would be prepared to accept is presumably one which, on a reasonable estimate of prospects, would be expected to leave both parties better off than they would be if the existing structure were retained.[5] But since both the prospects of the industry, and also the financial effects of the scheme, must always be speculative, there is clearly a wide scope for bargaining about terms. From the public standpoint, what is to be avoided is that compensation should take a form which leads to an increase in the costs of the surviving firms, as occurs with a levy on production or the creation of a new prior charge of any kind. In other words, it is desirable that the owners of the redundant plant should share in the equity of the survivors. It may be argued that, in fact, there is little to choose between these methods, since the difference in risk attaching to these various forms of compensation would be reflected in the nominal value attributed to each of them. Nevertheless, in view of the necessarily uncertain future of the industry, it is essential that the basis of risk-bearing should be as wide as possible, and that the industry should not start on its new career burdened with a load of prior charges heavier than in the past. The effects of an optimistic estimate of the industry's future will obviously be much less serious if an equity payment is made than if the arrangment takes the form of a levy on output or an issue of debentures.

A scheme which leaves unchanged the relative position of the shareholders in the various firms (running and closed alike), and does not raise the burden of prior charges, is much easier to work out in some industries than in others. Where it is desirable for technical and commercial reasons to bring about consolidation in the industry, then the holdings in existing companies can be exchanged for holdings in a new concern, or an allotment of ordinary shares can be made by the absorbing company to the absorbed. Where, however, there are numerous independent concerns, and where productive and commercial efficiency would not be served by a consolidation, but demands the retention of a multi-firm structure, the goal is not so easy to attain. For obvious reasons, it would be difficult, if not impossible, in peacetime to 'marry' particular retiring firms with particular survivors, as under wartime concentration, although where this was possible the financial method described above could be applied. In the more usual case, however, the least harmful solution would be to pay compensation to the 'closers' in the form of cash to be provided out of share capital by the 'runners'. In this case a company might be formed to acquire the plants of the closers, and the share capital of this company would be taken up by those that were to survive. The owners of the closed plants would then receive a cash payment which, ideally, would represent the preconcentration value of their interest, plus perhaps an additional sum equivalent to their capitalised share of the additional profit which the industry was expected to earn as a result of the scheme. The owners of the surviving plants would provide the money for the transaction, but in a form which would not leave their plants burdened with additional prior charges. The company could be wound up when the transaction as a whole had been completed. On the assumption that the above principles were expressed in the agreements reached, and that the estimates of the industry's prospects proved to be correct, the surviving concerns would find their profitability increased to a greater extent than the rise in their capitalisation.

It can at once be admitted that this last proposal does not avoid all the evils to which reference has been made, but it may be claimed that it is preferable to the method of the levy or the debenture issue. It will be asked, however, how the surviving firms could raise the cash necessary for this payment other than by a debenture issue, since it is highly improbable that firms in an industry suffering from the consequences of overcapacity could raise fresh share capital for the purpose. No solution along these lines would indeed be possible in most cases of this kind without the intervention of the government. It is suggested that if the government were convinced that the scheme was satisfactory on its technical side, and provided that the parties would agree to financial arrangements which accorded with the principles set out above, then it would be justified in giving financial assistance to the industry to tide over the period between the purchase of the closers' plants and the raising of the necessary share capital from the public.[6] The success of the latter operation would depend on the scheme having the results anticipated, and, by acting in the way suggested, the government would clearly be underwriting the risk. In some cases there would be justification for the government's action, in that the condition of the industry could be attributed mainly to official decisions. More generally, the justification would be the probability that, in the absence of such help, either no scheme at all or an unsatisfactory scheme would be forthcoming.

It may be argued that a government which was prepared to act in this way would be able to intervene more effectively than in the past for safeguarding the community's interests in matters of industrial reconstruction. For instance, we have seen that the main result of many of the so-called rationalisation schemes of the 1930s was to increase the power of producers to resort to restrictive practices; for, in the absence of a positive policy of its own, the government, faced with conditions of chronic depression in several major industries, frequently contented itself with endorsing schemes that the producers put forward. If it were to adopt a policy of the kind sketched here, however, it would be in a much stronger position than previously in countering restrictionism. It is not the intention of the writer to consider in this article the very large question of the possibilities and limitations of governmental policy directed towards the control of monopolies. But, in this context, it can at least be pointed out that measures designed to eliminate restrictive practices (except when permitted by licence) would form a highly significant part of any policy for the removal of excessive capacity and for adapting the structure of industries to permanent changes in technique and demand. Such measures would have a powerful influence in moulding the form of rationalisation schemes so as to bring them into line with what the public interest required, and in preventing the abuse of the monopolistic powers sometimes conferred by schemes which lead to the creation of close combines. They might also strongly incline firms which had hitherto responded to a fall in demand by resorting to production-quotas and price-maintenance arrangements, to reach agreements quickly for the removal of excessive capacity and for the creation of a structure adapted to the new conditions.

Some may argue that a vigorous anti-monopoly policy would of itself be sufficient to bring about the rapid transference of output from high-cost to low-cost producers that is required. It would be so in some industries, but one may doubt, for reasons already given, whether it would be true of all the trades that use much highly specific capacity. In any event, it is improbable that such a policy, if it were to stand alone, would have any chance of adoption in the political atmosphere of the immediate postwar years. It is certain that, in future, government will require to establish closer relations with industry than in the past because of economic policies to which it is already committed. Those relations would be extremely uneasy and unstable if it were to adopt a policy which industrialists would regard as hostile to them and completely unsympathetic towards their difficulties, Such a policy, however, if associated with positive measures of financial assistance, similar to those suggested above, is much more likely to win acceptance than if it stood alone. The implication of this argument is, of course, that it would be worthwhile for the State to assume some financial risk if, by doing so, it helped to restore efficiency to industries in need of reorganisation and to check the resort to restrictive practices, which are, in certain types of industry, the normal response to adversity.

8 Economic Planning and Private Enterprise[1]

Men appointed to newly created Chairs have to set their own standards of achievement; they must approach their duties with the confidence of pioneers. The tenant of an old-established Chair has a more exacting task than theirs. His responsibilities are to the past as well as to the future, for he stands in the shadow of his predecessors, and although he may not hope to match their achievements, he must try to avoid falling too far short of them. The previous holders of the Chair of Political Economy in this College have set the standard high, and I approach my duties with humility. I am, however, comforted by the thought that even they, should they be permitted to survey contemporary affairs, would look on them with perplexity. Some of my distinguished nineteenth-century predecessors, for example, would find in modern economic theory only traces of their once well-established structures; in applied economics they would be bewildered by many of the topics which preoccupy the present-day economist; and from the actual ordering of economic society they would all turn with dismay. It is true that Jevons might be heartened to see that a 'Coal Question' was still with us, although he would discover that it had assumed an unfamiliar form. Foxwell would doubtless be interested to find us grappling once again with the problem of inflation; but he would scarcely view our present troubles with the equanimity that he displayed in his own paper on the subject thirty years ago.[2]

One of the most striking contrasts between economic society as observed by most of my predecessors and that with which contemporary economists are concerned is to be found in the relations between the State and industry, and it is with this topic that I am to deal in my lecture. Before I do so, I ought to say a word about the place of the Department of Political Economy in the study of economics in the University of London. The oldest academic centre for this study in London is in this College; the largest centre is now, of course, the London School of Economics and Political Science, to which this Department owes a debt of gratitude for help generously given in the provision of library facilities and teaching. So far as economics and cognate subjects are concerned, the School is unmatched in the range of its special studies and in the magnitude of its teaching and student bodies. But University College has an important part to play in this academic field. A subject such as economics is likely to develop in different ways in different environments. There are advantages in an institution specialised to the social sciences, such as the LSE; there are also advantages of a different kind to be gained from its study in a College which is engaged in the pursuit of knowledge in all the various fields of science and the humanities. Obviously, both sets of advantages cannot be realised by one institution; but co-operation may be expected to confer mutual benefits. Lately, we at University College have been the chief beneficiaries, and the LSE may well be inclined to regard the facilities with which it provides us as being of the nature of 'unrequited exports'. In accordance with the spirit of the times, however, may I be permitted to express the hope and expectation that we shall steadily approach equilibrium in our balance of payments? A possible objection to this co-operation is that the student who sits at the feet of teachers in two institutions may from time to time be confused by a lack of uniformity in doctrine. Whether that will be so, I do not know. Anyhow, I am not perturbed at the possibility, remembering Montaigne's advice: 'Let diversity of judgment be proposed unto him; he will choose, if he can; if not, he will remain in doubt'.

Let me now turn to the subject indicated in the title of my lecture. As I have said, one of the main differences between the society which my nineteenth-century predecessors had to interpret and that in which we now live is to be found in the changed relationship between the State and industry, for this has meant a profound modification of the economic system of this country. The forces that have produced this change have been steadily growing in influence for many decades, and since the recent war they have received an immense accession of strength. The result is that economic liberalism, which once seemed so firmly rooted both in doctrine and practice, and which survived, though in a bruised condition, even the uncongenial weather of the interwar period, has almost withered away. Economists as such are not called upon to make judgments about the wisdom of political decisions, but they are closely interested in the economic problems to which such decisions give rise. The problems that spring from the State's new industrial policy are bound to engage the close attention of postwar economists. Several distinguished colleagues have already expressed their views on certain aspects of that policy. I myself have chosen to deal with it because I believe it to be of outstanding importance, and to constitute a field of enquiry which some members of this Department will wish to cultivate.

It is useful, to begin with, to glance at the long path which we have travelled since the time when the advocacy of *laissez-faire* and free enterprise was the mark of the progressive mind, and when economics, on the whole, assigned very narrow limits to government interference in economic processes. About the middle of the nineteenth century John Stuart Mill summed up moderate opinion, both among economists and laymen, in saying: ' . . . in all the more advanced communities the great majority of things are worse done by the intervention of government, than the individuals most interested in the matter would do them, or cause them to be done, if left to themselves'; and again: '*Laissez-faire*, in short, should be the general practice; every departure from it, unless required by some great good, is a certain evil'.[3] These propositions were generally in accordance with the policy of governments.

Sixty years later, on the eve of the 1914–18 War, both opinion and practice had undergone significant changes. The State had assumed control over important categories of transactions. It had built up a great code of factory and mining legislation; it had returned to the system of the public regulation of wages; and social insurance had become an accepted field of government activity. Further, the development of industries where the competitive check was necessarily absent—the 'natural monopolies'—had led to State intervention for regulating the prices charged to consumers, or in some cases, to the appearance of public corporations, or to the growth of municipal enterprise.

The main causes of this change of policy lay in a general recognition of the evils that had accompanied the material progress of the time, and in widespread agreement that remedies could be found only by State action. Few believed that unrestricted private enterprise was inefficient; on the contrary, it was commonly admitted that government interference might lead to some material loss which must be accepted as the price of social amelioration. There were some who thought the price too high, and feared that losses, not only of a material kind, might result. Such opinions were perhaps more common among laymen than among the economists of the period. It may be recalled that the National Health Insurance Scheme provoked Belloc to write *The Servile State*. About the same time Dicey, after discussing 'the general acquiescence in proposals tending towards collectivism', concluded that 'the combination of socialistic and democratic legislation threatens the gravest danger to the country'; and he even suggested that Old Age Pensions would make Englishmen unwilling to fight for their country even in a war of defence because of their fear that the government would be able to finance a war only by cutting the social services.[4]

The economists of the time, however, were by no means unsympathetic to the trend of policy. As long ago as 1870, Cairnes, in a lecture delivered at this College, had declared: 'The maxim of *laissez-faire* has no scientific basis whatever, but is at best a handy rule of practice'.[5] Later Jevons was quoted in the House of Commons in support of the proposition that 'the State was justified . . . in doing any single act which in its ulterior consequences adds to the sum of human happiness';[6] while the Cambridge economists were concerned with analysing situations in which, under *laissez-faire*, private net product differed from social net product, and with calling attention to circumstances in which action by the public authorities was needed to secure the optimum allocation of national resources. Thus, it seemed that intervention could sometimes be justified not merely to protect the weaker members of society, but also to promote a more efficient ordering of economic affairs.

Yet none of these changes, either in practice or in doctrine, seriously disturbed the presupposition that in *industry and trade* private enterprise was properly to be regarded as the rule. The State might introduce correctives at points where the system worked badly. But these were activities on the periphery. The heart of the system beat as before.

The 1914–18 War had less immediate effect on practice and opinion than might have been expected. The postwar governments hastily abandoned the wartime controls, and although minor breaches were made in the Free Trade system in the early twenties, and although there was intervention in certain industries, these could be justified by an appeal to special circumstances. They did not affront the general principle that industry was properly the sphere of private initiative subject to certain legal restraints. The substantial advance in the social services that took place at that time could be regarded as a continuation of a prewar trend; the same was true of the extension of government activity in respect of the public utilities. In the middle 1920s Keynes delivered some lectures entitled *The End of Laissez-Faire*—a rather odd title in view of all that had happened to the thought of economists and the practice of governments in the previous half century. In them he spoke favourably of the 'possible improvements in the technique of modern capitalism by the agency of collective action',[7] but he clearly did not regard the collective activities which he had in mind as being incompatible with private enterprise. The springs of action, he thought, need not be affected by them.

In subsequent years the disposition both of economists and of the general public towards these questions was deeply influenced, first, by the chronic depression in the staple exporting industries which produced the miseries of the depressed areas, and secondly, after 1929, by the rise in general unemployment that accompanied the world depression. Private competitive enterprise, it seemed, was incapable of dealing with either of these troubles. It came to be widely accepted that the structural adjustments required in industry as a whole, and the reorganisation of particular trades, could be brought about only by concerted action on the part of producers, or, where this could not be achieved by agreement, by State action for promoting the same result. The Balfour Committee was typical in its criticism of industrial individualism. It stated in 1927 that 'generally speaking, the greater the completeness and permanence of the fusion of interests, the greater is the opportunity of substantial economy'.[8] Official encouragement of so-called rationalisation schemes was given throughout the 1930s, and in some cases, as in coalmining, compulsion was resorted to. This was an important change. Interference had ceased to be confined to the introduction of general correctives; it was penetrating into the organisation and business policy of particular trades and firms. It extended not merely to manufacturing and mining industries, but also to fishing, agriculture and transport.

The policy received reinforcement in the early 1930s from certain advances in economic theory, although it is not to be supposed that it was in any way derived from them. It was a deduction from the theory of imperfect competition that, where such conditions existed, there was no reason to believe in the existence of a self-regulating economic force which could be relied upon to bring about the structural changes in industry that were required. Since imperfect competition was the rule, and since, as had long been realised, perfect competition was found only where deliberate efforts on the part of the State or organised bodies of producers had been made to bring it about (as in the organised produce markets), *laissez-faire* as a prescription for policy was deprived, so it seemed, of any vestige of theoretical justification. It would, of course, have been consistent with the analysis if State intervention had been directed towards removing the imperfections in the competitive system, at any rate where technical considerations in industry did not present too formidable an obstacle. But, in the prevailing temper, this possibility was ignored, and the opposite path was chosen. In the 1930s the influence of the State was used mainly to promote concerted action by industrialists, and to weaken still further competitive forces. In practice, the ostensible aim of promoting efficiency was soon lost sight of; the chief result of the policy was to improve the financial position of established producers by buttressing monopoly among them. After the introduction of the new protective tariff, this policy was extended into the field of foreign trade, and the government actively encouraged British participation in international cartels. Thus a result of the further departures from *laissez-faire* in the interwar period was the strengthening of private monopoly.

Meanwhile the high level of unemployment in the leading industrial countries had done much to create a conviction that the system of private capitalism was doomed. It seemed to afford evidence (to quote Professor Robertson) of a 'chronic and endemic tendency towards the stifling of enterprise and a consequent running-down of the whole system'.[9] The Keynesian analysis, however, suggested that the evil was remediable within the framework of the capitalist system. If, by an appropriate fiscal, monetary and investment policy, the State were able to maintain a constantly buoyant demand, then private capitalism could be saved. The State need not intrude into the sphere of particular decisions, and the pricing system would remain the chief regulator of economic processes. According to this view, therefore, the economic functions of government were to be enlarged, not with the object of superseding private enterprise, but in order to preserve it.

I am not concerned here with the question whether in fact 'full employment' can be maintained without detailed intervention, or whether measures for the maintenance of effective demand are likely to be adequate. I wish merely to emphasise that while the trend of economic opinion in prewar days was in favour of a more active intervention by the State in economic affairs, such intervention was not inconsistent with the preservation of the system of private enterprise; it was indeed deemed necessary for improving the operation of the system. Of course, not all of those who gave thought to these questions accepted these solutions as possible or desirable. While almost everyone who, during the recent war, reflected upon our reconstruction problems was agreed that the policy of the interwar period was unsatisfactory as a model for the future, there were those who, reviewing the failure of governmental corrective measures to deal with the *malaise* of private capitalism, came to the conclusion that the only way out of our difficulties was (in the words of an American economist) to institute public control 'at the point where things are being decided in the processes of industry itself'.[10] This conclusion points to some form of economic planning, which has been the solution favoured by our postwar government.

The term 'economic planning' is ambiguous. To some people it means the abandonment of the pricing mechanism, and the determination of productive programmes and of the allocation of resources by a central authority which uses physical controls for the purpose. It is rather difficult to decide whether this is the sort of planning that our official planners favour in the long run as contrasted with the present transitional period. Their statements have not been altogether consistent with one another. But to judge from acts rather than words, I should say that the system which is evolving in this country is not intended to be of this extreme type. Still less does it resemble the system which attempts to combine collectivism in the ownership of resources with a pricing system, a possibility to which certain economists have pointed. On the other hand, our economic planners demand much more from the State than that it should create, as Professor Robbins suggests, 'a system of laws and institutions' within which the market mechanism 'may be made to work the right way'.[11] Few would deny that the State should intervene to achieve certain aims, such as 'full employment' or an acceptable distribution of the national income, and that it should assist in promoting structural adjustments in industry when these are required, provided that the measures of which it makes use are mainly of a fiscal and financial character and do not disturb the working of the pricing system. But our present policy certainly goes much further. The State seeks on the one hand to assume complete control over an important, though limited, sector of the economy, and for the rest, for that part if it that remains in private hands, to furnish substitutes (though apparently only partial substitutes) for the compulsions of the market. These substitutes take the form of inducements, or priorities, or controls, which persuade or compel those industrialists or workers whose action the State wishes to influence to act in the way the central authority requires.

Even if we ignore the measures that are being taken to deal with our immediate troubles (and I am not now concerned with them), we can find many examples of this policy by which the government weights the scales in favour of projects deemed worthy of encouragement. For instance, the government invited the iron and steel industry as a whole to put forward a long-term reconstruction plan. The acceptance by the government of the plan that was drawn up has meant that priorities in securing the necessary materials and equipment are being granted to firms for carrying out *approved* projects. Again, in cotton-spinning, the government proposes to give subsidies for re-equipment, provided that the industry satisfies certain conditions and carries out the reorganisation which the government favours. Further, priorities, including building licences, are given to firms who are prepared to locate their establishments in areas where the government wishes to foster new enterprises. These are all measures of long-term policy which subtract from the authority of the pricing system, but are not intended entirely to supersede it.

I should now like to consider briefly some of the economic implications of policy in both of these fields, the public sector and the private sector which is being subject to what might be called halfway planning.

It is sometimes stated that the nationalisation of certain industries will not give rise to any important new economic problems, since that policy involves merely the replacement of private monopoly by public monopoly and one form of bureaucracy by another. This argument is not, of course, relevant to the whole field of nationalised undertakings. For instance, it may apply to the railways, but it cannot apply to inland transport as a whole; it is relevant to Cables and Wireless, but not to the purchasing of raw cotton. Yet even in the section of industry where the argument has some force, it ought not to be lightly assumed either on the one hand that important new economic problems will not be created by the transference of control from boards of directors to the State or, on the other hand, than most of the old problems will disappear. Let me give examples which illustrate both these assumptions. The anonymity of the great joint stock company, with its apparently impersonal methods of control, often disguises the importance of dominating individuals in its affairs. Both in the building up of great businesses and in their subsequent administration, authority, though formally invested in a board responsible to shareholders and exercised through a managerial bureaucracy, is sometimes intensely personal. Many great companies have depended and still depend, for their success on the initiative and organising capacity of dominant personalities. Unless such persons are attracted by service on government boards and are given scope for their qualities of leadership, nationalisation, at any rate in industries that depend to any extent upon innovation, will make a substantial difference to the way in which they are administered.

It is no doubt for this reason in part that the practice has been followed in the nationalised industries of placing control in the hands of boards appointed by Ministers instead of in government departments which are subject to day-to-day criticism in Parliament. But this policy, in attempting to meet one difficulty, runs into another. The managers of public enterprises cannot be irresponsible. If these industries are to serve the public interest, Parliamentary control cannot be reduced to a futility. In competitive industry the market is the regulator of business decisions and the consumer is the master of business policy. In private monopoly, or quasi-monopoly, these propositions cease to be true, although conditions in the actual world are seldom such as to invalidate them completely. The private monopolist is usually restrained in some degree by fear of stimulating competition or of provoking public criticism, which may lead to the imposition of some form of public control over his activities. Still, these safeguards are only partially effective. Transference of control to a public monopoly affords an opportunity of providing a complete safeguard against the abuses of economic power, but it does not guarantee that the opportunity will be seized. Moreover, dangers of a different kind make their appearance. In the operation of a public monopoly financial results cease to be regarded as the chief measure of administrative success. Decisions about the productive programme and investment are not likely to be taken primarily by reference to profitability. To give a free hand to the administrator in these circumstances is to confer on him a power unrestrained by the considerations of which the private entrepreneur must take account.

It follows that some form of effective Parliamentary control over the operation of the public monopolies is clearly necessary. It must be for experts in administration to devise suitable forms of control, if they can. I can make only one rather obvious suggestion in this connection. From the time of the rise of the great public company, where there is often a divorce between ownership and control, the State has tried to safeguard the interests of the shareholders by insisting on a certain degree of publicity for the company's affairs. Successive Companies Acts have tried to ensure that the published accounts shall reveal the true state of the company's finances, so that it is possible for the public to be able to form some estimate of the value of the shares which they are asked to buy. These attempts may not have been wholly successful, but the principle is well established. When the State takes over an enterprise and when the general public become in effect the shareholders, then this safeguard of publicity can be, and should be, made fully effective. There can be no possible justification for withholding from the people complete information about the operations of their own undertakings; without it informed criticism, inside and outside Parliament, is impossible, however many Consumers' Councils are formed.

There are many other important issues in connection with nationalised undertakings to which economists may be expected to give their attention. Pricing policy will be among the most intricate of the problems; and here I come to the cases in which nationalisation will not change the nature of the problems, although it may sometimes provide opportunities for reaching a rational solution of them. This is so, for instance, in the case of inland transport. As a recent writer has pointed out, the proper distribution of traffic between rail and road, unless it is to depend on quite arbitrary decisions, must be governed by cost comparisons of precisely the same type regardless of the nature of ownership.[12]

Now let me turn to the economic planning that is being applied to the private sector of the economy. This planning, as we have observed, is apparently intended to fall short of thoroughgoing planning. The pricing system, working within a legal and institutional framework, is no longer to be the chief regulator of economic processes; neither does the government propose to engage upon a detailed control of the whole of economic life. Rather it establishes priorities or, to use the current jargon, it sets up official targets, and it tries to induce people to aim at them instead of at those which private self-interest would have led them to select. These targets are confined to certain industries or certain categories of transactions.

It is easy to understand why in this country this middle way should have been chosen. Professor Schumpeter, in his book *Capitalism, Socialism and Democracy*, has argued that private capitalism has come to grief because in the course of its development it created a social environment hostile to itself, or more precisely, critical and democratic attitudes of mind that were unwilling to accept the conditions necessary for the efficient working of the system.[13] Those who believe in any form of planning would presumably not disagree with this view. But it may be argued with equal plausibility that a people nursed in the traditions of political democracy which private capitalism fostered would find intolerable the permanent restrictions on their freedom that are inseparable from a fully planned economy. It is understandable, therefore, why we in Great Britain should have tried to find a middle way.

Does such a way exist? Is it possible to combine a measure of consumer sovereignty exercised through a pricing system with a measure of centralised planning which expresses itself in targets and priorities? Some economists doubt whether it *is* possible. They have pointed to the damaging inconsistencies which arise when government decisions about the disposition of resources (decisions which men in their capacity as electors approve of) conflict with the choices which men make as individuals when they come to spend their incomes. They conclude that these inconsistencies can be removed only by a retreat from planning or by the loss of freedom. If this is so, the outlook is bleak indeed. For the motives that determine men's political choices may be as deeply rooted as those that determine their choices as individuals in the market. If Professor Schumpeter is right in his belief that private capitalism has been rejected because it does not satisfy men's social aspirations, and if at the same time a country with democratic traditions will not tolerate permanently the restrictions on personal freedom that a planned economy requires, then we reach a deadlock. The dilemma will not be apparent as long as government planning is limited in scope, but if its area is widely extended, the strains may become intolerable. In face of this prospect one is tempted to argue that Great Britain may be expected to find the middle way, even if theory cannot detect it, by practical evolution, just as she found the solution for many intractable problems in the past. But it is dangerous to lull ourselves with the murmur of *solvitur ambulando*, and economists certainly cannot be satisfied with an argument which rejects the services of critical intelligence.

I must now leave this question of whether the conflict in this sphere can be resolved, and I should like to address myself to some of the more immediate problems which the pursuit of the middle way has raised. The new system means the transference of important categories of decision from the individual to the bureaucracy, and this centralisation requires the State to have at hand immense masses of detailed, up-to-date information about economic processes in the fields upon which it is concentrating its attention, and also to establish an administrative machine capable of reaching speedy and wise economic decisions in those fields. Have we in this country confidence in the ability of the administration to undertake these great tasts, even though some of us believe that in principle it should be for the State to perform them? The following lines, which though time-worn, are apposite:

> . . . the democratic spirit does not object on principle to the performance of vastly increased duties by the State. On the contrary, it demands it, and it has confidence in the ultimate controlling power, which is the Legislature—that is to say, itself; but when we come to the execution of the work decided on by the Legislature, the democratic spirit does not feel confidence— on the contrary, it is exceedingly critical of all acts of the Executive, and we are confronted by the difficulty of an Executive summoned to all-pervading duties, but with agents who receive little popular support. The public demands inspection, but too often denounces the inspectors; the public demands regulations, but chafes at the red tape employed in carrying them out; . . . it demands organizations which require the appointment of vast numbers of clerks, yet the deficiencies of Government clerks and the expense of their salaries and pensions furnish endless food for popular declamation. Theoretically, the Executive Government is the all-wise and benevolent agent of the community, with an eye which is everywhere, and an untiring arm. Practically, in its working capacity, it is a body of over-worked, much-criticised gentlemen who are not trusted half as much as they ought to be.

This passage was written by Viscount Goschen in 1883.[14]

Another difficulty that attends the journey by the middle way is that of economic discipline. No economic system can work without rewards and penalties. Under the pricing system, the rewards and penalties, the pressures or the stimuli to which persons are subject are mainly financial in character. What is to replace these former means of discipline when they are weakened, as they must be, under the new system? The coercion and regimentation that form the substitutes in totalitarian countries are rejected by democratic communities. Is there any alternative?

Recently, the idea has found favour that the solution lies in the creation of a kind of partnership between the government and organised bodies in industry. According to this view, the government is to determine the broad aims of policy, while industry or organised labour, after being persuaded into acceptance, will then assist in devising the means for achieving those aims. In other words, there is to be a Gentlemen's Agreement between the State and organised industry and labour. The idea is not unattractive, and experience during the war, as Sir Oliver Franks lately pointed out, suggests that much may be done by this means.[15] Wartime experience is not, of course, wholly relevant to peacetime conditions, for obvious reasons. Yet, even in peacetime, this method, which requires acquiescence by industry in the government's plan and help in its execution, has been widely used. The administration of location policy and price control depends to some extent on this method. So does, in part, the realisation of the government's export targets. The Chancellor abandoned what amounted to a tax on advertisements in return for a Gentlemen's Agreement with industry for carrying out an advertisement policy that would yield the same result. Among the means chosen to combat inflation bargains between the government on one side and organised industry and the trade unions on the other are given an important place.

On the whole economists have not shown any marked enthusiasm for this method of economic administration. For my part, I think that we shall be so hard put to it to find help in our journey along the middle way that we should not reject any method which offers even moderate prospects of success. However, I certainly think that there are narrow limits to the application of Gentlemen's Agreements, which are, moreover, attended with certain dangers.

In the first place, the force of a Gentlemen's Agreement depends upon the willingness of both parties to carry it out, even if circumstances change. Now, whatever may be said of industry, gentlemanly conduct can hardly be expected of governments. Whenever the welfare of the State, or the community as a whole, is concerned, a government may sometimes be compelled to go back on understandings reached with sectional interests. Industry is fully aware of this, and industry in consequence has to be cautious in committing itself to agreements which the other party may fail to carry out on the unanswerable plea that the general interest must come first.

Apart from this difficulty, our view of the method must be contingent to some extent on the nature of the bargains for which it is used. It may be valuable when employed to provide correctives in cases where the unregulated pricing system works badly, as (I suggest) in industrial location, or where large structural adjustments in particular industries need to be made quickly. The case is very different, however, when the method is employed in such a way as to displace the price mechanism, not merely to correct a bias in its working. If it is so used over a wide area of transactions, then, though the proposed path is novel, the destination is familiar—a fully-planned State. This condition apparently, is not what we desire; and, for several reasons, one of which I have already given, it is doubtful whether in such a State we could look to Gentlemen's Agreements to save us from the prescriptions of Commissars.

So much for the limits to the application of this method. I now come to certain dangers which, in a half-planned system, are inherent in it. These agreements have to be made with large representative organisations, such as trade associations, and they must usually provide for uniform treatment for all the members of an organisation. The greater the reliance of the government on bargains of this sort, the stronger become the organisations on which the government counts for the expertise needed to carry out its policy. In such organisations the newcomer usually has only a small voice, just because he is a newcomer; and in them the conservatism of the ordinary run of industrialist is likely to carry the day against the innovator. The *status quo* becomes strongly entrenched in them. Uniform treatment, which representative organisations insist upon, is a deadly principle in industrial life, for there progress depends upon favours going to those who are most alert in making or seizing opportunities.

Economic planning (even of the milder sort) here encounters a serious obstacle. A progressive economic system must be readily adaptable to changes in circumstances, and such changes are generally unforeseen and incalculable. The history of particular areas, or of whole countries, demonstrates the transformation that occurs, often in a short period, in the relative importance of different trades and of different firms within each trade. In a few decades industries which were insignificant and products which were hardly known may become the leading activities of a community. It is impossible for any economic inquiry, however penetrating it may be, to detect such changes in advance. They depend on habits of demand which have not yet been formed, and on new technical devices which may be only ideas in the minds of inventors or entrepreneurs. Sometimes they depend on nothing more than the chance that a Ford or a Morris may be born at a time when a combination of circumstances favours the exercise of his talents, or that a Hirst and a Holden may meet and take each other's measure at a critical moment in an industry's growth. The transformation in the industrial structure that occurs is sometimes the result of a multitude of minor adjustments in the scope of particular businesses.

Now that a knowledge of industrial technique is widely diffused over the world, the economic position of any country which, like Great Britain, lives by serving foreign markets, must depend largely on its alertness in moving into new fields of enterprise as it loses its former relative advantages in the old. Anything that handicaps the innovator, anything that checks the development of new types of enterprise or the adjustment of the old to altered circumstances must have damaging consequences. Government is liable to frame its policy with its eye on large organisations, on well-established producers or well-defined industries. Its methods of administration on the whole tend to weight the scales in favour of the average business man, and it tends to discriminate against the original and enterprising man from whom progress often proceeds. Government must plan on the basis of past trends and experiences; and in so far as it grants priorities to the well-established producers or trades, it may stifle the enterprises which are as yet hardly born, but might in a market economy become great businesses. To my mind, one of the most difficult tasks that confront governments engaged in planning the disposition of resources is to leave the way open to such enterprises. This, of course, is not a plea for returning to *laissez-faire*. I am trying to point to one of the major difficulties in operating the new system, and I am thus led back to the question which I raised a few moments ago, and which I now frame in the particular context of industrial development. Is it possible for the State to formulate far-reaching plans for the disposition of economic resources, plans which are intended to promote objectives of which men in their political capacity approve, and at the same time to afford adequate opportunities in the industrial sphere for 'the free and miscellaneous movements' of the mind and will, without which, if the experience of the past is any guide, progress in this country—and not only material progress—is in jeopardy?

9 The Efficiency of British Industry[1]

A nation specialised in manufacturing industry and dependent for its prosperity on world markets can never, for long, experience repose and stability. Even in the nineteenth century when Great Britain enjoyed industrial predominance, it appeared from time to time to contemporary observers that our position was being gravely threatened by developments elsewhere. Yet although we lost our leading place in some industries in which we had been pioneers, our industrial production as a whole continued to grow substantially. The progress was possible because we were able to shift our resources from trades where we had lost our former relative advantages to new trades which offered favourable opportunities. As Lord Beveridge once wrote: 'In the heyday of her early start [Great Britain] had gone successfully into many lines of business for which she had no enduring advantage. Once competitors entered the field, she came under growing pressure to discover and maintain those branches of work for which she had the greatest aptitude and to withdraw the rest'. His comment was a reference to the structural changes through which British industry passed in the last quarter of the nineteenth century. A contemporary observer of the same period, Sir William Ashley, writing in 1902, took a gloomy view of the probable outcome of those changes. We were coming to depend in our foreign trade, he thought, on exports of coal, a wasting asset, and on the products of cheap unskilled labour. The remainder of our industry was likely to decay in face of the scientific achievement of the Germans and the mass-production methods of the Americans. The gloom was soon dispelled. Between the turn of the century and 1914 there occurred a remarkable expansion of industrial production and a steep rise in the volume of our staple exports. The prophets of decay seemed to have been discredited.

After the First World War the international economic environment became unfavourable to the British export trade, and for a variety of reasons this country was obliged to make widespread modifications in the structure of her production. The great staple industries (textiles, coal, shipbuilding, and some branches of iron and steel and of mechanical engineering), which had hitherto provided the bulk of the exports, lost part of their foreign markets, and some of them (cotton, for example) entered upon a period of continuous decline. Yet, although the years between the wars were marked by violent industrial change and heavy unemployment, and although the volume of exports remained well below the 1913 level, this was not a period of stagnation. Many industries which had been small in 1914 became substantial during the next twenty-five years, and the volume of industrial production was far greater at the end of the period than at the beginning. On the eve of the Second World War the real income per head of our population was probably about thirty per cent higher than it had been before the First World War, a rise attributable mainly to the increased productivity of labour. Output per man-hour, it has been estimated, rose by some fifty per cent in the period. Thus, although industrial supremacy— the *relative* superiority of Great Britain as a manufacturing nation— had long passed, in an absolute sense (and this is after all the important sense from the standpoint of economic welfare) productive achievement was greater than ever before.

Is there reason for supposing that the future will reproduce, in broad outline, the experience of the past, and that those who predict decline can be disregarded? Are our troubles merely temporary—a consequence of wartime dislocation and of changes in the world economy to which we have not yet had time to adjust ourselves? Or has the international scene in which British industry plays a part, altered so profoundly as to make the task of adjustment beyond our powers? Are our difficulties due mainly to changes from without? Or can they be attributed to changes in ourselves, a loss of initiative, a decline of energy, a failure of nerve? These are fundamental questions which no-one at present can answer with assurance. Even an approach to them would require a survey far wider than can be attempted here. It may be useful, however, to consider one of the factors that will exert a powerful influence on our future, namely, industrial efficiency.

It is a commonplace of economic discussion that the way out of our present difficulties lies in increased production—that is, the more efficient use of the resources (the manpower, capital equipment and materials) at our disposal. It is also claimed that Britain's industry is behind that of many other countries in its methods of production. This criticism is not new. The loss of exports during the interwar years was often attributed in part to this cause. At that time critics sought to demonstrate the force of their arguments by comparisons between the organisation of certain British industries (especially those that were depressed) and that of their foreign counterparts. The individualistic structure of the British coal and cotton industries of the 1920s, it was said, made those trades incapable of taking the concerted action needed to meet the competition of their highly organised rivals abroad. Many government reports, notably the Balfour Report, pointed to the desirability of unification of control in industry (or rationalisation) as a means of securing the economies of large-scale operation and of effecting rapid adjustments in methods of manufacture. The government itself actively encouraged manufacturers to rationalise their trades, and foreign example had an important influence on this policy. Today, the observer who looks back on the results of industrial policy during the 1930s finds that rationalisation as practised here served to increase the control of producers over prices rather than to reduce costs; and that experience suggests that international comparisons of organisation, if they are to be used as a guide to policy in this country, must be approached with caution.

It is obviously useful to seek by inquiry from abroad for information about how others, especially the more successful among our competitors, run their trades. But it does not at all follow that because in Germany, the United States, or Japan, a particular industry that happened to be prosperous was organised in a certain way, therefore the corresponding British industry would have been well advised to follow that example. The very term 'corresponding' begs the question, for it is seldom that industries that go by the same name in different countries produce precisely the same type of goods for the same markets. Where there are differences in products or markets, those differences may well justify divergences in forms of organisation.

An illustration of this argument may be illuminating. In the early 1930s the horizontal organisation of the British cotton industry where spinning and weaving are normally in the hands of specialist concerns, was contrasted unfavourably with the vertically integrated organisation of the Japanese cotton industry which, it was alleged, operated with large combined spinning–weaving mills. Further inquiries showed, however, that it was only one section of the Japanese industry which was organised in this way, namely, the section which produced cheap standardised shirtings and sheetings for Eastern markets. The weaving sheds that turned out fancy goods and higher-quality goods were usually smaller than their British counterparts, and they were not associated financially or technically with the spinners from whom they obtained their yarns. Further, from 1931 to 1937, the section of the Japanese cotton industry which was advancing most rapidly, both in production and in the export trade, was the section composed of these relatively small independent weaving sheds. The great combined mills were meeting with increased competition in the lines of goods in which they were specialised, and Japan was shifting to the higher quality diversified goods for which the independent weaving sheds were the most efficient units of production. The types of goods produced by Lancashire bore a much closer resemblance to the products of the independent weaving sheds than to the products of the combined mills. It is ironical that at a moment when a large section of the Japanese cotton industry was assuming a structure similar to that of Lancashire, Lancashire should have been advised to create for itself an organisation modelled on that of a relatively declining section of the Japanese industry.

Even if products in the countries being compared are roughly identical, it does not always follow that there should be an identity of organisation. If the relative prices of different kinds of labour vary between the countries, or if the supply of capital for investment is more abundant in one than in the other, then this will affect the way in which it pays industrialists to organise the production of a commodity.

Again, the size of the unit of control may sometimes be due to circumstances that have nothing to do with productive efficiency. Combination in Germany during the 1920s, which led to the emergence of giant concerns, was stimulated by the need for replacing from abroad working capital lost during the inflation; for a large rationalised unit stood a better chance of obtaining foreign capital than a number of smaller independent producers. These arguments are not intended to suggest that all was well with British industrial organisation during the interwar years, nor that foreign example had not a great deal to teach us. The lesson is rather that an uncritical acceptance of foreign types of organisation as the norm is as foolish as insular complacency. Our task is more difficult than that of following foreign example. It is to work out improvements based on our own special circumstances.

The modern approach to the problem of comparative efficiency is via the channel of relative productivity. This approach is more direct than that which proceeds by way of comparisons of organisational forms; but it finds itself confronted by many of the same difficulties and by others also. The lack of identity between the products of the same industries in different countries is the most obvious difficulty common to both approaches. Other problems are more complex and may be illustrated by a few examples. The Platt Report on the Cotton Industry revealed that output per man-hour in nearly all processes in that industry was much higher in the United States than in Lancashire for the products chosen for comparison. 'With normal staffing British P.M.H. . . . is less than the American by approximately 18% to 49% in spinning, by 80% to 85% in winding, by 79% to 89% in beaming, and by 56% to 67% in weaving'. Does this mean, on the assumption that the product was substantially similar in the two countries, that the American industry was more than twice as efficient as the British, or that labour in the American industry was to that extent more efficient than in the British industry? Certainly not. Before we could draw the latter conclusion, we should have to consider whether labour in America was working with similar equipment to that used here (and of course it was not); and before we could draw the former conclusion we should have to take account of the differences in the resources available in the two countries. For instance, if in one country skilled labour is scarce and dear while capital is plentiful, then industry in that country will use a relatively large amount of capital equipment in its industrial processes. In another country where skilled labour is relatively cheap, it will pay employers to make extensive use of that labour and to invest less in elaborate equipment. In the former country output per man-hour will almost certainly be higher than in the second, but it does not at all follow that its industry is more efficient in the sense that the output for a given input of resources is greater. The latter comparison can, of course, be effected only in terms of money costs, since it is not possible to add together physical units of capital, labour, and natural resources. Here we encounter a formidable obstacle, since a comparison of money costs involves the rate of exchange between the currencies of the two countries, and that rate is determined by things that have little to do with productivity in a particular industry. Any comparison of productivity, must therefore, be tentative.

Even if we manage to reach conclusions about the relative productivity of particular industries in two countries, we still have to take account of another important aspect of the subject; for the efficiency of a country's industry depends in part upon the way in which its capital, labour, and natural resources are distributed over the economy as a whole. A country where capital and labour flow easily towards uses in which productivity is rising, and away from uses where productivity is falling, or is stationary, is more efficient in one sense than a country where such changes are brought about slowly or not at all. It is only by comparing returns from *all* activities in two countries that we can get an idea of relative efficiency in this larger sense. Such a comparison reveals its results in terms of income per head, subject to certain qualifications which need not here be discussed.

What, then, do we find if we turn to the estimates that have been made of productivity and income per head in different countries? The estimates of Mr Rostas and others suggest that before the recent war physical production per head in manufacturing industry was more than twice as great in the United States as in Great Britain, while in mining it was about four times as great. In Germany production per head in manufacturing was roughly the same as in this country. Since output is the basis of income, it might have been expected that income per head in these countries would stand in the same relationship as productivity. In fact, however, income per head in the United States was only slightly higher than here, and in Germany it was much lower. There are several reasons for this apparent paradox, but the most important is to be found in the different distribution of the occupied population in the three countries. Manufacturing industry, in which comparisons of productivity are so favourable to the United States, occupied before the war only twenty-five per cent of the American working population, whereas in Great Britain the proportion, was thirty-six per cent. For other branches of production the American superiority was much less marked. In particular, the American productivity in agriculture was only slightly greater than ours. Here we come to the heart of the explanation. In almost all countries production per head in agriculture is far lower than in manufacturing industry, and whereas in this country a very small proportion (less than five per cent) of the working population was engaged in agriculture, in the United States about one-fifth was so engaged. Thus, while Britain's production per head in manufacture and mining was much less than the American, she made up for this to a large extent by a more effective distribution of her occupied population. The same explanation holds for the comparison with Germany also. This shows that it is just as necessary for a country to choose the right industries as it is to be efficient in the industries actually chosen.

Further, demand and technique are always changing, and since these changes frequently require a rapid shift from old types of production to new, an efficient industrial system must be mobile or adaptable. This condition is more easily satisfied by some countries than by others. New industries often grow out of old ones by a series of adjustments in the scope of production of existing firms. For instance, in several countries the manufacture of bicycles was originally developed by small-arms manufacturers, and more recently petroleum companies have played a large part in the creation of the synthetic rubber industry. In this country the jute industry grew out of the linen industry, and many branches of the motor accessories trade out of the 'lighting' brass foundry trade. Some industries, however, can adjust themselves more readily than others to changes in demand. Industries which use equipment of a specific kind and employ labour with specific skills find greater difficulty in transforming the scope of their production than do those in which the processes employed are common to the manufacture of a wide range of goods. It was easier for the Midland hardware trades to change over to new products when their old markets declined than it was for the cotton spinners or the shipbuilders or the pig-iron producers. One of the problems of British industry in the interwar period was that many of the staple industries whose traditional products were losing favour worked with highly specific equipment and with labour that had specific skills. But even in such industries alertness in detecting incipient changes and willingness to invest in new types of equipment and in the retraining of labour can do much to accelerate the transition, and these qualities are distinguishing marks of industrial efficiency. It may well be that employers and workers in the older staple industries were slow in reponding to change. Government policy, as we have seen, must bear some responsibility for this, for in the interwar years it was directed towards maintaining wages and profits in the depressed industries rather than towards stimulating a shift to new activities.

It has also been claimed that mobility was impeded in this country because of the specialisation of certain of the industrial areas. As long as the industries located in those areas were growing, there were advantages in specialisation. But when, as in the inter-war period, the older industries of South Wales and the North decayed and the newer industries grew up in the Southern half of the country, the result was the appearance of the depressed areas, for workers could not easily transfer themselves to districts in which new employment was offered. The Development Area policy has been designed to make these transitions easier by encouraging the location of new industries in the hitherto specialised areas and, if wisely administered, it can make a useful contribution to mobility. But new industries cannot always operate as efficiently in the older centres as in new ones, and a migration of labour cannot always be avoided if we are intent on producing at minimum cost. An efficient industrial system cannot expect to maintain all its old centres of employment any more than it can expect to preserve all its old industries.

There are thus three aspects of efficiency which we must view. There is the efficiency with which a firm or industry uses the resources available to it; there is the efficiency with which the industrial system as a whole allocates its resources over various uses; and finally there is the speed with which the system responds to change.

Many British industries have been criticised under the first heading because of their relatively low output per man-hour. This mediocrity of performance has been attributed to a number of causes, such as inferior management, the rigidity of trade union regulations, and failure to use up-to-date equipment. Much emphasis has recently been placed on the last-mentioned deficiency, and attention has been called to the small amount of capital per worker in certain British industries when compared with that in 'corresponding' American industries. In the last quarter of a century the disparity seems to have widened. So far as the old staple trades are concerned, a failure to invest in up-to-date equipment is easily understood by reference to their chronic depression during the interwar period. But it is sometimes alleged that the cause is more deepseated, and the age of our industries is held to be responsible for the deficiencies from which British industry suffers in this respect as in many others. This charge requires investigation. Persons associated with an old industry are likely to have immense resources of experience and skill. These resources, which the older British industries can certainly claim, may sometimes enable them to compete successfully with newer industries overseas which have been started with superior equipment. On the other hand, old industries may suffer from inertia. Experience shows that when fundamental technical change occurs, the older centres of production sometimes decline not wholly because they lose their former physical advantages of location, but simply because of their reluctance to adopt the new methods. The decay of certain traditional centres of industry at the time of the industrial revolution has been explained in this way. In our own time, the British iron and steel industry has been criticised on the grounds that it failed to effect the changes in organisation and location which were required by new technical conditions. It remained tied to the old centres, so it is claimed, when it should have shifted to the newer ore fields. Even the proposals for reconstruction contained in the Report of the British Iron and Steel Federation to the Ministry of Supply were of necessity influenced by the conditions which the industry has inherited from the past. Since a large production of iron and steel will be required during the next few years, it is impossible to plan the postwar industry as if it were a 'green field' project. Much of the investment is necessary for patching the old plants in the old localities. To this extent the organisation and location of the industry will be determined by what was economical in the past rather than by the requirements of the present. In the same way, economies of operation may be difficult to achieve in some industries because wage systems are based on past conditions; an example is to be found in the cotton industry. Obviously, such handicaps may be surmounted; but the weight of tradition is not one which a newly industrialised country has to contend with, and it must be set against the advantages which an 'old' country possesses in its greater experience and skill.

It is not only the older British industries that have been the target for adverse criticism. Indeed, output per head shows up even less favourably, as compared with America, in some of the newer industries than in the old. Here the deficiency is sometimes attributed to the relatively small size of plants and firms in this country, and to a lack of standardisation and specialisation on the part of British producers. Too much weight should not, however, be given to the former explanation; for such inquiries as have been made have failed to detect any close correlation between size and low costs. It does seem true, however, that one reason for the low British productivity compared with the American is to be found in the lack of standardisation of British products. The motor car industry provides one of the best examples of this contrast. In the United States the production of motor cars in 1939 was ten times as great as in Britain. The three leading American companies were responsible for nearly nine-tenths of the total production, whereas in Great Britain the three leading companies turned out only two-thirds of the much smaller output. The contrast in the variety of engine-types and models was even more striking than in the degree to which output was concentrated in the two countries. The popular argument that lack of standardisation in Britain is to be explained by the smaller size of the market compared with the American has little substance, for in many products the British market is quite large enough to enable producers to achieve the full technical economies of large-scale organisation. The reason is rather that the British demand is less uniform than the American. Does this provide grounds for criticising British industry? If the British consumer demands variety– even though this means that he has to pay a relatively high price—it may be contended that British industry must organise itself to provide the variety. Variety in production, however, may sometimes be due not to the insistence of consumers but to the efforts of each manufacturer to carve out for himself a market in which he has a partial monopoly. British firms may prefer to enjoy the security that such a monopoly confers, even though the market for each product is limited, rather than to compete on price for a mass demand.

Even if we do attribute the British variety in production mainly to consumer insistence, it may nevertheless be a serious handicap to Great Britain in catering for a world demand for cheap mass-produced goods. Whether this is so or not depends in part on conditions in the outside world. If our relative advantages in international trade are held to lie in the supply of quality goods (as is probably true), then it would not be wise for us to reorganise our industries with the object of competing in markets for mass-produced goods where other countries have already established a superiority. The answer to the question must ultimately depend on a judgment about whether the market for quality goods is likely to be extensive, and this in turn depends on the prospects for material prosperity in customer countries. So the problem is an extremely intricate one and no general solution is possible. The right course to pursue in any particular trade can be decided only by those who have an intimate knowledge of it.

Let us now consider the efficiency that arises from the optimum distribution of resources among different industries. Obviously a country that has been able to allocate its manpower and capital so that no unit of them is employed in an occupation in which the value of its output is less than it would be if employed in some other activity, has reached an ideal solution of the problem. One of our difficulties at the present time in approaching this ideal is that the allocation of manpower and investment required to meet our immediate troubles is unlikely to be the allocation that a long-run view of our economic situation requires. We are at present directing a large part of our manpower and new investment into a few of the older industries (coal, cotton, iron and steel), where shortages of supply are seriously handicapping the whole of our reconstruction effort, especially in exports. Yet, while an enlargement in our production of (say) cotton goods would be an immense advantage to us in this time of world deficiency, it is most unlikely that, when production has recovered in other parts of the world, we shall be able to rely to the extent that we did in the past on exports of textiles. This is probably true of other staple industries which are now receiving priority. Since our capital resources are narrowly limited, heavy investment in those trades must mean that less is available for the newer industries upon which our future trade is likely to depend. Thus we are being compelled to sacrifice industrial efficiency in the future to our immediate necessities.

Finally, there is the question of resilience—of adaptability to change. If, as is probable, the future of Britain will turn on her success in moving to new forms of enterprise as old products meet with competition from elsewhere, then this aspect of efficiency is of first-rate importance for us. Industrial resilience can exist only in the presence of right attitudes on the part of industrialists and workers. With changes in economic circumstances, both groups must be prepared to shift readily to new products and to new occupations. For the industrialist to act as if he had a right to profits in the line of business in which he is at present engaged, or for the worker to insist on his right to work in his present job and his present locality, is fatal to industrial resilience. Unfortunately, these attitudes had become manifest even during the interwar years, and long experience of government controls has confirmed them. During the war industrialists lost their function of risk-bearing and became mere administrative agents of the government. Since the war they have had little opportunity of resuming their former rôle. Even at present some materials are allocated to firms on the basis of prewar usage, and the effect of this is to check the transference of business from high-cost to low-cost producers and to weaken financial inducements to greater efficiency. As long as the controls last—and they cannot be abolished while inflationary pressure continues—a serious brake on efficiency will remain. It is all the more necessary to remove it at the earliest opportunity, because our economy is being affected by long-term influences that are unfavourable to resilience, such as the ageing of the population.

Since the war the government has taken a hand in the promotion of industrial efficiency, namely, by establishing the Institute of Management, by encouraging industrial research, by stimulating investment in new equipment where there is an obvious deficiency (either by subsidy or by providing new facilities for raising capital), by developing a regional advisory service for small firms, and by making provision for the establishment of development councils where manufacturers can co-operate in the solution of common problems. These measures probably represent about as much positive action as can be expected from the government in this field. For, in the end, industrial efficiency must depend, on the one hand, on the initiative and intelligence of manufacturers and workers themselves and, on the other hand, on the existence of an economic environment congenial to enterprise. State intervention may even do harm to efficiency, and especially to industrial resilience, if it consolidates the power of established producers and by so doing reduces the opportunities for new types of undertakings. The government's most useful activity in this connection is negative in character. It should aim to remove the barriers to initiative and to destroy any force hostile to innovation that appears in industry itself. Under the first head, its taxation policy, as well as its use of physical controls, is clearly important. Under the second head, it can attempt (as it is now proposed to a limited extent) to take action against restrictive practices. But it cannot *compel* us to be enterprising nor oblige us to exercise the pioneering qualities upon which our former industrial greatness rested and without which we cannot hope to resume our economic progress.

10   Industrial Prospects in the Early 1950s[1]

During the latter part of 1951 certain important British industries, for the first time for over ten years, were faced with a shortage of demand for their products, and since then many business people have suffered the shock of realising that a sellers' market is not a permanent feature of the postwar economy. Only a very rash prophet would state with confidence that the deflationary forces in the world were now stronger than the inflationary forces which for so many years dominated economic affairs. Yet recent experience suggests that the world economy as a whole, and the British economy in particular, are much more vulnerable to attack by the forces of recession than seemed probable only a year ago. This proposition would be admitted even by those who believe that the depression in the textile industries is to be regarded as a necessary part of the process by which resources are being diverted to rearmament, or who confidently expect that the fall in the demand for various kinds of consumption goods will shortly be reversed.

The situation can be interpreted at three levels. Superficially it would seem reasonable to suppose that the depression in textiles came about mainly through heavy buying in anticipation of price increases during the first half of 1951, and the withdrawal of customers from the market as soon as their price-expectations changed. According to this view the depression is likely to continue until stocks have been cleared. Indeed, it may deepen and spread to other industries in the course of this year if the restrictions imposed by customer-countries on our exports throw increased supplies of 'frustrated exports' on the home market before Britain's own import restrictions have had time to reduce substantially the quantity of foreign goods for sale here. On a short-term view, therefore, the outlook for a considerable sector of the economy seems to be deflationary. If one looks beyond this short period, however, the prospects are very different. Expenditure on rearmament is expected to grow steeply; large claims for wage-increases are looming ahead; and the solution of our present balance-of-payments problem may demand further steep cuts in imports. On what may be called a middle-term view, therefore, the prospects are inflationary. But about the timing of the resumption of inflationary trends there must be serious doubt. Expenditure on rearmament is lagging behind what was expected; the effects of the dearer-money policy are pervading the economy as a whole; and at present, over a part of the industrial field, conditions are such as to make employers more strongly resistant than hitherto to demands for wage increases. Economic trends in the United States are also uncertain. Thus, it is possible that the rise in monetary demand will be delayed for some time. Beyond this middle period the dangers are of another sort. The long-continued inflation from which this and most other countries have suffered since the war has produced distortions in the structure of costs and prices and the creation in some industries of new capacity that cannot be sustained without further, and perhaps continuous, inflation. The precarious basis on which much economic activity now rests would be clearly revealed if armaments expenditure were reduced, as it presumably will be when the present plans have been carried through—and perhaps even before the period is over. If this interpretation is correct, the world may well face a depression in the middle 1950s, and whether governments really have the capacity to apply adequate corrective measures in such circumstances is, to say the least, uncertain.

These are all debatable judgments of the present situation. Whether or not they are acceptable, however, it is evident that we have reached the end of a clearly marked phase in postwar economic history. This is, therefore, a convenient moment at which to make a broad survey of the condition of British industry as it confronts the doubtful future. To begin with, a comparison of the trends in industrial development since the recent war with those of the interwar period may be illuminating.

The years between 1919 and 1939 saw a profound change in the structure and composition of British industry. As is well known, certain of the older industries suffered a steep—in some cases a continuous—decline in output and employment. These included the older textile industries (especially cotton), coalmining and ore-mining, shipbuilding, certain branches of mechanical engineering (such as textile machinery, railway equipment and prime-mover manufacture), and some sections of the iron and steel industry (such as pig-iron production). In all these industries a leading cause of the decline, in some cases the only cause, was the loss of foreign markets either through the successful competition of overseas industries, or through the introduction of substitutes (as of oil for coal in ship-propulsion). On the other hand, a large number of industries, including many which had been very small at the end of the 1914–18 War, expanded substantially. Among these were the motor and cycle trades, electrical engineering and apparatus, rayon, hosiery, carpets, furniture, building, a multitude of miscellaneous consumption-goods industries, and many 'service' trades. Some of these industries, notably the electrical engineering and apparatus trade, developed large export markets; but most of their increased output was sold at home.

The coincidence of a decline in the staple trades, which were much concerned with export, and a rise in other industries, which disposed of most of their output in the domestic market, meant that Great Britain was engaged during these years on the difficult process of diverting a large part of her resources from manufacture for export to manufacture for home use. In fact, the proportion of industrial production that was exported is estimated to have fallen from thirty-five per cent in 1913 to twenty-seven per cent in 1924, twenty-two per cent in 1930, and fifteen per cent in 1938. This switch in resources was made possible by two circumstances: first, the movement of the terms of trade in favour of Great Britain during the period—a unit of manufactured exports bought far more imports in 1938 than in 1913—and, secondly, the reduction during the 1920s and the cessation during the 1930s of (net) overseas capital investment by Great Britain. It was thus possible for Great Britain to import all the food and materials she required in order to sustain a considerably improved standard of life, in spite of the steep fall in the volume of her exports. She did not, however, effect the re-allocation of her industrial resources with complete success. A measure of her failure was the heavy unemployment which clouded the country's economic and social life throughout the 1920s and 1930s.

Since the end of the Second World War industrial development has taken a different course. In the first place, the tendency for exports to decline has been reversed. In 1951 the volume of British exports was about seventy-five per cent greater than before the war, and the proportion of British industrial output exported had also risen steeply. In this respect the wheel of change has turned a full circle since 1913. The reasons for this renewed concentration on exports are well recognised. These larger exports are not a symptom of economic prosperity, for they have been made necessary because of this country's weakened economic position in the world. First, the terms of trade have moved sharply against manufacturing countries, and so a unit of British exports no longer buys as much imported food or raw materials as it did during the 1930s. Secondly, as during the war Great Britain lost a large part of her foreign investments (the interest and dividends on which paid for over one-fifth of her imports in the 1930s), she can obtain essential imports only be exporting more goods. The repayment of foreign debts, accumulated during the war in the form of 'sterling balances', has also been possible only through increased exports.

It had been realised, even before the end of the war, that unless Great Britain were to succeed in raising her exports, she would have to reduce her imports drastically, with grievous effects on her standard of life. But at that time it was not easy to pick out the industries which might be expected to furnish these exports, nor indeed was it possible to feel much assurance that the markets for the necessary quantity could be found. In the event, the task has been made easier through the absence for several years of Britain's two chief competitors. Germany and Japan, from the world's markets, and also through the generally inflationary conditions that have prevailed. The diversion of so large a part of our productive capacity to export might have been expected, in itself, to have led to a fall in the standard of life. That this has not happened can be attributed, in part, to the increase in Britain's production, and, in part, to the using up of our reserves and to aid furnished by the United States and Canada.

How has the renewed concentration on exports affected the development of the various industries—in particular, their relative importance in the British economy? What has happened certainly cannot be described simply as a reversal of trends. It is true that certain industries that were declining before the war have regained much of the ground which they lost. This applies especially to the shipbuilding industry, which after twenty years of shrinkage has, since 1945, recovered approximately to the size at which it stood in 1913. Some formerly declining branches of the metal and engineering trades, for example, pig-iron and textile machinery manufacture, have also made a substantial recovery. Furthermore, in the inflationary conditions of the last few years, no industry could attribute—until very recently— a failure to expand to a shortage of demand, as it could in prewar days. Nevertheless, although the economic environment has been very different from prewar, the changes in the relative importance of the various industries have on the whole closely resembled those of the interwar period; that is to say, with some qualifications, the interwar trends in industrial development have persisted. The corollary is that the increased exports have been provided in the main not through the revival of the staple exporting industries that shrank in the interwar period, but through the enlargement of the exports of the newer trades, which were relatively prosperous even at that time. Among these trades there are some which formerly sold most of their output at home, but which since the war have found large markets abroad. To a large extent the rise in exports has been brought about by the increase in the exporting activities of a group of industries which for several decades have been expanding.

These general statements may be illustrated by a few examples. Let us take, first, two of the older staple industries which suffered from a chronic depression in the interwar period chiefly through a loss of foreign markets—coal and cotton. The manpower in these two industries diminished between 1913 and 1939 by about one-third and two-thirds respectively. During the Second World War the industries suffered a further loss of labour, for workers left them for employment in the munitions industries and for the armed forces. After the war, policy was directed towards rebuilding their labour force so that they might cater for the urgent postwar demand for their products. These efforts, however, were only partly successful, and so the output and manpower of both industries have failed to regain even the levels of 1939, which, as we have seen, were far below those of 1913. In both coal and cotton, then, the absolute decline has persisted since 1939.

Meanwhile, the metal and engineering group of trades, especially the newer branches of that group, has gone ahead very rapidly. This group, which was growing in relative importance before the war, expanded further during the war, and after 1945, benefited by the heavy demand for capital goods both at home and abroad. The motor industry, which before the war sold most of its products on the domestic market, has become predominantly an exporting industry, and there has been a great increase in the size of the electrical, chemical, aircraft and non-ferrous metal industries. Among textiles the rayon trade, which was expanding rapidly during the 1930s, suffered comparatively little during the war and has grown greatly since 1945. The conclusion that emerges is that, in spite of the violent fluctuations in general economic conditions over the last thirty years, the broad changes in the relative import- ance of the various British industries have been consistently in the same direction. The most striking results are the lessened relative importance of coalmining and the older textile industries and the rise in the importance of the metal and engineering group, especially the newer members of that group.

The chief question raised by these reflections upon the past is whether the British industrial structure is now stout enough to face the storms that probably lie ahead. In seeking an answer to this question, we must first turn to consider the problem of foreign competition. Before the war the three chief exporting countries were Great Britain, the United States and Germany; together these were responsible for about one-third of total (world) exports. Three-quarters, or more, of the British and the German exports, in value, consisted of manufactured goods, while about half of the American exports fell into that category.

Although these three countries competed with one another in many classes of finished products, to a large extent each of them specialised in particular classes of goods. For example, in 1937 over a quarter of Great Britain's exports consisted of textiles; coal and manufactured fuel accounted for about one-tenth, and machinery and vehicles (including ships) for rather less than one-fifth of her total exports. Germany, for her part, specialised in chemical, metal, machinery and vehicle exports, and the United States, so far as manufactured and mineral products were concerned, in oil, metal, machinery and vehicles. For neither Germany nor the United States were exports of textile goods nearly as important as they were for Great Britain; the value of the yarn and piece-goods exports of these two competitors taken together amounted to well under half that of the textile exports of Great Britain. It was, of course, Japan that constituted this country's chief rival in international trade in textiles, and Japan's competition had proved keenest in cotton goods of the kind sold in the Asian, low-priced markets. In the trade in machinery and vehicles, which was important for all three major exporting countries, each country specialised to a consider- able extent in particular types of goods (except perhaps for electrical machinery and apparatus, where the exports of all three were of the same order of magnitude). Thus, the United States was far ahead of the other two countries in motor car exports, while the German and the American exports of machine tools were much greater than the British. On the other hand, Great Britain led in prime-movers and boilers, and she and Germany far outstripped the United States as exporters of ships and textile machinery. If we were to break down these large categories of goods, the degree of specialisation would become even more obvious.

The specialisation applied also to markets. Germany sold the greater part of her goods to Continental Europe and easily led in exports to Central and Eastern Europe. The United States found her chief markets in the Americas and Japan; while the United Kingdom was ahead of the others in distant markets—Africa, Oceania, India and China.

Now, since the war, the increase in the British export trade has not come from an expansion in the exports of those products in which she formerly specialised (such as textiles and coal), for her overseas sales of those goods have declined. It has come from the growth in her exports of metal and engineering goods and chemicals, in which the lead was formerly held by one of the other great exporting countries. Thus, she has become the chief exporter of motor cars—a class of product in which her trade was formerly quite small—and she has re-established a large export trade in ships —a trade in which she had been overtaken by Germany during the 1930s. In 1950 machinery, vehicles and electrical goods made up two-fifths of Great Britain's total exports, compared with only a quarter in 1938 when the total volume of exports was much smaller. The metal, engineering and chemical groups, as a whole, accounted for nearly fifty-five per cent of total British exports in 1950 and 1951.

Circumstances have been very favourable to Britain in building up her export trade in these goods, for the United States has been preoccupied in supplying the urgent demands of her domestic market, and Germany has been slowly recovering from the effects of defeat and economic dislocation. In spite of the claims of rearmament, however, American productive capacity is now such as to make her a more formidable competitor in those classes of products in which Great Britain has been especially successful since the war; while Germany's output and exports of engineering and chemical products have grown very rapidly during the last year. It would seem, therefore, that Great Britain will have to fight hard to hold her own in the fields in which she has gained most during the postwar period. It is significant, moreover, that the pattern of specialisation in foreign trade that existed before the war has been partly destroyed as a result of Great Britain's encroachment on the specialities of her rivals. We must expect, therefore, that competition among the three will become even keener than it was before the war. It is improbable that the intensity of the struggle will be mitigated by a return to the prewar pattern of specialisation, for this would require a large expansion of Britain's exports of textiles. In the chief branch of the textile trade (cotton) the indications are that the long-persistent trends will continue; that is to say, the probability is that the chief consuming countries will become increasingly self-supplying in cotton manufactures and that international trade will shrink further. And, in this diminishing field, Great Britain will have to compete with the Japanese who have now rebuilt their cotton industry.

Similar changes have occurred in the distribution of the markets served by each of these countries. To a considerable extent the geographical pattern of specialisation has been destroyed by the war, and it is not likely to be reformed. In particular, Western Germany has lost her markets in eastern, and south-eastern Europe, and she will, therefore, have to strive to sell a larger proportion of her exports in overseas countries where she will come into competition with British goods. There is a similar situation in the Far East. The Japanese have lost—for the time being at any rate—their former chief markets in China and north-east Asia. Yet their need for a large export trade in manufactured goods will be as urgent in the years to come as it was before the war. If their markets in China and north-east Asia do not recover, Japanese exports will be directed into other areas where they will probably offer increased competition with those of Great Britain.

The renewal of competition with British goods in foreign markets would not be a reason for disquiet if we could look forward confidently to a continued buoyancy of international trade as a whole. Whether we can assume this or not, however, the question of the efficiency of British industry must become increasingly important as we move into an era of vigorous international competition. This question has certainly not been ignored in Great Britain since the war. Numerous inquiries have been carried through by the various Board of Trade Working Parties and by the Productivity Teams sponsored by the Anglo-American Council on Productivity; while the concern of the government with problems of industrial organisation and re-equipment has been expressed in many innovations in its policy towards industry since 1945. Increased efficiency, it has long been realised, was the chief means by which this country might hope to offset the consequences of its loss of foreign assets and its worsened terms of trade during the late 1940s, and increased efficiency is the means by which it can hope to counter renewed foreign competition during the 1950s.

What can be said about improvements in British industrial efficiency since the war? It is not easy to provide general statements on this subject, but it may be useful to refer to some of the statistical evidence which, imperfect as it is, throws some light on the problem. The volume of manufacturing production in Britain in 1951 (excluding building) was probably about forty per cent above that in 1938. This represents over the period an annual rate of increase much the same as that of the period between 1924 and 1937. It is more difficult to estimate changes in industrial productivity (output per man-year) over the same term of years; but the improvement between 1938 and 1951 was probably of the order of twelve or fifteen per cent. The changes in productivity have differed considerably from industry to industry. The largest increases appear to have occurred in the engineering, metal and chemical industries. They have been small in cotton, while productivity in the coal industry and in building is lower than in prewar days.

This rise in productivity is one of the most hopeful, as it has been one of the most persistent, trends in our industrial system. It was chiefly the rise in productivity in the interwar period which made possible the improvement in the British standard of life, in spite of the heavy unemployment of those years. The Second World War arrested the process, but only temporarily, and our chief hope of material progress in the future depends upon this factor. Improvements in productivity, however, are not to be regarded as inevitable. They depend upon a complex of circumstances, but the outstanding causes are, first, advances in applied science and technology and, secondly, the enterprise of our industrial leaders in introducing new types of products and in finding cheaper ways of producing existing types. Generally (though not always), the application of the discoveries of science to industry and the introduction of new methods of manufacture require increased capital investment, and so advances in productivity in any economy are usually closely associated with a rise in the quantity of capital per head. Applied science, enterprise and capital—these lie at the foundations of industrial progress, and the economic policy of any government should be to foster them if it aims at raising the material wellbeing of its citizens.

In any estimate of the industrial future of this country it is necessary to consider whether the general economic environment and the policy of the government are likely to be favourable to these three agents of industrial progress. In this context the question of applied science can be dismissed with only a brief reference, for the methods of promoting scientific research and the application of its results to industry have been widely discussed and governments have been active in fostering improvements in this field. There is, of course, controversy; but it is over methods rather than objectives. It is frequently argued that this country's massive achievements in fundamental research have not been matched by its success in the practical application of the results of that research. In so far as this criticism is just, however, it can be resolved into a criticism of industrial leadership, a claim that where we have fallen behind is in enterprise. The recent past provides evidence which bears this out. The most ominous feature of the interwar period was not that our older staple industries, in which we had formerly led the world, were in decay, but that other countries had taken the lead in the new industries which were then developing. Our position in certain of the newer branches of engineering, for example, motorcar production, did not compare with the position which we had once held, and still largely held, in the older branches such as railway equipment and shipbuilding. Among the textile trades, we were still in the first rank in cotton, wool and linen; but other countries had far outstripped us in the production of rayon.

Now it may well be that since the war British industry has recovered the enterprise which formerly distinguished it; but at the same time it may be doubted whether either the government or industry has yet acquired the attitude towards innovation which has been such a powerful influence in establishing the industrial leadership of the United States. In Great Britain what might be called the 'architectural' conception of industry is still very common and has had an influence on the policies both of the government and of industrialists themselves. It is characteristic of this conception that every industry should hold that it has a prescriptive right to its existing place in the economic structure and should claim that the government ought to buttress it if the need should arise. The assumption which is sometimes made by the trade unions that every type of worker has a right to maintain his customary place on the wage-ladder has its parallel among manufacturers in the view that every industry, once established, has a permanent right to its niche in the economy. As a corollary, the members of an industry often feel indignant if a firm hitherto engaged in some other line of production takes up the manufacture of their types of products and breaks into their preserves. Yet history shows clearly enough that economic progress is usually attended by the destruction of some established positions, and that constructive innovations often proceed from firms which see advantage to themselves in 'muscling in' upon an old trade, especially if the existing firms in it have become conservative in their methods and policies.

If this 'architectural' view is allowed to influence policy, economic progress may be seriously menaced. It is not that policy can, in the end, arrest the changes in the relative importance of firms and industries that are brought about by alterations in demand and technique. Those forces are far stronger than any political measures that are taken to defeat them can be. But if the maintenance of the *status quo* plays a large part either in the government's industrial policy or in the policy of powerful associations of producers, then the resilience and adaptability of the economy may be reduced. Policy should work with the grain of economic development, not against it. Thus, it may be questioned whether, at a time when this country was very short of industrial capital, the government was well advised to subsidise investment in the cotton industry, as it did after the war. Our exiguous supplies of new capital, it might be thought, could have been more advantageously invested in industries with long-run prospects superior to those of the cotton trade. It is a matter of serious concern, also, that the government and the National Coal Board, in deciding on the distribution of capital expenditure over the next decade among the various coalfields, should apparently have been influenced by a policy of maintaining the *status quo* among them nearly as much as by considerations of the most economical sources of coal supply. Some critics take the view that the postwar Development Plan of the iron and steel industry conceded too much investment to the older high-cost centres of production and too little to the more newly developed areas where there are cheap ore supplies.

The dangers of misdirected investment are always especially great during periods of inflation, and it may prove that the inflationary conditions of the postwar years have led in many lines of production to the expansion of capacity which cannot be sustained. In this and in other ways inflation has led to waste; while the heavy taxation which has been introduced to curb it has not merely reduced incentives to individuals but has also made it difficult for both individuals and firms to save for further industrial investment, or at times even to maintain their capital intact. This is serious enough for established concerns; but it may be disastrous for new enterprises. Innovations do not always originate in large concerns. Many new devices and products have in the past been introduced by small firms, and as large organisations tend to be cautious, opportunities must be afforded to forceful pioneers if economic progress is to continue. Experience shows that new industries often spring from small beginnings and, since we cannot tell where the next advance will start, we must beware of so rigidly ordering our industrial life as to leave no chance for unconventional and unofficial enterprise. If, in the future, private finance is not available for the pioneer in the early days of his career, and if, because of heavy taxation, he cannot build up his capital resources quickly through the reinvestment of his profits, as was usual in the past, then one of the main avenues through which material advancement has come will be closed.

All this is highly relevant to the question of Great Britain's industrial future. Ever since she became industrialised, this country's progress has depended largely upon her taking the lead in new developments, for her natural resources, apart from coal, have never been very great. Throughout the nineteenth century, as competitor-nations appeared, she succeeded in adapting herself to the new conditions and in shifting her resources to fresh activities. During the interwar period, as we have seen, she appeared to have lost some of this resilience, and other countries succeeded to her rôle as the chief industrial pioneer. Great Britain's economic future will depend to a great extent on whether she can recover her former resilience and adaptability; in other words, on whether she can show capacity for industrial leadership. And her performance in this capacity will be determined by whether she can produce industrialists of imagination and initiative on the one hand, and, on the other hand, whether she can provide an economic and social environment congenial to the exercise of business talent.

11   Economic Progress, Retrospect and Prospect[1]

The economists of today are no less ready than their predecessors to proffer advice on the ordering of affairs. Indeed, if there are any among our administrators who think that this advice is important. they must be embarrassed at its profusion, and they may well feel every sympathy with the plight of the Confucian disciple of whom it was said: 'When Tzu-lu heard any precept and was still trying unsuccessfully to put it into practice, his one fear was that he might hear some fresh precept'. I shall not add to their embarrassment, for although what I have to say has some relation to economic policy, the precepts that I have to expound are mellow with great age.

The presumption that, once a country has transformed itself into a modern industrial society, its continued material progress is assured (in the absence of a political cataclysm) seems to have long survived the loss of belief in progress in general, and until recently it appeared to be undisturbed by all the disorders of our time. We might not be prepared to go quite so far as Mill who declared in 1848:

> Whatever may be the other changes which the economy of society is destined to undergo, there is one actually in progress concerning which there can be no dispute...there is at least one progressive moment which continues with little interruption from year to year and from generation to generation; a progress in wealth; an advance in what is called material prosperity.[2]

But it was at any rate possible for a distinguished authority in 1944, when a bleak view of our future might well have been held, to suggest, on the basis of certain assumptions which he presumably thought to be reasonable, that it would be possible for the British people in 1948 to consume nineteen per cent more goods and services than in 1938, to invest twenty-five per cent more and to produce enough exports to pay for all the necessary imports.[3] In the event, things did not turn out quite so well; but the experience of this country in the decades before the war did not suggest that such a forecast was unduly optimistic. Economic statisticians have estimated that between 1880 and 1913 the real income of this country more than doubled and that average real wages rose by about two-fifths. Further, they tell us that, although this progress was interrupted by the 1914–18 War, by 1924 real income had almost recovered to its prewar level, while real wages were about twelve per cent higher. We look back on the interwar period as one of economic distress. Yet the estimates are that between 1924 and 1938 aggregate real income rose by about a quarter, and average real wages by over a fifth.[4] All this confirms the common observation that we were a good deal better off on the eve of the Second World War than we had been before 1914. To this progress many factors had contributed, including, of course, our more favourable terms of trade. But the main cause was the rise in industrial production, which was estimated at eighty-four per cent between 1907 and 1937. This was equivalent to an increase in output per wage-earner of forty-seven per cent and, since the length of the normal working week had been reduced during the period, to an increase in output per man-hour of sixty-five per cent.[5] Most of this advance was achieved after 1924—in the years of industrial stagnation, so-called. As was suggested of another period that has a bad name in economic history, that from 1815 to 1850, the events which most impress themselves upon the attention of contemporaries are not always the most representative of the period.[6] Economic progress (in the sense of a rise in production and real income per head) may sometimes make less impression on opinion than the instability which attends the advance. It was, of course, the persistence of heavy unemployment that had given the interwar years a bad name. Since, however, substantial progress had been made in spite of that unemployment, and since it was thought that we had discovered how to avoid it in the future, there appeared to be justification for the confident extrapolations of 1944.

Yet many of the wise men of the past had, in the relatively favourable conditions of their own time, inclined to the view that material progress, like happiness, never continues long in one stay. The shadow of Malthus hovered over the economy of the early nineteenth century, and in the Victorian heyday Jevons had created some despondency by pointing to the probable effects of the disappearance of one of the main natural advantages upon which British industrial progress had depended. With the exhaustion of easily accessible coal 'the cost of fuel must rise', he said, 'perhaps within a life-time, to a rate injurious to our manufacturing and commercial supremacy . . . and the check to our progress must become perceptible within a century'.[7] Nearly fifty years later Marshall, after referring to the rise in real wages during his lifetime 'at a rate which [had] no parallel in the past and [might] probably have none in the future', expressed fears for what the coming years had in store for us—fears based largely on the probable worsening of our terms of trade with primary-producing countries. This was, he said in 1907, an 'age of economic grace' which 'may run out before the end of the century'.[8]

Some of these misgivings have been justified, although not always in the way that their authors expected. It is true that the Malthusian devil appears finally to have left our shores for the more congenial demographic climate of Eastern Asia. But we no longer enjoy superiority in natural resources; the age of dear British coal has come, and we have fewer advantages than many other countries in access to supplies of alternative sources of power. As for the terms of trade, after two decades in which cheap imports had placed a cushion under our elbows, they have moved against us at a critical time, although of course it would be very rash to assume that the present relationship between the prices of primary and manufactured products will persist for a long time. These changes, however, have not been responsible for the most serious damage to the foundations upon which economic progress in the past was believed to rest. The breakdown in the system of multilateral trade, the disappearance of an international monetary standard, the abandonment of a freely working pricing system, the spread of monopoly both private and public, the establishment of burdensome taxation systems, all these would have seemed to the nineteenth-century observer to poison the springs of progress. Now it is believed that we can dispense with some of the props which our fathers thought to be essential to a progressive system; but many of them are still deemed to be necessary, and it is the object of policy to set them up again. At the end of the war, however, it would have been very optimistic to expect any quick success in reaching this result, and at the same time it was obvious that our own relative position in the world economy had gravely deteriorated. How is it then that our faith in the continued material progress of this country was so largely unimpaired? Our hopes for the future depended, I think, upon two factors, first, the continuance of those improvements in industrial technique and organisation which have been the chief proximate cause of economic progress so far and, second, the preservation of full employment for a long time ahead. There seemed no cause for doubting that applied science would continue to yield its fruits in higher production, and with full employment firmly within our grasp, there was no reason why we should throw away a large part of the benefit that technical progress made possible, as we had done between the wars. A state of full employment has been maintained since the war; but, in spite of that, our economic position has become precarious. It was natural, therefore, that increased attention should be focused on the former of the two factors on which our hopes rested, namely, technical progress and efficiency. This interest has been stimulated by numerous inquiries into our industries, inquiries which have brought to light serious deficiencies in some of them. These are now being underlined by the various productivity teams which are the fortunate beneficiaries of American instruction and American hospitality.

The conclusions that have been generally reached are that, while our industries made considerable technical advances between the wars, the advances were less rapid than those made by our competitors, and that if we are to balance our international accounts and even to maintain the present standard of living, massive improvements in technique and organisation are necessary throughout industry. One of the reasons for the backwardness of our older industries (so it is urged) is their unsatisfactory equipment. The higher capitalisation of American industry, the fact that the American worker in most trades is assisted by a greater amount of power machinery than the British, is held to be a major cause of the disparity in productivity between the two countries. The remedy, it seems, lies in heavier industrial investment. Now there is little doubt that differences in capitalisation correspond very closely to differences in productivity, both between countries and between periods. Economic progress, it has long been a truism to state, is closely correlated with the rise in capital per head. This proposition, however, does not take us very far. Why do these differences exist? Why has Britain become inferior to some other countries in this important respect? Is it merely an injection of fresh capital into our industrial system that is required? These are fundamental questions which I should like to discuss.

In the first place, it seems to me that, in this diagnosis, attention has been confined to symptoms and that the deeper causes of

economic disparities have been ignored. I am led to this view because I observe that for several of our industries in which comparisons of productivity are unfavourable to us, the cause, or part
of it, is to be found elsewhere than in a disparate growth in capital
investment. For example, the steep rise in output per man-shift in
the German coalmining industry during the 1930s, a rise which left
the Germans far ahead of the British in this respect, was not attributable mainly to the use of more mining equipment, for the mech-
anisation of German mining had been almost complete before 1930.
The chief reason given for the advance was the better organisation
of mining operations. It was not that the industry was provided with
more resources, but rather that it made better use of those which it
already possessed.[9] Again, the far higher productivity of the
American building operative when compared with the British in the
erection of roughly similar buildings does not depend on a much
greater use of capital equipment. The chief causes are to be found,
first in the method by which the Americans organise the whole
complex of operations between the time when the contract is let and
the time when the building owner takes possession, and, second, in
the different attitude of the American operative towards his work.[10]
Then, I am told of a company which operates almost identical
plants in the United States and here and which gets substantially
higher productivity from the American one. The recent experiments
that have been made in the cotton industry show that large
increases in productivity can be obtained without additional
investment and merely by the reorganisation of the mills—the
rearrangement of the machines and the 'redeployment' of the
workers.[11] These examples suggest that high productivity is often
the result of the way in which the capital resources are used, and is
not determined solely by the quantity of them. The key, in other
words, is to be found in organisation.[12]

Even when we compare industries where the capitalisation in
America is much higher than it is here, and where the productivity
appears to be closely correlated with the amount of capital used,
the causes of the disparity remain more interesting than the fact.
In some cases, failure in this country to adopt more capitalistic
methods is apparently due to institutional arrangements. In the
British cotton industry it is alleged that wage systems based on
the conditions of the past and the objections to multiple-shift
working have made the widespread use of more modern types of
machines unprofitable. Sometimes the inferiority of our business

organisers to the American has been given as an explanation. This is a point to which I shall return. There is, however, another type of argument which is more difficult to handle. Static analysis normally explains the differences in capitalisation and in organisation between countries in terms of the relative scarcities of the various factors of production. Where skilled labour is cheap and capital expensive, it is to be expected that firms will use less capitalistic methods than they do in a country where the reverse relationship applies. The result may be that the two countries in our comparison specialise on different qualities of the same good; the first is likely to concern itself with high qualities and specialities, and the latter with mass-produced goods. While this reasoning is satisfactory in explaining the contrast that exists at any moment, and while it also indicates that it would be dangerous for us to play the 'sedulous ape' to the Americans, it does not justify complacency, for the argument scarcely touches the dynamics of the problem. No doubt one reason why the Americans in the middle of the nineteenth century were pioneers in the adoption of the 'interchangeable method' of production in engineering, was that, in the absence of a large supply of skilled labour, they had perforce to seek for means of economising its use. Hence the standardisation of products and processes and the employment of highly mechanised methods of manufacture. Once these methods had come into use, however, a chain of consequences followed. The initial standardisation of components and, to some extent, of finished products also, was brought about by the lack of skilled labour. But standardised output influenced consumers' tastes in the direction of uniformity, and a uniform demand thus provided opportunities for mass-production methods. In a particular context, it can be seen how what might have been originally regarded as a deficiency was later put to glorious gain; for when the motor car production began, the existence of parts-making industries accustomed to working on the 'interchangeable principle' provided advantages to the American car manufacturers that were not present in this country. It was thus the enterprise of the Americans in overcoming an initial disadvantage which won for them benefits which time showed to be cumulative.

The conclusion is, then, that while material progress is affected by numerous circumstances, fertility in resource and imaginative enterprise lie at its root. Where these qualities are present in a population and are given opportunities to exercise themselves, obstacles to progress are readily overcome. In the presence of enterprise, moreover, the capital needed for high productivity is seldom lacking. It is erroneous, in my view, to look to the side of savings for a leading cause of any deficiency in capital equipment, for enterprise generates its own savings out of the higher incomes which it makes possible. In the old civilisations of Asia, what has retarded economic progress is the lack of native entrepreneurial ability far more than a shortage of capital or skilled labour. As a result, in India and elsewhere, until very recently, the not inconsiderable savings of the wealthy were used in the creation of consumers' capital or in loans for consumption purposes, and material progress was largely confined to those sectors of the economy in which foreign entrepreneurs participated.[13] In the one Asian country where entrepreneurial skill was available (Japan), industrial progress was remarkably rapid as soon as it was allowed freedom to exercise itself, in spite of the initial shortage of capital. I suggest, therefore, that the capitalisation of industry is a function of enterprise, and that the higher productivity which the extensive use of capital makes possible, depends ultimately on the supply of entrepreneurs.

This conclusion brings me to another stage in my argument. Economic efficiency refers not merely to the relation between input and output in particular industries. It has also to do with the way in which the whole resources of a community are distributed among the different uses to which they can be put. One reason why our income per head before the war was not far short of that of the United States, in spite of their superior productivity in manufacturing and mining industry, was that a larger proportion of our workers was found in those industries which in all countries have a relatively high productivity. The consequence of our having carried industrial specialistation to an extreme limit, was that in 1939 only five per cent of our working population was engaged in agriculture (which in every country is a low-productivity industry) compared with twenty per cent in the United States. This specialisation was one of the reasons for our material progress in the past. At present, when the change in the conditions of international trade is forcing us at great cost to retrace our steps, we may wonder if this specialisation did not mean our giving too many hostages to fortune. Still, up to 1939, we reaped great advantages from it, and whether in the long run the policy will be counted wise may not be told until our story is finished.

The efficient allocation of resources is not a once-for-all operation. An economic system cannot progress unless, with the inevitable changes in circumstances, it alters that allocation. A readiness to do so is especially important for a country that has owed part of its material wellbeing to superiorities that time destroys, such as those that come from exhaustible natural resources, or to an early start. In such structural adaptability Great Britain once showed great skill; but her achievements in this respect during the last thirty or forty years have not matched those of her past, nor indeed those of other countries. Our industrial weakness during the inter-war years was demonstrated far more by our failure to secure a substantial share of the new trades that rose during that time than it was by the probably inevitable decline of our older staple manufactures. Lack of resilience may be regarded as a serious cause of misgivings about the future, for economic progress is associated far more with a capacity to take the lead in new industries than it is with steady technical progress in the old. This is particularly true of a country that occupies a position like ours in the world. With our superiority in natural resources gone, and with the knowledge and experience of established industrial technique widely spread among the peoples, we can hope to maintain a high rate of progress only if we show imagination in scouring out new channels.

I now come to the proposition which lies at the heart of my theme. It is that economic progress springs less from the detailed improvements effected in the methods of established industries than from massive innovations which lead to the creation of new ones. In other words, the rise in material wealth depends not so much upon steady progress in turning out familiar things (although, of course, that is important enough) as upon the discovery of new ways of producing those things and upon finding new things to produce. If this proposition is true (and I believe that the history of any period in which there has been a striking advance in material wealth supports it), then it means that of all the forces that make material progress possible, industrial leadership is the most powerful. The key to progress is held by the man who is capable of effecting novel combinations of resources, often for the creation of fresh classes of goods. I do not think that anyone who studies the development of an economically progressive country over the last century can fail to agree about the major part that has been played by a comparatively small group of forceful pioneers. They have not always been entrepreneurs in the classical sense, that is to say, independent businessmen working with their own resources. Many of them have been salaried officials. What has distinguished them has been their capacity for imposing their authority on their organisation and of persuading others to entrust them with the resources necessary for new ventures. This type of man is the true entrepreneur, as distinct from the ordinary run of businessman who treads the path beaten out for him. Professor Schumpeter has made us familiar with this distinction, which he used in expounding his theory of economic development; but other economists—as well as most businessmen themselves, no doubt—have observed it. Marshall, for example, drew a contrast between those businessmen who 'have prospered by steady adherence to affairs, largely of a routine character; with but little use of the higher imagination . . .', and the leaders 'on whose work the progress of industry most depends'.[14] A recent investigator into business behaviour has laid emphasis on the special importance of the part played in industrial progress by the 'surging energy of the founder-type of personality'.[15]

In his rôle as the chief contributor to material progress, the industrial leader is not concerned merely with meeting existing demands by fresh combinations of resources. His equally important function is the creation of new demands.

Innovations in the economic system do not as a rule take place in such a way that, first, new wants arise spontaneously in consumers and then the productive apparatus swings round through their pressure . . . It is the producer who as a rule initiates economic change and consumers are educated by him if necessary; they are, as it were, brought to want new things. . .[16]

Professor Knight has expressed the same idea:

It is common to think of the economic process as the production of goods for the satisfaction of wants. This view is deficient in two vital respects. In the first place, the economic process produces wants as well as goods to satisfy existing wants, and the amount of social energy directed to the former . . . is very large and constantly growing.[17]

A German student of industrial organisation is following the same line of thought when he states:

> Industrial development is not merely the result of a passive adaptation to technical progress and market conditions. On the contrary, modern industry . . . actively influences markets . . . in order to mould them according to its requirements.[18]

Thus, although as Adam Smith said: 'Consumption is the sole end and purpose of all production', large increases in consumption usually result from the initiative of producers who persuade people to want new things, and who themselves act as if production were the end of economic activity. According to this view then, the changes which contribute most to progress arise from impulse within industry rather than from impact upon it.

These industrial leaders set the pace in industry as a whole, for they draw after them the 'routineers' whose old markets are destroyed or whose methods are rendered obsolete by innovations. Those who cannot follow fall out of the race. So it may be said of the true entrepreneurs as was said, in a more elevated context, of the greatest nation of innovators in history: 'They were born into the world to take no rest themselves and to give none to others'. Whether this striving for material progress is a good thing, whether Mill was right in looking forward wistfully to the coming of a Stationary State, are questions that do not concern me here. All I need say is that however much the present generation is repelled by some of the manifestations of material progress, it seems firm in its belief that higher real incomes are among the most desirable benefits to which mankind can attain. Again, no one would deny that the process of creating new wants, or of diversifying existing wants, is attented at times by waste. But whether in such a society as our own we need to charge our bureaucrats with the responsibility of protecting us against that waste and of saving us from the possible social disaster of getting what the innovators and their publicity agents make us think we want is a question which, fortunately, lies beyond the scope of this paper. I steer my discourse warily away from these speculations towards a purely economic question upon which the argument may throw some light. Traditional economic analysis commonly proceeds on the assumption that a businessman, when acting rationally, enlarges his output to the point at which his net profits are maximised; but this assumption seems to be refuted by the common observation that the general run of businessman is content to stop short of that point. His aim is rather to ensure to himself over a long period an income which enables him to maintain a customary standard. Now, in an unprogressive society, or even in a protected sector of a progressive society, he is no doubt able to follow such a policy. But the intrusion of a few restless, ambitious and exceptionally capable innovators into the system forces the comfortable and the psychologically well adjusted out of their routine. They must become economic men or go under. The appetites which drive the innovators forward may, it is true, be quite other than the conscious desire to maximise profits; indeed, their motives are obscure. Yet since pecuniary gain provides a clear demonstration of their success, their activities are likely to produce a result in conformity with theoretical expectations in their own case, and the result for industry as a whole (or for that part of it that is being affected by their innovations) may not be very different from what it would be if the theorist's assumptions were correct.

These results will occur, of course, only in a society in which the activities of innovators are not seriously impeded. Where law and public opinion are favourable to free enterprise, the routineers must adjust themselves to change or go out of business. But whenever defensive action by the routineers is possible, they will take it, as can be seen by many examples drawn from both before and since the 'age of economic grace'. If such defensive action is supported by the State, then a powerful brake may be imposed on material progress. The action may take forms familiar to us in our own day, restrictive practices of the kind associated with cartels and trusts, product differentiation and the like. The object of these practices is not usually the exploitation of the consumer in the crude sense, but rather the provision of insurance against a sudden change of circumstance. The practices may win considerable public sympathy, for although the results of economic change are welcomed, the change itself is disturbing. Yet a society where defensive action in support of threatened interests is generally successful is not a society that can expect conspicuous advances in material wellbeing. It may, therefore, be a true instinct among the Americans, who of all people are still the most avid of material progress, to see in cartels and monopolies the canker at the heart of the economic system.

If they are right, it is not mainly for the reasons given by static economic analysis. Economists usually object to departures from their ideal competitive system on the ground that imperfect competition and monopoly lead to higher prices, lower output and less employment than would exist if industries were conducted under conditions of perfect competition. Apart from the fact that perfect competition is usually an unreal alternative in the actual world, it may be suggested that this conclusion is not of primary importance in the consideration of a dynamic system. The substitution of monopoly for competition may certainly involve waste; but as long as the industrial system as a whole is moving forward under the impetus of technical discoveries applied by creative entrepreneurs, the wastes that can be detected at any moment in particular areas of the system as a result of monopoly are likely to be dwarfed by the progress elsewhere, and are in any case likely to be temporary. The real danger of monopoly arises when it is used to impede change. A society that keeps the channels of innovation clear need have little fear of the waste that arises from monopoly or imperfect competition in *established* industries. It is when these channels become choked that material progress slows down. If we look back on the metal industries of the last quarter of the nineteenth century, we can see that from the standpoint of economic progress the significant fact was not the extent to which the output of wrought iron was then restricted by the imperfections of competition among the producers, each with his famous brand of iron, but rather the entire destruction of the older forms of production by the coming of mass-produced steel. In the same way, I suggest, material progress in so far as it depends upon a supply of cheap textile materials will be bound up less with the success or failure of official schemes in the United States and elsewhere for keeping up the price of raw cotton than with developments in the manufacture of synthetic or semi-synthetic fibres—developments that have already brought down the price of staple fibre below that of raw cotton.

I return to a consideration of our own affairs. Because of our precarious international position, not merely an advance in our material prosperity, but even the preservation of our existing standards, depends upon our demonstrating a capacity for industrial leadership. Yet, in spite of the achievements of our scientists and inventors, there can be little doubt that during the last few decades we have fallen behind other nations in successful industrial innovation. We have seen the undermining of our position in established industries by developments that have taken place abroad rather than at home. I can refer to only a few of the numerous causes that have been responsible. One of them, without doubt, has been the preoccupation of policy with the buttressing of threatened positions rather than with clearing the way for fresh enterprise. But policy reflects social opinion, and it may be contended that this opinion has been hostile to the exercise of industrial leadership. Sixty years ago Marshall noted that while economic progress did not necessarily require the maintenance of those rights of property that lead to extreme inequalities of wealth, it did depend upon the existence of a social milieu sympathetic to the exercise of free, individual responsibility.[19] Later, in his *Industry and Trade*, he pointed out that the United States was satisfying that condition more completely than this country:

> As arts and sciences flourish best where their followers work for the approval of brethren of the craft . . . so business flourishes most where the aim of the business man is not to shine in elegant society, but to be held in respect by those who are the best judges of his special form of strength.
>
> This exclusive devotion to one pursuit involves some loss of life to the individual, but the constructive economic force which it gives to America at this phase of her development is unique.[20]

Although it can scarcely be said that the British businessman today is distracted by a desire to shine in elegant society (for in contemporary England he would have difficulty in discovering that particular firmament), his 'special form of strength' is not one which at present wins social approbation, and he is under even more insidious temptations to dissipate his energy. Consider the advisory committees, working parties, councils and associations, both official and unofficial, that have proliferated in recent years!

Centralised economic planning, moreover, necessarily restricts the functions of the industrial leader, for it leaves little opportunity for what has been called the very essence of free enterprise, namely 'the concentration of responsibility in its two aspects of making decisions and taking the consequences of decisions when put into effect.'[21] Under planning the businessman cannot on his own responsibility create new combinations of resources; he becomes merely the administrator of such resources as are allotted to him for given purposes. Professor MacGregor in his latest book draws a distinction between policy and plan. 'A policy,' he says, 'is directive; a plan is executive.'[22] Applying this principle to our present arrangements, he argues that only a small part of our economy, the nationalised sector (which according to Mr Morrison is to be only twenty per cent of the whole), is to be planned, while eighty per cent of it will remain private and so subject to the method of policy. This definition may have its uses; but it conceals the real nature of planning. To my mind the distinctive feature of planning when compared with free enterprise is that the businessman is unable to create fresh combinations of resources unless he first obtains the permission of the central authority whose decision follows from the plan which it has made. In that sense our present-day economy is largely planned, although how far these conditions are to be regarded as permanent and how far as arising out of our special postwar difficulties is not easy to determine.

Now it does not follow that if the private entrepreneur in this country has had his day, the function of innovation can no longer be performed at all. An alternative agency is the State, and we are thus led to consider whether government is, or can be made, competent to discharge this function which is so essential to material progress. I have little time to give to this question, but I should like to make a few comments upon it. In some countries the government has played a very important rôle as an innovator, and through its initiative the economic life of whole nations has been transformed. But its most notable successes have been achieved in introducing into primitive societies, where experienced private entrepreneurs have been scarce, the technique and forms of organisation already worked out in advanced countries. We cannot yet find, I think, any example of a State's having been responsible for developing successfully industries of an entirely novel kind in advanced societies, except perhaps those that serve military needs. When the government intervenes in such societies, it concerns itself with what is already established. It plans in relation to what exists, not in relation to what may be called into existence. Its tenderness for what already exists may even jeopardise the birth of new ventures, for economic advance frequently involves the destruction of established positions and the decay of industries that have become obsolete. A government can hardly be expected to take up new and untried ventures and to persist, in spite of disappointment and public criticism, in carrying them over the harassing period of experimentation until they have come transformed into new industries. The concentration of attention on established firms is damaging to economic progress because new developments do not always, or even usually, spring from the more obvious origins. In this country it was not a firm in the major textile spinning industries, nor in the chemical industry, that built up the rayon industry, but a silk-weaving firm which happened at a critical moment to be employing an imaginative chemist in its dyeing department. It was not the great engineering firms that took up motorcar manufacture, but small firms in the bicycle, tinplate-ware, electrical apparatus and sheep-shearing machinery trades. Further, in many lines of production, there seems to be no unique solution to the problem of efficient organisation. An equally good result can be achieved in several different ways, and it is difficult to belive that a government would deliberately promote a diversity of this kind, even if it went so far as to recognise that diversity is itself fertile. The immense variety in the methods by which a woollen manufacturer may achieve a given standard of efficiency was noted by the Wool Working Party.[23] Diversity of method is even more characteristic of new industries in their early days than of old industries, and the superiority of any single method (if that ever emerges) is only brought out *ambulando*.

In the end the problem for government as for private enterprise becomes that of selecting the right person and of giving him scope for the exercise for his powers. The State may make such a selection just as competently as private enterprise for established under-takings, but it is not easy to see how it can perform this function in the case of ventures which are in process of being born, because the men who are likely to do best in them are generally still young, unknown and untried. Any alternative to the older system must provide, to quote again from Marshall, 'some reasonably efficient substitute' for the freedom which that system offered 'to constructive genius to work its way to the light and to prove its existence by attempting difficult tasks on its own responsibility and succeding in them; for those who have done most for the world have seldom been those whom their neighbours would have picked out as likely for the work'.[24] One must not, of course, press this argument too far. If the supply of private initiative shows signs of failing, either through a decline in energy or through the creation of an environ-ment uncongenial to its exercise—and the latter may come about through changes in social policy which the public requires—then the State must step into the breach. The time has not come for a final judgment on the issue. It would be rash to condemn novel kinds of economic arrangements because they pay little regard to the conditions necessary for the successful operation of past systems, which themselves had plenty of faults. Still, I feel justified in stating the following conclusion. One of the chief agents of economic progress during the last hundred and fifty years is likely to have little scope for its activities in this country during the years ahead, and at present there is no clear indication of how an adequate substitute is to be provided. Since this country is as firmly convinced as ever of the desirability of material progress, and since that progress in my view will depend upon its success as a pioneer in producing and marketing new kinds of industrial products, there is serious cause for concern.

Apart from whether the government is competent in a technical sense to exercise industrial initiative, there remains the question whether the society whose resources it has taken upon itself to administer really wishes for innovation, not merely in the sense of being prepared to enjoy its fruits, but also in the sense of accepting the conditions for their harvesting. The question which Berkeley posed two centuries ago is highly relevant to government planning in a democratic society: 'Whether it be not the Opinion or Will of the People, exciting them to Industry, that truly enricheth a Nation?'[25] An investigation of the ultimate causes that produce great outbursts of energy (as distinct from the instruments which they use), and a discussion of the conditions which make those outbursts creative and not destructive of the society in which they occur, would take us far beyond the subjects with which economists usually concern themselves. I shall content myself with a few reflections. Great industrial changes mean the disruption of older ways of life, and are not always compatible with social peace. As Knight says: 'The more vital problems are not problems of economy, but of maintaining social unity in the face of economic interests.'[26] Economic progress thus depends upon morale, which permits a reconciliation of innovation and social stability. As to the forces that have driven men to the furious pursuit of material progress, they lie, in the main, beyond the realm of cool, economic calculation, although calculation may be their tool. The investigators of American economic superiority, after listing the technical and administrative causes, find an unexplained residuum which they attribute to 'the American way of life'. The productivity teams, for instance, make much of this quality in their reports. The inference that British industry is supposed to draw from the explanation is not always clear; but that 'the American way of life' supplies much of the driving force to the American economic machine cannot be gainsaid. To go farther afield, soon after I interested myself in the economic affairs of the Japanese, I noted Marshall's comment on their country's extraordinarily rapid economic development after their centuries of isolation came to an end:

> Their quick rise to power supports the suggestion, made by the history of past times, that some touch of idealism, religious, patriotic or artistic, can generally be detected at the root of any great outburst of practical energy.[27]

In our own early industrial development the relationship that existed between nonconformity and the rise of capitalist industry was once a commonplace of historical writing. In that connection, since I am speaking in Birmingham, may I be allowed to quote a passage which many years ago I gleaned from the records of one of the City's own great innovators, the firm of Boulton and Watt? This quotation is from a letter written in 1795 by an 'adventurer' in the Cornish mines, Richard Mitchell by name.

> I will venture to assert that, of all men for the last five hundred years, no two men have been of so much use . . . to the county as the Reverend J. Wesley with respect to Religion, and Mr. James Watt with his automatical machineries. Mr. Wesley . . . taught the vulgar to be sober, honest and industrious. . . . He not only taught them to live well, but to do well; therefore, he has now his reward in Heaven. Mr. Watt, after Mr. Wesley had taught them to be industrious, within the last twenty years has taught and helped them to get at the vast treasures, which Providence till then had hidden in the bowels of their county, by his fire engines for working deep mines, without which thousands on thousands of pounds of tin and copper must have remained there forever.[28]

The diversity of inspiration is striking; the American way of life, emperor-worship, John Wesley. Fortunately, an economist is not required to probe into these mysteries. He notes their existence, and for the rest he must content himself with expressing in his own jargon the substance of the familiar though (it is to be feared) ambiguous lines:

> Time and the ocean and some fostering star
> In high cabal have made us what we are.

12 Restrictive Practices in the Copper-Mining Industry[1]

The history of the combination among the producers of copper between the years 1785 and 1792 offers an early example of a modern type of combination, and the course of its development during the seven years of its existence presents a parallel to that of many recent combinations. A short description of the state of affairs in the copper-mining industry during the years which immediately preceded the formation of the combine will be sufficient to indicate the causes which brought it about, and will in addition show the way in which Boulton and Watt became so intimately connected with the industry. That connection, as will be seen, was fraught with serious consequences.

About 1780 there were two main producing centres of copper ore in this country, Cornwall and Anglesey. They were bitter competitors, and the conditions under which copper was mined in the two counties were so different as to deserve notice. While the two mines of Anglesey (the Paris and Mona Mines) were recent discoveries and were worked at small expense, most of the numerous Cornish mines were deep and in continual danger of becoming waterlogged. Copper-mining in Cornwall would in fact have been an almost impossible undertaking, if there had been no pumping engines to free the mines from water, and throughout the eighteenth century Savery's and Newcomen's engines had been employed for that purpose. By the 1770s, however, these were proving inefficient and very expensive to work, because of the increasing depths of the mines, and it seems probable that it was only the appearance of Watt's engine which saved the industry from extinction. In 1777 his engines were introduced into Cornwall, and installed by most of the mining companies of 'adventurers'. A considerable saving in coal and a much greater efficiency in working resulted. This reduction in the cost of producing the ore gave a stimulus to Cornish mining, and the revival of old mines and the opening of many new ones came as a direct consequence. The result was an increase in the supply of copper in the 1780s, which, being un-

144

accompanied by any appreciable increase in demand, brought about a fall in price which again reduced the mines to their previous unprofitable position. It is in this connection that Boulton and Watt came to exercise an important influence on the future history of the industry. As they relied for their income, not only on the sale of their engines, but also on the monthly dues or 'savings' paid to them by those adventurers who had made use of their patent, this fall in price, which endangered the continued existence of many of the mines, threatened Boulton and Watt with a loss of their patent dues. Since, moreover, at this time the Cornish mines provided practically the only market for their engines, the ruin of the industry would have brought disaster on the partners. Realising that the mines must be kept going at all costs, Boulton at first attempted to encourage the adventurers to continue to work the mines by taking shares in them—a practice which was followed by the other contractors to the mines whose interests were in many respects coincident with those of Boulton and Watt. Although the latter lost money by these investments, they more than recompensed themselves for such losses by the profits on their engine business. Boulton soon found, however, that this method would be inadequate to prevent the mines from ceasing to work, for during the early 1780s their financial position became desperate. His next step, therefore, was an attempt to improve the management of the mines, and he used his power as a shareholder to eliminate the waste and inefficiency, of which there were many glaring instances in the mine administration. More interesting, however, were his attempts to reorganise the copper trade on its marketing side, attempts which led ultimately to the formation of the combine of 1785.

The nature of the problem which Boulton set himself to solve was twofold. Firstly, it was essential that the relation between the Cornish adventurers and the various smelting companies should be changed; and, secondly, the competition between Cornwall and its rival Anglesey had to be restricted. The methods by which the Cornish ores were disposed of during the eighteenth century to the Welsh smelters, who marketed them, were indeed unsatisfactory. During the 1770s and early 1780s the ores were purchased at 'ticketings' by eleven different smelting companies. 'These companies were perpetually contending with each other as well as with Anglesea, and the method of combating each other was by lowering the price of copper, which generally produced a proportionate effect in the price of ores, to the great detriment of the miners.' It seems that at this time the prices which the adventurers received from the smelters for the ores were even lower than the depressed state of the copper market warranted, and the miners were unable to hold out for higher prices, partly because they were disunited, and partly owing to the fact that their capital was small when compared with the great expense of working the mines. Consequently, they relied on the proceeds of each monthly sale to enable them to meet the expenses of the following month, and they were, therefore, not in a position to refuse the low prices which the smelters offered. Thus the trade was wholly in the power of the smelting companies, and Boulton realised that the miners' fortunes could never improve while this method of marketing their produce was maintained. In his attempt to wrest the control of the copper trade from the smelters, Boulton was supported by Thomas Williams, the manager of the two Anglesey mines, who had no cause to love the smelting companies, since they were his bitter competitors. It may be noted that the Anglesey miners, although they were at one time 'oppressed by the copper companies' just as Cornwall was, had taken steps to set up smelting works of their own and to market their copper themselves. They were especially successful in developing foreign markets. The increase of Anglesey's production at this time was even greater than that of Cornwall's. In 1778, Anglesey produced 1200 tons of copper compared with its rival's 3000 tons; in 1785 the respective amounts obtained at the two centres were 3000 tons and 4400 tons. In these circumstances there can be no wonder that there was a glut on the market, and that the centres suffered from mutual competition. Between 1780 and 1785 both Boulton and Williams had suggested many schemes to the Cornish adventurers, by which the latter might free themselves from the smelters' control and come to some agreement with Anglesey for the purpose of maintaining an acceptable level of prices. It was not till 1785 that these proposals began to receive general support in Cornwall, but in the autumn of that year a thorough reorganisation of the copper trade on its marketing side was effected.

The initiators of the 'copper revolution', as it was called, realised that if the Cornish miners were to control the smelting and marketing of their ores, fresh capital would have to be introduced into the industry, and a new organisation set up, which could co-ordinate the activities of the numerous mines. To this end the Cornish Metal Company was established on 1 September 1785, with a nominal capital of £500,000, £130,000 of which was immediately subscribed. A large proportion of it was advanced by Boulton and his friends, and by the other contractors to the mining companies. The objects of the Metal Company, it was stated, were 'to keep up the price of copper ores at a proper standard and to contract for the smelting of all ores as should best promote the interests of the mines'. The Company agreed to buy all the ores raised in Cornwall from 1 September 1785, to 1 September 1792, and to sell the copper in a metallic state. The associated miners of Cornwall, for their part, agreed to sell all their ores to the Company at such prices as should be fixed by the Governor and by the thirty-six directors, two-thirds of whom were to be nominated by the miners. They also guaranteed, to the subscribers to the Company's capital, interest at the rate of eight per cent per annum. Thus after September 1785 Cornwall possessed a central selling agency which controlled the marketing of all the ores raised in the county. It was now in a position to come to an agreement with Anglesey by which prices could be maintained at a high level to the benefit of all copper producers.

According to the price agreement between the Cornish Metal Company and Anglesey a minimum price for all the copper produced by the two centres was fixed, and from this price both parties bound themselves not to depart under a penalty of £100,000. Cornwall's share of the total sales was to be three-fifths, Anglesey's two-fifths. It is to be remarked, however, that no attempt was made at the time to set any limit to the total amount of production. The agreement also stipulated that, after the ore had been smelted, the metal was to be sent for sale to warehouses at London, Birmingham, Bristol and Liverpool. Anglesey was given the right of serving Liverpool, Cornwall that of supplying the Bristol consumers; while both at Birmingham and London there was to be a general warehouse, to which both centres were to send their copper. Each party was required to present the other with weekly accounts of its sales. and five merchants were to be appointed 'to govern and direct the trade for the mutual benefit of each party'. The operation of the contract was to begin in May 1786; after that date the price of copper was to be £86 a ton. This price was about £12 higher than that of May 1785. It was now expected that high prices could in the future be paid for Cornish ores, that Boulton and Watt's engine dues would be secured, and that large profits would be gained by all who were concerned in the copper industry.

The optimism which greeted the formation of this combination was hardly justified by results. Just as the introduction of Watt's engines had first brought salvation to the miners, but later had failed to prevent the recurrence of their troubles, so the prosperity which accompanied the Metal Company in its first few months of life was productive of forces which ultimately led to disaster. The formation of the combine brought about an immediate rise in the price of copper, and this rise, together with the knowledge that the price would be £86 a ton after the next May, caused the directors of the Metal Company to be generous in the prices at which they bought ores from the miners. The increase in the price of ores 'threw a temporary gleam of sunshine on the miners and encouraged them to erect new engines in deep mines at great expense'. The result was that a greater quantity of ore began to be produced than the Metal Company could dispose of in a metallic state, and so a stock of unsaleable copper soon began to accumulate.

It was not, however, the excessive production which alone caused this accumulation of copper. The stocks of the metal in the hands of some of the old smelting companies were 'much greater than had been computed'. Further certain other mining companies, which posssessed rich mines and large stocks of copper, had not been included within the price association. The production of these 'outsiders' was stimulated by the high prices which ruled at this time, and they and the smelting companies sold copper considerably under the price stipulated by the agreement between Cornwall and Anglesey. By 1787, moreover, foreign copper from Hungary, Sweden and Holland began to flow into England, as well as into the foreign markets previously supplied by Cornwall and Anglesey. One instance is well worth mentioning. A quantity of unrefined copper, 'which had lain for years at Cadiz while low prices were to be had', was bought by an English firm, shipped to this country, refined, and sold under the price fixed by the agreement. The danger of foreign competition had been foreseen by the promoters of the combination, even before it had become immediate, for in March 1786 there was an unsuccessful attempt to induce the Swedish copper producers to enter into the price association.

The effect of the competition on the fortunes of the combination was evident in the Metal Company's accounts presented in October 1787. By this time practically the whole of the Company's capital was represented by a stock of copper in its warehouses, even though an additional subscription of £11,000 had been raised a few months before. The Company, moreover, was deeply in debt. When it had found that its initial capital was insufficient to enable its contract with the miners to be carried out, recourse was had to a temporary form of loan. A contract was made between the Company and the smelters, by which the latter, instead of receiving a fixed sum for smelting, agreed to pay for the ores, when delivered to them by the Company. These ores, though in the possession of the smelting houses, were still to be considered the property of the Company, and were really a security for a loan advanced to it. At the end of the 'regulated time of smelting ores' the copper was to be returned to the Metal Company, which then repaid to the smelters the money advanced together with interest at the rate of eight per cent. Although this method was meant to be only a temporary expedient for raising money, in actual fact more and more advances had to be obtained from the smelters, so that by 1787 these advances had become practically permanent loans and amounted to £228,500. This sum was secured by 2677 tons of copper in the smelters' possession, while in the Company's own warehouses were 4027 tons. The total value of the whole stock was over half a million pounds.

At the Company's meeting in October 1787 it was estimated that this stock was at least equal to a two years' supply, and so it was declared that the Company would have to deduct from the prices paid to the miners for their ores a sum equal to two years' interest on the capital invested in their purchase. It was evident that this would make the burden on the miners intolerable. A few small mines had already been stopped and all were losing by this time. A further reduction would complete the ruin of the industry. Meanwhile, disputes with Anglesey had broken out. Since Williams was a skilful salesman, he had managed to obtain the principal sales for his own mines, and Cornwall was unable to make up its due proportion of the total. Williams, however, refused to restrict his sales in any degree—to the wrath of the Cornishmen.

Boulton saw clearly enough that the only possible way of preventing the ruin both of the Metal Company and of the miners was to restrict production. This course he strongly urged on the adventurers during the autumn of 1787, but for some time without effect. Mutual jealousies among the adventurers made it difficult for them to decide which mines should be closed, but another and more potent reason prevented the Cornishmen from adopting his plan. The adventurers were frightened of the 'working' miners. The latter, on hearing of the probable cessation of work in some mines, had revolted and attacked Truro, where the Company's offices were situated. The mob was dispersed only with great difficulty, and 'no mine dared give up' for fear of another riot. If the mines stopped, moreover, considerable numbers of the 'working' miners would be thrown out of work and would become a charge on the local communities. As they 'could not in that county get their bread by any other means, they would prove an intolerable burden to the parishes to which they belonged'. So the adventurers informed Boulton that 'they might as well sink their money in employing the poor as maintain them without working'.

The state of the Company's finances, together with the fact that Anglesey had sold more than her fair share of copper, induced the adventurers at the meeting in October 1787 to decide to break their agreements both with the Metal Company and with Anglesey, and to revert to the old methods of sale. In order to prevent the Company from further depressing the market by attempting to sell its huge stock, the adventurers agreed to pay the subscribers £17,000 a year for five years provided that the Company did not sell more than 1300 tons of copper a year. The result of this breach of the contract was disastrous. Anglesey immediately lowered the price of its copper, which still more reduced the sales of Cornish copper and it seemed that Cornwall was now doomed as a copper-producing centre.

The renewal of competition was disliked, however, by Anglesey almost as much as by Cornwall, and before the end of the year another agreement was made, by which the Cornish Metal Company's position was re-established and its contract with Anglesey renewed with modifications. In this new contract attempts were made to avoid the defects of the former combination; but prolonged negotiations were necessary before the following terms were accepted by both parties. In order to avoid mutual suspicions and breaches in the agreement, it was decided to place the sale of all the copper produced in Cornwall and Anglesey in one hand until September 1792. Thomas Williams was made the joint agent of the two centres. He was to reside at London, to direct the course of the trade from there, and, in return, to receive a commission of two per cent on the amount of the sales. The price of copper was to be fixed at joint quarterly meetings at London; but, to avoid the danger of unforeseen competition, there was to be a certain amount of elasticity in the price. It was also stipulated that both Cornwall and Anglesey should restrict the production of copper to 3000 tons each per annum, and, although for 1788 Cornwall was to be allowed to sell twice as much as Anglesey, in subsequent years the sales were to be equal. The price of copper, moreover, was reduced to £80 a ton.

One suggestion, which received much support about this time, is worth recording. It was that a Bill should be introduced into Parliament to bind the contracting parties, and that 'five commissioners should be appointed by this Act to see it put into execution, and to be ultimate arbiters in all disputes'. Although there was much talk about this Bill, it does not seem evident that Parliamentary sanction was actually sought for the new combination.

It was chiefly due to the efforts of Boulton and Williams that the agreements had been resuscitated, and during the early months of 1788 they used their influence in the trade to enforce a restriction of output, which was so necessary for the success of the combination. Only with utmost difficulty, however, could the Cornish adventurers be prevailed upon to give up their mines or reduce their production. Although several mines stopped working in 1788 because of their heavy losses, the Metal Company found it necessary to bring about a further decrease by granting 'a compensation to such mines' as would discontinue working, 'equal to 40s for every ton of copper annually produced'. It was not, however, till October 1789, after the cessation of several large mines, that the desired reduction had been brought about, and that the Metal Company could dispose of any part of its enormous stock which had been accumulating up to that date.

Although the Metal Company had been saved from complete ruin, the position of all those concerned in the copper-mining industry was in 1789 still serious. The Company was burdened with large stocks, and could not, therefore, afford to give reasonable prices for the ores. So nearly all the mining companies of Cornwall were losing money. The merchants who supplied them with materials had to consent to a reduction on their bills, and Boulton and Watt were unable to obtain the payments of their engine dues from many of the mines. Where the mines had stopped working the partners' loss was, of course, permanent. Among the labouring miners the direst poverty and distress were the fruits of the Metal Company's failure. The reduction in the 'get' of ore, and in its price meant that thousands were thrown out of work or reduced to starvation wages. Among these miners at this time 'the spirit of violence was upon the ferment'. When it was decided to close one mine in the autumn of 1789, they 'intimated a visit to take down the greatest house in Truro'. The mine did not close! For some time past all that Boulton had been able to suggest as a remedy was that 'Mr Pitt' should 'send orders for 3000 tons of copper', or, as an alternative, 'a press gang'. There seemed, in fact, no possibility of getting rid of the huge stock by which the Metal Company was burdened, and yet its sale was the only means by which the prices paid for the ores could be raised.

The next year, however, Cornwall was saved as if by a miracle. The great store of copper ore in Anglesey, which had been mined so cheaply, was by 1790 becoming exhausted. Its decay was apparently quite unexpected by those interested in the Cornish mines, for Boulton often declared, just before this time, that Williams' ultimate aim was to supply the whole of the copper market, and that his alliance with Cornwall was merely a temporary policy to keep up prices until he could so so.

This decline in Anglesey's production enabled the Metal Company to dispose of some of its surplus stock during 1790, and so to give considerably higher prices for the ores. Yet, in spite of the improvement in the situation, the burden of the stock, which amounted in 1790 to 5500 tons of copper, valued at £400,000, lay heavy on the adventurers. Several of them began selling to the excluded smelting companies, which, having no dead stock, could offer higher prices for the ores than the Metal Company could. In order to induce the adventurers to keep to their contracts and to maintain the combination intact, Williams in July 1790 offered to smelt the ores at the Anglesey works 'upon lower terms than is in the power of the old companies'. He declared that the market at that time would take only 6500 tons of copper, but he was prepared to allow Cornwall to supply 4000 tons of this to Anglesey's 2500 tons. He also offered to the shareholders of the Metal Company a douceur of $2\frac{1}{4}$ per cent on their capital in order to induce them to keep the Company in existence beyond the date fixed for its dissolution. By this means he hoped to retain a control over the copper trade even after Anglesey had been reduced to impotence as a producing centre. The result of the entire scheme is doubtful; but it is certain that he was not successful in his attempt to prolong the life of the Company, for it came to an end early in 1792.

By that time the Metal Company's position had much improved. It had sold the whole of its stock; it had wiped off its debts; and by March 1792 it possessed practically intact its subscribed capital. This achievement was only possible, as one writer says, because 'the reduced produce of the mines of Anglesea, in conjunction with the ruin of several Cornish mines, had the effect of raising the price of copper from £80, at which it stood in 1790, to £90, which was its price in 1791'. By 1792 copper stood at £100 a ton. Thus the Metal Company was able to get rid of its stock at a high price on a market from which its most dangerous competitor had been removed. The clause in the price agreement that the sales of both Cornwall and Anglesey should be equal after 1788 was, of course, ignored, when Anglesey proved unable to supply its quota.

It might be thought that the Cornish production of copper would have rapidly increased after 1790; but this did not immediately occur. The explanation is to be found in the fact that, once the mines had been closed, it was always a long and expensive business to set them to work again. Extensive floods, moreover, which occurred in 1791, made any such attempt useless. Thus all favoured the Metal Company, once its fortunes had changed.

Boulton was by no means so pleased with the improvement as might have been expected. His interests by 1790 had undergone a change. Before that date they had been, in the main, linked with those of the producers of copper; afterwards he became interested in the copper industry as a consumer. The change was attributable to the development of his coining business. He had embarked upon this manufacture when the price of copper was low, and in 1788 he had made a heavy purchase from the Metal Company in order to relieve it of part of its excessive stock. After 1790 new markets for Watt's engines were opened up, and Cornwall ceased to be of such vital interest to the partners as it had once been. On the other hand, Boulton's coining business was becoming substantial and, with the shift in the centre of his interests, his attitude to movements in the price of copper changed. Thus Boulton, who had striven to form the combination to put up prices, found himself adversely affected by the organisation he had himself done so much to bring into existence. It was possibly because of his influence that the Company came to an end in March 1792, even before the expiration of its contract with the Cornish miners.

From this time onwards the demand for copper rapidly increased, as a result of the extension of manufacturing industry in general, and of the growth of the navy during the French war. In spite of the large increase in the 'get' of ore after 1792, and although the old methods of sale were reverted to, prices rose almost without interruption until the end of the century. So combination and restrictive practices no longer seemed necessary to the adventurers, and the Cornish Metal Company had no successor.

13 Policy Towards Competition and Monopoly[1]

When governments have addressed themselves to the question of monopoly they have usually found little difficulty in working out a reasonably satisfactory policy towards restrictive practices that depend on agreements among independent firms, that is to say, towards the activities of cartels. But they have had little success in devising, and pursuing, a consistent and generally acceptable policy towards monopolies of scale or mergers (regarded either as a process or an established structure). Even in the United States, where the policy has a long history, there have been many changes in objectives and much vacillation during the last seventy years. Early in the century mergers leading to monopoly were strongly condemned and several giant combines were broken up. Between the wars the Courts tended to distinguish between 'good' and 'bad' monopolies and to reserve their strictures for the latter. After the Second World War they reverted to their previous view that 'power and its exercise must necessarily coalesce', and they insisted on the supreme importance of maintaining competition. They were, however, less inclined than at the beginning of the century to find remedies in the actual breakup of combines. Attention was directed mainly to practices and market behaviour.

Britain was very late in introducing legislation for dealing with monopoly and restrictive practices. Those advocates of the competitive system who think that the British government after the Second World War was timid and inconsistent in its approach to the problem should reflect that, until 1948, Britain had virtually no policy at all towards monopoly and restrictive practices. We now accept such a policy as a necessary part of economic administration, but very few people in the years immediately after the war saw any need for it. As a temporary civil servant at the Board of Trade during the early 1940s, I recall the shocked surprise with which most of the older permanent officials greeted the initial proposals of the enthusiasts who held that Britain's future industrial efficiency depended on restraining monopolistic practices. It was, of course, natural that they should cast a cold eye on the proposals, since many of them had been actively engaged before the war in promoting the cartelisation of the staple industries. I recall also the reaction of a group of Manchester industrialists when I suggested to them that an anti-monopoly policy was likely to find an important place in the postwar government's economic measures: 'We will have none of it', they asserted, 'businessmen must be allowed to protect themselves against the excesses of competition'. This attitude was general at that time. If the Monopolies Commission in the first ten years of its existence did nothing else, it at least persuaded the business world that monopoly and restrictive practices were matters of serious public concern and could not be left wholly to the decisions of the monopolists themselves.

The government's initial approach, as expressed in the Monopolies and Restrictive Practices Act of 1948, was more tentative than some proponents had hoped, but, viewed in the perspective of later years, it was prudent. In the late 1940s the British public were even more dubious than they are now about the virtues of the free market, and businessmen would have keenly resented any policy based on principles similar to those that had informed the American anti-trust legislation. At the outset, the task of the Monopolies Commission was simply to investigate the practices and structures of the industries referred to it, and to analyse their economic effects. No virtue was ascribed in the Act to competition as such. The Commission was charged with the task of judging whether the 'things done' were, or were likely to be, contrary to the public interest and (if so requested) of proposing remedies for any offending practices. Its conclusions and recommendations were then submitted to the government for executive action. Now, it is at first sight strange that, although the concept of the public interest was central to the Commission's deliberations, no helpful definition of that concept was provided by the legislation. The references to it in the 1948 Act were platitudinous. Subsequent Acts, including the Monopolies and Mergers Act of 1965, were equally vague, and the Code of Conduct issued later failed to dispel the darkness. In my twelve years of experience on the Commission, I do not remember any occasion when the members referred to the public interest clause for guidance. Nevertheless, the Commission found little difficulty in reaching agreed conclusions about the effect of various practices on the public interest, despite the fact that the members were by no means all believers in the virtues of free competition or were ready to condemn monopolistic practices in principle. Where they disagreed (and it was not often), their lack of accord turned on the recommendations for remedies.

The criticisms of business conduct made in the reports were little concerned with the exploitation of consumers, as they were in the shortlived enquiries into monopolies after the 1914–18 War, and they were mainly directed to the damaging effect of restrictive practices on industrial efficiency. Throughout the first period of the Commission's life (1948–56), the most important references consisted of industries governed by cartels. The practices investigated were price-fixing agreements, resale price maintenance, market sharing and exclusive dealing arrangements, collusive tendering, to mention the most important. In all these cases the Commission had to be convinced that the manipulations of the market they had discovered were justified by industrial performance before they could be allowed to continue. It almost invariably condemned practices that deprived newcomers of access to markets, practices that suppressed enterprise and innovation. But it was not doctrinaire in its judgments. For instance, there were cases in which it was willing to allow price-fixing arrangements if there was reason for believing that these were necessarily associated with useful technical collaboration among the parties. Similarly, the Commission invariably condemned the collective enforcement of retail price maintenance, on the grounds that it left no freedom of choice to individual traders about their way of doing business, but it seldom ruled out retail price maintenance as such.

It may be contended that the Commission's reports, while they may have influenced opinion, exerted only a modest effect on business behaviour. In the main the reason was that the government failed to carry out its recommendations expeditiously, in some cases not at all. Still, its conclusions set out in some twenty reports, persuaded the government in 1956 to enact fresh legislation, the Restrictive Trade Practices Act. The attitude of the law towards monopoly now ceased to be neutral, as hitherto. Interferences with free competition, from this time onwards, had to be justified by reference to certain precise criteria. Competition was accepted as the norm and any departure from it by collusion among traders or manufacturers was suspect. At the same time, for restrictive practices, though not for close combines, a judicial procedure was substituted for the previous administrative procedure that involved investigation and report.

The shifting of the onus was a logical result of the Commission's work. As to procedure, the business world strongly objected to that laid down in the 1948 Act. Firms resented being used as guinea-pigs for experiments designed to find out the effect on the public interest (undefined) of certain kinds of business behaviour. The Commission was accused of exercising the functions of both prosecuting counsel and judge. Businessmen preferred to be charged with a specific offence defined by law. Whether they would have been such enthusiastic advocates of a judicial procedure if they had been aware of the content of the 1956 Act in advance may be doubted, for it was very hostile to restrictive practices and its consequences were far reaching.

According to the reports of the Registrar of Restrictive Practices, market forces were strengthened as a result of proceedings under the new Act, and many prices became more flexible than formerly. It cannot be claimed that the Act unleased vigorous competition throughout the economy, but it loosened a previously rigid structure. The Restrictive Practices Court condoned certain 'practices' in a few industries, but in general the classical type of cartel was dismantled. On the other hand, it must be admitted that the gaps left by the former restrictive arrangements were sometimes closed by information agreements, recommended pricing, and discussions among competitors about tenders and 'cover' prices. The lack of a satisfactory follow-up procedure weakened the effect of some of the Court's decisions. In recent years, however, these blemishes have been removed in some degree. For instance, the Resale Prices Act (1964) powerfully reinforced competitive forces in the retail trade and put the United Kingdom in the van of countries that have legislated against resale price maintenance. The Restrictive Trade Practices Act of 1968 was aimed at preventing information agreements from frustrating the intentions of the 1956 Act.

Let me now summarise the conclusions of this brief survey. Government policy towards restrictive practices in manufacturing industry and trade has become clearcut and it has without doubt had the effect of strengthening competitive forces in the economy. This policy was not based on any *a priori* assertion of the value of the competitive principle by the government, but it emerged from an examination of a long series of particular cases. It is to be regretted that no systematic appraisal of the results of the policy has so far been undertaken, but one is now in train.[2] The law on restrictive practices has now, in all probability, done as much as can be expected of it to encourage efficiency in the formerly cartelised industries and to release competitive forces from restraints. What is now chiefly needed is postoperative investigation and a more systematic enforcement procedure. The policy has not satisfied political idealists, but, even they, if they consider that twenty years ago Britain had no anti-monopoly law on her statute book, must admit that there has been progress. In future, policy towards restrictive practices must be directed towards ensuring that the intentions of the law are not circumvented by new devices and that enforcement is adequate.

It is when we come to monopolies of scale and mergers that policy still remains inconsistent and uncertain. Economic theory affords little help here. Even the Americans have won few successes in their efforts to deal with such monopolies, although they start with the initial advantage of a definite principle of action, namely that on the whole more competition is 'good' and more monopoly 'bad', and that (at any rate according to the view prevailing since the war) a monopolistic structure is *ipso facto* 'bad', irrespective of the behaviour of the monopolist. In the absence of any such principle, the Commission charged with investigating close combines and mergers in Britain has been left to make up its own mind about whether firms have operated, or are likely to operate, against the public interest. The wide oscillations of informed opinion on these structures demonstrates the lack of any organising principle.

The reasons why the government has not been able to provide any guiding rules are easy to understand. For one thing, the term 'merger' covers processes, or structures, that differ profoundly in economic significance. The motives that inspire mergers are very various and the economic effects of mergers differ from case to case and often bear little relation to the motives which led to their establishment. The mergers that have excited the harshest public criticism are those which have led to the concentration of the production of a particular product or group of products in one or a few hands; in other words, those which have brought about market domination by the group of merged firms. But these mergers are in a minority. Most mergers occur among relatively small firms as part of the process of continuous economic change, and do not lead to any significant modification of the nature of the market. Others involve the taking over by large or growing firms of unsuccessful competitors who are on the way out anyway. In such cases the merger is part of the process by which efficient firms grow; in a sense, it supplements internal growth and it may be regarded as a civilised alternative to the bankruptcy of the unsuccessful firms. (As we know, the initiative in such mergers does not always proceed from the firm that is acquiring the firm absorbed.) Other mergers (including those among large firms) may owe their origin to a search for the economies of scale; technical or marketing changes in the industry, or changes in the conditions governing research in it, may be the compelling force behind such mergers. I emphasise 'marketing changes', since it is the economies in *production* that attract most public attention. But there may be notable economies to be obtained from bringing together manufacturers of diverse products if they are then able to use a common marketing organisation.

Professor D. H. MacGregor referred to mergers prompted by an effort to secure access to economies of scale as a process by which some industries achieve a 'higher organisation'.[3] Here we meet with a major problem, a problem that the Monopolies Commission and similar bodies frequently encounter. A merger formed ostensibly to promote efficiency by opening up access to the economies of larger-scale production may, incidentally, secure a position of market dominance, just as a merger which may have been formed with the object of curbing what the members of the industry regard as 'excessive' competition may find itself with the capacity to realise certain economies of larger-scale production once it has been formed. Those who have promoted the merger may not have bothered to draw this distinction if the merger has improved the group's profits; but to those who are required to give a judgment about how the public interest has been affected, the distinction is crucial. They must ask: has the merger in fact realised the economies which it was supposed to achieve, and how has the newly won power over the market been used? We know that some mergers have not improved efficiency, either because of defects of management and a failure to reconcile diverse interests, or because of a preoccupation with the exercise of market power. On the other hand, there is no doubt that in some industries it is only by enlarging the scale of production (by concentration) that advanced techniques in production, marketing and research can be introduced. In other words, it is not the fact of concentration, or the size of the merger, that calls for criticism, but rather the realised or anticipated results and the way the market power is used. It is behaviour rather than structure itself that is most significant, and behaviour cannot always be inferred from structure.

It would, of course, be going too far to contend that structure is quite unimportant in this context. Obviously, in general, a highly concentrated industry offers more opportunities for the exercise of monopolistic power than an industry composed of a large number of firms. Where the opportunities exist, there is always the danger that they will be seized at some time or other, even though the conduct of those at present in control is economically impeccable. It seems that the Monopolies Commission was moved by these considerations when it recommended that the Imperial Tobacco Company should be required to sell its once large holding in Gallahers, in spite of its being satisfied that Imperial had not used its financial power to influence Gallaher's policy. Yet there are occasions when more concentration may well bring with it increased competition. The arrival of Hedleys in the detergents industry in this country led to the disappearance of a number of small firms, but it provided a powerful rival for the formerly dominant Unilever. Again, an industry composed of many small firms with markets fragmented by high transport costs may be less competitive than a concentrated national industry faced with vigorous international competition.

The reports of the Monopolies Commission, both before the 1956 Act and since (when its duties have been concerned mainly with the investigation of monopolies of scale), seem consistent with these views. This is true at any rate of its inquiries into monopolies *in being*. Its criticisms have usually been directed against behaviour prejudicial to the public interest, whatever the structure of the trade might be. Indeed, it has had very little choice, for Parliament has not ruled that a competitive structure is always to be preferred to a monopolistic structure. So the Commission has picked out for condemnation such devices as price discrimination, exclusive dealing arrangements, the sharing of markets by agreement, and other practices intended by the monopolist to strengthen his position, or to eliminate sources of possible competition. When it has addressed itself to performance, the Commission's conclusions have been tentative. Performance is related to the provision of goods at 'reasonable' prices, the absence of exceptionally high profits, efficiency as reflected in costs or in movements in costs, and alertness in innovation. On these matters it is extremely difficult for outsiders to come to assured conclusions, especially in cases where performance is not being tested in the market. This is especially so when the monopolised product under investigation is being turned out by a multi-product firm. In such cases precise costs cannot be assigned to particular products. 'Once we recognise that overheads may have to be assigned in an arbitrary way to various products because they are part of the general costs of keeping the firm as a social organism in being, then we must recognise that the firm's internal cost situation may give no unique price for a particular product'.[4] In such circumstances, the Monopolies Commission's investigation of prices and costs is a doubtfully useful undertaking. The difficulty applies also to conclusions about profits, even if the profits of the business as a whole are assessed and not merely the profits earned on the monopolised product. It has been the habit of the Commission to compare the profits of the firm under investigation with average profits of manufacturing industry or an appropriate section of manufacturing industry. What is the value of such an average for this purpose? Since the average is made up of many diverse particulars, any conclusion reached when comparing the profits of the business under investigation with the average must involve judgments about the degree of risk and the extent to which the profits of the firm are to be explained by its relative efficiency. Of course, after a prolonged investigation, the Commission naturally gains some broad impressions of the risk to which the firm's business is subjected and the efficiency with which it conducts its operations. But it is very difficult, if not impossible, to quantify its conclusions.

An example may illustrate the difficulty. In the course of an enquiry the Commission found that a certain firm, with a complete monopoly in this country, was earning exceptionally high profits on capital employed. The first reaction was to find that these profits were excessive, but on further investigation the Commission discovered that most of the firm's sales were overseas where it met with keen competition from other producers. The high profits, in other words, were justified by the firm's efficiency, efficiency tested in an internationally competitive market. Clearly, there were no grounds for condemnation, Yet, if the Commission had been required to declare the 'right' level of profits in these circumstances, it would have been unable to reach any precise conclusion. Again, the leading firm in the fertiliser industry informed the Commission that, while it tried to earn as much as possible on products sold in competitive markets, it was content with modest profits in the monopolised sector. The Commission was naturally well disposed towards this price policy in principle. But there are degrees of competition and monopoly; there is no clearcut division between them. How could the Commission decide whether in a particular case there was a sufficient infusion of competition to justify a certain rate of profit?

Only in extreme cases can a judgment be taken with confidence. For instance, a firm with a dominant position in the manufacture of sparking-plugs claimed that its high profits were justified by risk, the risk that technical innovation might well render the sparking-plug obsolete in the foreseeable future. The Commission considered that this contingency was likely to occur, if at all, only in the long term, and rejected the argument. In another industry a dominant firm was found to be maintaining several small, high-cost plants the losses of which were being covered by the high profits on the rest of the business. Here the absence of 'workable' competition had evidently had an adverse influence on the firm's efficiency, and the Commission felt justified in taking this fact into account in putting forward its recommendations. Thus, in a few cases, it is possible to take a fairly confident view of the performance and conduct of monopolists, but even where this is so, the evidence that leads to this conviction is not precise statistical evidence. The conclusions emerge only as a result of the convergence of many facts and impressions gained in the course of a prolonged scrutiny. A forthright critic of the 'Monopolies Commission in Action' has argued that many of its inconsistencies and errors could have been avoided by rigorous analysis (and measurement) of the factors at work and the results of alternative courses of action.[5] This criticism overlooks the extreme difficulty of obtaining convincing evidence of performance. The Commission has always been well aware that measurement is desirable, but it would have been irresponsible if it had made a pretence of exactitude when hard evidence was not available. So most of its conclusions have been, and must necessarily be, qualitative. If this is so for verdicts on existing monopolies, how speculative is the Commission's task when it is asked to pass judgment on a *proposed* merger?

An investigator into the history of British mergers concluded first, that mergers were unlikely to be successful in the long run unless they yielded economies of scale, and, secondly, that they were only likely to occur when those economies were difficult to realise without a merger.[6] This comfortable conclusion fails to bring out the fact that, although the defects of some mergers ultimately brought their breakup or demise, in the process very large resources were probably wasted. Moreover, the records of past experience are of little help to investigators who are set the task of deciding here and now whether a *proposed* merger is likely to be a good thing or not. It is difficult enough to reach a judgment on a combine in being. The evidence that enables one to affirm with confidence that the industry is being carried on more efficiently than it would have been if the process of combination had not taken place is seldom available. Trying to judge what is likely to happen as the result of a *proposed* merger is formidable indeed.

In spite of these difficulties I consider that, on grounds of expediency (since investigatory resources are limited), the examination of proposals for mergers should be regarded as of more urgency than that of close combines already in being, except when there are strong reasons for believing that the practices of the latter are very restrictive. This is because the effects of reversing the process of combination once completed are incalculable. In other words, it is easier to find convincing reasons for stopping a merger in the 'national interest' than for breaking up an established combination. The different views taken by the Monopolies Commission of two great firms, Pilkingtons and Courtaulds, may be ascribed in part to this distinction. Pilkingtons emerged from the inquiry into its activities without censure, whereas Courtaulds attracted some adverse criticism. One reason for the divergence of judgment was that Courtaulds was then in the process of *extending* its control over the textile industry.

Since the passing of the Monopolies and Mergers Act of 1965, the Commission seems to have asked itself two questions before proceeding to a judgment on a proposed merger: first, is the merger likely to reduce competition, and, secondly, is it likely to improve efficiency? There is no difficulty when the answer to the first question is 'Yes' and to the second 'No'. But when the answer to both questions is 'Yes', any solution proposed may arouse controversy, for in such a case the Commission's recommendations must depend not only on its estimate of the firm's performance, but also on an analysis of the uncertain effects of particular kinds of market behaviour. For instance, such common practices among monopolists as the charging of uniform delivered prices or of price discrimination sometimes raise subtle problems of economic judgment, as they did for the Commission in its inquiries into chemical fertilisers and electrical accessories for motor cars.

To these inherent difficulties in reaching decisions, there have been added those that have arisen from the confusion of aims in government itself. At times two opposite policies seem to have been pursued, as when the Industrial Reorganisation Commission and the Ministry of Technology were encouraging mergers and the Board of Trade and the Monopolies Commission were looking askance at them and had even vetoed some of the proposals. The inconsistency was not, in fact, quite as glaring as it appeared. There is a real distinction between mergers that may reasonably be expected to promote efficiency and those that, in the main, simply strengthen market domination. The distinction is there. Whether any body of outside investigators can draw it in particular cases is, however, debatable. Their judgments will be fraught with un-certainty until the government is ready to furnish them with a guiding principle, for example, that free competition is the pre-ferred way of administering economic resources in a mixed economy like our own. Those who support this principle are satisfied that some form of competitive pressure ('workable' competition, so-called), is essential to efficient performance over the greater part of industry and that this proposition is attested by experience. Accordingly, policy, while not condeming all mergers, should en-sure that alternative sources of supply are available, and that attempts to eliminate these alternatives should be resisted. As al-ready shown, combination does not always lessen competition. As long as independent sources of supply remain, it may sometimes increase the fierceness of the rivalry between different groups. But the onus should be on the promoters of mergers to demonstrate that what they propose will have this effect or, if not, will confer positive benefits on the public, as by eliminating obvious forms of waste. It may sometimes be preferable to preserve several independent sources of supply and initiative in an industry, even at the expense of higher unit costs in the short run, although each case would have to be considered on its merits in the light of the principle stated above.

This approach to the problem is, of course, challenged by those who hold that the maintenance of competition is a hopeless task in the modern world, that competition is incompatible with the presence of giant firms and the magnitude of the public sector. The interests of the people, so it is argued, can be safeguarded only by extending the area of government supervision over private business or, where monopoly exists, by the establishment of centres of countervailing power. These may provide the only solutions for industries that are supported financially by the State or for which the State is the chief customer. Yet, even in the nationalised industries, competition rears its head. Those who see only a steady progression towards monopoly, public or private, ignore the industries where once-powerful monopolistic positions have been eroded. When, more than twenty years ago, a State monopoly was created in the coalmining industry, that industry was the source of nearly all the power used in Britain. Today, there is a four-fuel economy. Similar developments have taken place in transport. The State-monopolised steel industry has lost part of its former market to new materials, such as plastics. New forms of competition have appeared in the retail trade. The advent of container ships may well be damaging to some of the liner conferences. So, if one looks at industry in a historical perspective, one finds that monopoly, public or private, is not so secure as it appears at any moment, and that in a country rich in enterprise, the position of even powerful monopolists is often insecure. Competition remains a force to be reckoned with in every dynamic economy. It would be stronger still if the authorities tried consistently to sustain it.

Unfortunately State policies and actions have been equivocal. In the attack on private restrictive practices through legislation, such as the Restrictive Trade Practices Act of 1956, the Resale Prices Act of 1964, and the Restrictive Trade Practices Act of 1968, the government has done much to maintain 'workable' competition. Economists who believe that one cannot dispense with the market test without endangering efficiency must applaud those measures. It is true that when one enters the area of monopolies of scale and mergers, the policy cannot be applied without qualifications, because in some industries firms must be very large in order to have access to economies of scale and resources adequate for extensive research and development. But, in a period of rapid technical change and commercial innovation, competitive forces can thrive even in that sector of the economy, provided that government policy is biased in their favour. This proposition does not mean that all dominant firms are to be regarded with suspicion, or that all mergers should be frowned upon. It implies, however, that the behaviour of such firms towards customers and rivals must be scrutinised by an independent body and that practices designed to strengthen market domination disallowed, whenever they can be identified. The maintenance or infusion of competition should be accepted as the organising principle of policy, and should be applied whenever there are not overwhelmingly strong reasons against doing so.

What is disquieting about the trend of policy in recent years is that, although the government has been reluctant to commit itself firmly to any such principle, it has been eager to throw a net of bureaucratic control and supervision over ever-widening areas of industry. Its alacrity in this respect is an example of the tendency of modern governments to neglect the important tasks which only they can fulfil, while they make a pretence of discharging elaborate and farreaching functions of a kind that are beyond the capacity of the most competent bureaucracy. This pretentiousness and arrogance on the part of governments are among the most deplorable features of public life in our time, endangering as they do the efficiency of a large part of our industry.

* * * * * * *

A NOTE ON MONOPOLY AND ECONOMIC PROGRESS[7]
In his article on 'Monopoly and Economic Progress', in the August number of *Economica* (1953), Professor Jewkes called attention to the retarding influence that monopoly appears to exert upon technical progress and, in support of his thesis, he stressed the tendency to inertia frequently associated with 'established authority'. Further, he provided some interesting examples of the historical fact that important innovations have often come from outside the great aggregates of industrial power; many more examples of a similar character could be adduced. Yet, although Professor Jewkes left no doubt where his own sympathies lay, he put forward his conclusions somewhat tentatively and he urged the need for further empirical study before his case could be taken as proved. It is, indeed, clear that no more than tentative conclusions are possible at the present time, for there is a sharp conflict of expert opinion on this matter. In the course of his article, Professor Jewkes quoted from the writings of several distinguished economists who, far from regarding monopoly as a hindrance to innovation, consider it an essential condition of technical progress in the modern age. It is well known that, under the influence of Professor Schumpeter's work, the attitude of many economists towards monopoly has become much more favourable than it was only a short time ago.

Among contemporary economists, Professor Galbraith has come forward as a notable champion of monopoly, and Professor Jewkes commented upon his views.

What is perhaps the most curious feature of the debate is that it is from among economists in the United States that these favourable judgments of monopoly have mainly proceeded. English economists, accustomed to find in American law and public opinion the most uncompromising hostility to monopoly, have been astonished to discover this complacency among many of their American colleagues. Unless one is discourteous enough to find an origin in academic perverseness, these views must be attributed to observation of the contemporary American business scene and they cannot be lightly dismissed. The outcome of the debate is of importance both for economic science and for economic policy, and the present writer has been provoked by Professor Jewkes's article to venture into the field.

In the first place, he suggests that the issue is even more highly complicated than it appears. It may well be that the conflict of opinion cannot be resolved on the plane of broad generalised statements at all. It is possible that no conclusion which is generally applicable can be reached and that the consequences of monopoly for technical progress may differ greatly according to the type of society or the economic environment with which the enquirer is concerned. The irrelevance of the conventional static analysis to this problem is commonly acknowledged; but it is not clear from current writings that there is also a realisation of the danger of treating this issue in economic dynamics without close reference to the particular societies in which it is found.

In a country in which a high proportion of the most able men follow a business career, in which incomes are rising fast and capital accumulation is proceeding rapidly, and in which consumption habits are fluid, the appearance of monopoly in certain sectors of the economy may give rise to few of the deleterious consequences that are normally associated with it. In such a society it is not merely easier for entirely new enterprise to find adequate scope, but there also even large established businesses are alert in seizing opportunities for 'muscling in' on lines of trade which have hitherto been the concern of other firms. 'The gale of creative destruction' that blows through the society leaves few chances for monopolistic stagnation. The great firm has not merely the means to be progressive, but in that environment it has the will to be so; for without the will it cannot survive. This, admittedly, is the view of Schumpeter rather than of Galbraith, as Professor Jewkes points out; for Galbraith, having argued that monopolistic organisations alone command the resources required for many types of industrial innovation today, looks to the creation of 'countervailing power' in the competitive sector to offset the danger to the public interest of the established monopolists. The two economists certainly derive their complacency towards monopoly from very different lines of argument. Yet they may not be so fundamentally inconsistent as at first appears. Implicit in Schumpeter's view of economic development is the assumption that innovation normally proceeds from new combinations of capital and new firms, whereas Galbraith appears to assume that most innovations arise, after a certain stage of economic development has been reached, *within* existing firms which change their scope and type of activity under the impulse of progressive forces internal to themselves, or under the impact of the activities of other great firms, or of combinations that exert 'countervailing power'. In practice, innovations seem to come from both directions in modern industrial societies, and what is common to both economists is their implicit reference to a society that is avid for change, devoted to the prosecution of applied science, and fickle in habits of consumption.

The appearance of monopoly in any sector of industry may have very different consequences for a poorer and less fluid society where the flow of new savings is small, and where the rapid enlargement of incomes, though desired, is subordinated as an end of policy to the preservation of status. There monopoly once established in any sector of industry may be difficult to disturb, either by the incursion of new firms or by the encroachment of one great firm on the province of others. In such a society, within which the disposition of established authority towards inertia finds a congenial environment, monopoly may well constitute a powerful means of reinforcing an already existing tendency towards stagnation, and it may succeed in repressing innovators who, in its absence, would be able to launch new ventures. European, or at any rate British, economists may thus have valid reasons for being more sceptical of the virtues of monopoly than their American colleagues.

The contention that conclusions about the relation of monopoly to technical progress have only a local validity may be supported by a further illustration. In an 'underdeveloped' country that is intent upon industrialising itself quickly but is dependent upon the outside world for advanced technical knowledge, a high concentration of economic power may be required to stimulate a rapid process of capital formation and to mobilise effectively the scarce technical knowledge and entrepreneurial skill. The modern economic history of Japan furnishes a good example of rapid industrial development which took place in circumstances of the extreme concentration of resources and initiative in the hands of great concerns. It is significant that these aggregations of power, which were broken up by the Americans during the period of the Occupation, are now being reconstituted as a matter of deliberate policy. It would be rash to conclude that, in the circumstances in which Japan now finds herself and in the light of her previous industrial experience, this policy is mistaken if the rapid reconstruction of the country's industrial capacity is to be promoted. In bringing about the establishment of joint ventures between Japanese (or the nationals of any developing country) and foreigners in industries that depend upon advanced technique and large capital investment, or in the import of foreign 'knowhow', the great concern is likely to have a very important part to play, as past experience shows, and it is doubtful whether a structure composed of numerous small firms would attract the cooperation of foreign enterprise and capital to the same extent.

These considerations suggest that while, as Professor Jewkes maintains, monopoly is to be judged chiefly for its effect on technical progress, that effect is likely to vary widely with the type of economic society and the kind of economic purpose within which the monopolistic organisations are operating. If this is so, it is useless to abstract from those conditions and purposes when one is treating the problem. We must be content with conclusions that have a local and temporary relevance.

14 Britain's Economic Performance in the 1960s[1]

Economic prediction has seldom been more difficult that at the present moment. The amount of statistical information now available about the economy (much of it fairly reliable but some not as good as we once thought) provides the diagnostician with an apparently surer basis for his forecasts than his predecessors enjoyed. But the problems of interpretation remain as formidable as ever. During the last year (1964) these problems have been particularly perplexing. Some of the trends shown by the various statistical series have seemed inconsistent with each other, and policy-makers have fumbled, in part, because of their doubts about the chief causes of our troubles. The future is even more obscure, for, to the difficulty of judging how we have come to be where we now are, there are added uncertainties about British policy in the months ahead and the reactions of foreign countries to British policies already announced.

Let us begin the hazardous task of prediction by glancing at the course followed by the economy during the recent past. In 1963, things went well. Industrial production and exports rose substantially, and NEDC's postulated annual average rate of growth for 1961–66 was exceeded for the first time. When the Chancellor introduced his Budget in the spring of 1964, it seemed probable that a fairly high rate of growth could still be maintained without inflation or trouble with the balance of payments, and the Chancellor's measures accorded with that view. Yet, as we all know, difficulties soon began to accumulate. After the first quarter of the year, industrial output and gross domestic production ceased to grow, exports declined, imports soared, and the balance of payments deteriorated at an exceptionally fast rate. In the same period, money incomes and prices rose sharply, while unemployment declined to such an extent that by the autumn of 1964 the number of unfilled vacancies exceeded the number of those seeking jobs. So, there was every reason for believing that the economy had become 'overheated' and domestic demand excessive.

Yet the government and many expert observers were reluctant to draw this conclusion. What, it was asked, was the source of the alleged excess of demand? Consumer expenditure in real terms was stationary in the first eight months of the year (according to the statistics), exports had fallen and the rise in government expenditure was at a lower rate than that forecast in the Budget. The continuing buoyancy of investment seemed insufficient to produce an overstrained condition, while the classes of goods of which the import had grown most rapidly were not those of which the home sources of supply were in general unduly stretched.

These objections, however, may themselves be refuted. It is acknowledged that the growth in output within the more progressive sectors of the economy has for some months been limited by the shortage of skilled labour and by other bottlenecks. The fact that production in some other industries (or in certain areas) was being restricted by a lack of demand rather than by a shortage of resources was irrelevant to the question under discussion, since the resources of those industries (or areas)—being immobile—were not available for transference to the progressive sectors.

What may have happened is that rapid growth during 1963 had already brought the economy near to the limit of its resources (given the existing standard of capacity-utilisation and mobility). In these circumstances, a relatively slight subsequent increase in demand may have been sufficient to carry it over the brink, and the rise in investment may have provided this impetus. It is also probable that the recent improvements in the technical efficiency of certain foreign industries (Japanese shipbuilding, for example) exerted their full competitive effects on the trade of their British rivals just at the moment when the British economy was becoming 'overheated'. This relative increase in the competitive power of foreign industries may well be considered, in retrospect, to have been the most important influence of all. It is, of course, well known that other factors, besides the deterioration in the visible trade balance, have converged to produce the large deficit in the balance of payments for 1964. Private investment overseas has been high, largely because of a few exceptional capital transactions, but the alarming increase in government net spending abroad must bear a heavy share of responsibility, for this expenditure which is likely to account for over half the deficit, was thirty per cent greater in 1964 than in 1963 and twice the average amount for the late 1950s. It now constitutes one of the most serious obstacles to the restoration of economic viability.

In the light of this diagnosis, let us now consider the outlook for 1965 as it appeared in the later months of 1964. In the absence of corrective measures, no sufficient improvement in the balance of payments could have been expected. It is true that imports seemed likely to decline from the high level reached during the pre-election restocking boom and that exports, to judge from the evidence of order books, would rise. But one could not have expected that the recovery in exports would have been adequate to restore equilibrium. This is because, while domestic demand was likely to grow under the impetus of rising consumers' and government expenditure and of higher investment, the growth in the gross domestic product (in real terms) was unlikely to be much more than three per cent over that of 1964. The justification for this estimate is based on the view that production had reached the limit of capacity early in 1964 (given the productivity then attained and the mobility of resources found practicable) and that in consequence the scope for a further advance in real output would have depended on the additions to capacity made since then. Of course, there would have been other formidable obstacles to an adequate rise of exports, namely, the advance in the technical efficiency of overseas competitors, already referred to.

In a different climate of opinion the government might have been expected to counter these adverse trends by exerting deflationary pressure on investment and consumers' expenditure through a credit squeeze, higher purchase taxes and reductions in its own ambitious programme of expenditure both at home and abroad. Although these old-fashioned measures would have gone some way towards moderating the boom, they would have done little to correct the deepseated troubles of the British economy. But, if they had been applied in the early autumn of 1964, they would probably have succeeded (as they have done before) in restoring equilibrium in the balance of payments before the middle of 1965, while in the interval the continuing deficit would have been financed by the flow of short funds to London.

Such measures, however, were incompatible with two current popular doctrines. First, it had become fashionable to attribute most of our economic troubles in the postwar period to the government's mismanagement of demand which was most clearly demonstrated (so it is asserted) by the stop–go policy. It followed that deflationary measures associated with the 'stop' phase of that policy were to be avoided at almost all costs. Secondly, the recent obsession of politicians and publicists with comparative international rates of economic growth, together with the British government's essay in 'indicative' planning, created a frame of mind in which failure to achieve NEDC's four per cent would have been regarded as a sign of extraordinary economic ineptitude. No policy hostile to such a growth rate was acceptable, and the conventional remedies were, therefore, spurned by the late government as by the present one. Yet there is no evidence to show that stop–go has had more than a marginal effect on the rate of growth during the postwar period. As to the relevance of the policy to our present crisis, it must be stressed that, however firmly one may reject 'stop–go' in principle, once the 'go' phase has carried the economy into inflation, the 'stop' cannot be avoided, at least if devaluation is ruled out.

Furthermore, the acceptance of a four per cent rate of growth as an aim of practically certain attainment persuaded the late government to commit itself to a long-term programme of lavish public expenditure. Yet the basis of the original forecast was insecure. Throughout the postwar period the annual rate of growth has averaged only about two-and-a-half per cent, and even this compares favourably with Britain's achievement before the war. Comparisons with other countries are not to the point. During the last decade high growth rates have been reached only by countries with access to large supplies of underemployed labour (or labour employed in low-productivity occupations) which could be transferred to the modern and highly capitalised sectors of their economies. Britain passed through this phase when she was scaling down her agriculture during the second half of the nineteenth century. This is not to deny that ample opportunities exist for the redistribution of British resources along lines of greater productivity, but, up to the present, progress has been frustrated by official support accorded to established industries and institutions whenever these have been threatened by innovation. As long as policy is governed by this dislike of change, a growth rate of two-and-a-half per cent is about as much as we can hope to achieve, and it is prudent to frame financial and economic programmes accordingly.

Since the old-fashioned 'stop' devices were suspect, the new government at first preferred others, but the crisis of confidence which its policy helped to provoke presently compelled it to arm itself with the most conventional of weapons, a high bank rate. Let us consider how the measures taken as a whole are likely to influence the economic situation in 1965. In this connection, we must remember that the government's economic policy is intended to serve three purposes. The first is, of course, to correct the present balance of payments deficit. The second is to overcome inflation, both as an immediate danger and as a continuing threat, without checking development; hence the importance attached to an incomes policy. Finally, the government seeks to stimulate industry to greater efficiency, to redistribute resources so as to foster the export trade, and to attack such fundamental weaknesses in the balance of payments as result from excessively heavy overseas expenditure. Few economists will quarrel about the importance of these aims. Disagreements are likely to centre on the means employed to achieve them, for certain remedies appropriate to our immediate troubles may exert a deleterious influence on wellbeing in the long term.

The import surcharge, the export rebate and the high bank rate are clearly designed exclusively to deal with the immediate problem. The first of these should bring about a fall in imports once existing contracts have been worked off, and the second may provide a modest stimulus to exports which were likely to rise anyhow. With a considerable lowering of the trade gap, the monetary measures should prevent any speculation against sterling during the next few months. But this result will depend largely on how domestic demand is affected by what has been done. The success of the surcharge (and of the export rebate) will be achieved at the expense of intensifying inflationary pressure, although to the extent that imports subject to the surcharge continue to flow in, the effect will be the opposite. If we take account of the higher petrol duty and dearer credit, we may conclude that the net effect of all these measures will be mildly deflationary. If, as is likely, stocks are run down to a considerable extent in the immediate future, the deflationary effect will be strengthened.

In the short-run therefore, the measures have much to commend them. But the long-run consequences will be less agreeable. If the surcharge were to last for more than a few months, retaliation would be almost inevitable, and any benefit derived from the export rebate would be more than counterbalanced.

So it would seem that the government is relying on forces independent of the surcharge to maintain a precariously restored balance of payments after the spring. If the above analysis is correct, however, its confidence would be justified only on the condition that inflationary pressure is relieved by the continuance of high interest rates, heavier taxation and a reduction in government expenditure. It has already been announced that the April Budget is indeed to present us with higher income tax and insurance contributions, but these will not offset existing inflationary pressures since they will be required to meet the rise in pensions.

Thus, if the Chancellor is effectively to curb expenditure and to divert resources to exports, he must go beyond what he has already announced. It is true that he is to introduce a new capital gains tax and a corporation tax, but the former will not bite for some time and the latter may do little more than redistribute the burden. Of course, if one could believe in the imminence of an effective incomes policy, it might be possible to dispense with higher taxation and dear money. The TUC and the employers' organisations may be persuaded to give their assent to such a policy, but their support would not commit the great mass of their members. Unless inflation were brought firmly under control, agreement at the centre would be nullified by wage drift, especially in those industries where earnings are settled mainly on the shop floor. Much the same view may be taken about the control of prices which is to form an integral part of an incomes policy. Experience suggests that price control is fully effective only where it is combined with detailed controls over production (as in the wartime utility schemes) and with rationing. However, one must not be too pessimistic. Even if the upward trend in money incomes is merely damped down or retarded, the policy would be worthwhile, and it is not unreasonable to expect this modest achievement.

Unfortunately, none of the measures so far adopted, nor of those that will be necessary in the spring, is calculated to promote industrial efficiency, the third aim of the government. Higher import duties which relieve industry from foreign competition in the home market are hardly likely to achieve this result, while the prospect of long-continued high interest rates may well have a discouraging effect on industrial investment. The import surcharge, the petrol tax and the new insurance contributions will raise costs in the short run. The ultimate effect of a corporation tax which is likely to discriminate against distributed profits must be to increase the rigidity of the industrial structure. To throw the weight of fiscal policy on the side of a further concentration of capital in established firms with the inevitable result that the supply available for newcomers is reduced, is hardly the way to usher in the new world of enterprise.

It is not easy to summarise these speculations. The probability is that by the late spring the balance of payments will again be moving into equilibrium. Exports should be increasing and imports should have been sharply reduced. But the surcharge must then come off if foreign co-operation with the British authorities is to continue, and it is unlikely that Britain will be able to pay her way during the succeeding months unless further constraints on spending, both public and private, are imposed. These will probably take the form of credit restrictions, which will reduce private investment, and higher taxes on consumption. The severity of these restrictive measures, in the absence of any really effective incomes policy, will depend on how far the government succeeds in reducing its own expenditure or in diverting its investment into productive channels. The 'stop' phase is likely to be with us for some time, and the continuing necessity of measures to deal with the balance of payments will handicap the efforts that might otherwise be made to improve the long-run efficiency of the economy. Industry will be subjected to additional strains, since the contraction of certain types of spending and the redeployment of resources are likely to have significant structural consequences. It would be surprising if there were not some increase in unemployment.

The only satisfactory way out of our troubles is to be found by following a hackneyed prescription, namely, an improvement in efficiency. Such an improvement must apply not only to the methods by which particular undertakings in the public and private sectors conduct their operations, but also to the allocation of resources throughout the economy.

Here the government can play an important part. Excessive tenderness towards established industries, whether they are viable or not, has been a feature of British economic policy for many years past. Large public investments have been directed into the cotton industry in vain attempts to maintain its size; the taxation system has been used to ensure that oil is expensive for the benefit of the coal industry; the railways have been prevented from introducing lower freight rates in order to sustain high-cost coastal shipping. Examples of the way in which governments have frustrated efficient enterprise by bolstering up the obsolete and incompetent are legion. The wastage of capital and labour resulting from such policies is matched by the effect of restrictive practices in private industry (despite the blows recently administered by the Restrictive Practices Court) and by that of restrictive labour practices which no government and few employers have yet had the courage seriously to challenge. It would be erroneous to suggest that these blemishes in our industrial system are general, but their presence in some large and important sectors of industrial and commercial life are in a considerable degree responsible for Britain's competitive weakness at a time when economic efficiency is advancing quickly in rival countries. This diagnosis is now widely accepted, but it is doubtful whether the public realise the revolutionary effects that a wholehearted pursuit of economic modernisation would exert on the structure of industry, trade practices, industrial relations, the distribution of labour and relative incomes.

Many of our troubles have arisen because we have pursued ends that are incompatible. We are all in favour of rapid economic growth and higher incomes, but we are not all ready to accept the conditions necessary for the attainment of those benefits. The key question, which must now be faced, is whether the British people can be persuaded to content themselves with a place in the world and a standard of living commensurate with their present mediocre productive performance or, alternatively, whether a few leading spirits in government and industry can cajole or coerce them across the threshold of the modern world.

15 A Critical Appraisal of Galbraith's Thinking[1]

The classical economists and most of their successors and critics in the nineteenth century addressed themselves to an audience of educated men interested in public affairs. But when economists discovered more refined methods of analysis and called on mathematics for aid in their exposition, their audience changed its character. Professional economists now began to write primarily for fellow-specialists and, if they touched on questions of immediate practical interest, they were increasingly inclined to leave to economic and financial journalists the task of conveying their ideas to the general public. There were exceptions, but even Keynes's major contribution owed its wide influence almost as much to the writings of popularisers as to his own. Today much of the published work of contemporary economists in their professional journals is incomprehensible to the ordinary educated reader. Against this general trend towards obscurity the most effective voice raised in recent years has been that of Professor J. K. Galbraith. Galbraith has asserted that 'there are few, if any, useful ideas in economics that cannot be expressed in clear English'; accordingly, it is for an audience of men of good general education that he has written. Towards economic theorists (the élite among professional economists in their own estimation), he displays only contempt. Most of them, he thinks, waste their intellectual powers in the refinement of theories that are without relevance to the modern world. But he is not merely a destructive critic of the economic establishment. Whatever one may think of his sallies against the theorists, his work deserves close attention because he has directed his lively and forceful mind to the analysis and solution of some of the most important economic problems of our day. The questions he asks are the right questions.

His work covers a wide field. He began his long list of postwar writings with a study of the economics of price control; he followed this in 1952 with his book on *American Capitalism* in which he introduced the concept of 'countervailing power'. Then came, in

1954, a widely read book *The Great Crash 1929*. *The Affluent Society*, a bestseller which brought a new vogue word into our vocabulary, was published in 1958. I pass over a number of other publications that preceded the appearance in 1967 of his most important book *The New Industrial State*, of which a revised second edition has recently been issued. His ideas have been further developed in his latest book *Economics and the Public Purpose*. The influence of his books has deepened with the passage of years, not least because all his writings are infused with an economic philosophy of which the outlines in the last decade have become firmer, just as his conclusions have been more emphatically asserted. Even in the earliest of the books mentioned, *The Theory of Price Control*, Galbraith takes a stand, with which his readers are now familiar, against the conventional assumption among economic theorists (or so he supposes) that free competition normally prevails in a modern society. His fellow-economists, he observed, disputed the possibility of effective price control in wartime on the ground that the fixing of prices by government at a level lower than the equilibrium price would drive goods from the market. Galbraith shows that, in fact, most manufactured goods are sold in markets where some degree of monopoly exists. Here prices are not settled by competition but are 'administered'. In such conditions it is eminently practicable for the authorities to fix prices, since they are, in effect, already fixed! In *American Capitalism* he demonstrates, to his own satisfaction, the futility of anti-trust legislation designed to preserve, or restore, competitive conditions in industry. Modern technical methods can be applied efficiently only by very large firms the size of which enables them to dominate markets. So, some degree of monopoly is inevitable in many modern industries. In these circumstances, the only way to deal with the dangers of exploitation without jeopardising efficiency is to confront a monopolist with another monopolist (or monopsonist); in other words, to establish a position of 'countervailing power'. The application of this principle may sometimes require persons or firms menaced by the power of large concerns deliberately to create their own monopolistic organisations, or such bargaining bodies as trade unions or agricultural co-operatives. The State may often be justified in lending a hand to help the weaker members of society by supporting their efforts to organise themselves. Such, in Galbraith's view, are the only practicable means of restraining private monopolists.

In *The Affluent Society* he moves on to consider the social conse quences of the growth of an industrial system dominated by great firms with access both to advanced technology and to market power. In poor communities, he argues, production is limited to what is necessary to supply essential needs, the consumers' demands determine what shall be produced, and the producers are subject to the discipline of the market. In wealthy communities, on the other hand, where the satisfaction of essential needs makes only a modest demand on productive capacity, the consumer, left with a surplus of income, falls a victim to the persuasive arts of the advertiser and marketing expert, with the result that resources are increasingly used to satisfy trivial wants. All this occurs within the private sector. Meanwhile, the public services, which furnish much that is essential to civilised living in an urban society, are starved of resources, for these services depend on provision from public funds. Thus, such communities reach a condition of 'private affluence and public squalor', a condition that can be alleviated only by a large expansion in collective demand financed by taxation. Finally, in *The New Industrial State* Galbraith brings together many of the ideas that he has expounded in other books, associates these ideas with other significant trends in economic organisation and policy that he has identified, and sets before us a coherent and comprehensive view of modern industrialism. It is this book to which I shall now direct most of my attention, for it represents an epitome of his writings.

At this point I must refer to a characteristic of Galbraith as a controversial economist that he shares with Keynes. Keynes claimed that his *General Theory* constituted a break with economic tradition, although in fact it would have been more correct to say that he had built a new edifice on old foundations. He has been excused for this perversity on the ground that only by insisting on the novelty of his doctrine could he attract sufficient attention to influence events. Galbraith likewise exults in rebelling against academic tradition and trounces 'orthodox' economists for their blindness to the facts of economic life and for their timid conservatism in basing their analysis on assumptions long out of date. I think that his impatience with modern economic theorists has some justification. The preoccupation of many of them with the *apparatus* of inquiry and 'the fascination of what is difficult' have often diverted their attention to irrelevances. But, because some theorists have ignored economic realities, this does not mean that economists in general (including several leading theorists) have failed to interest themselves in the movements and trends which Galbraith regards as significant.

Let me give some examples. First, there is Galbraith's proposition that the old type of individual entrepreneur, in control of the undertaking for which he has provided most of the capital, has been replaced over much of industry by a 'technostructure' composed of professional managers, technologists, accountants and other experts. In consequence, the character of the industrial system and the motives that govern business decisions have been transformed. For one thing, the great company is not, as the entrepreneur-capitalist is supposed to be, a 'profit-maximiser'. The prime concern of the technostructure is with the security and growth of the organisation it controls. Of course, Galbraith is aware of the continued existence of small and medium firms which still conform to the model of the entrepreneur-capitalist. But in industry they are in retreat before the advance of the giant firms which determine the *modus operandi* of the modern economy.

None of this is new. The divorce between ownership and control has been recognised and its significance discussed by economists for half a century. The same applies to Galbraith's argument that the rise of the great companies has destroyed the former dichotomy between public and private enterprise. He points out that the methods of administration in a great company closely resemble those in public corporations or government departments, and that the ends they seek are much the same. Now precisely these points were made in one of the best-known studies of the British economy in the 1920s. The Report of the Liberal Industrial Inquiry, entitled *Britain's Industrial Future* (1928), argued that in a modern economy there was a steady gradation from the small private firm managed by its owner to the great public company where boards of directors, though nominally responsible to shareholders, were in fact self-elective, and where the maximisation of profits was only one of several motives actuating those in control. Between the private company and undertakings run by a government department there were many intermediate forms of enterprise in which the profit motive was qualified by other considerations. The public corporation was one of these forms. Like Galbraith today, the authors of this book argued that because of these developments the struggle between private and socialised enterprise had become a sham fight In the 1930s, Berle and Means[2] analysed in detail the organisation of industry in the United States and reached similar conclusion about the extent to which control has passed to what Galbraith has called the 'technostructure'. So this part of Galbraith's argument has long been accepted doctrine.

Let us now turn to his analysis of the decline in competition in the modern economy. When firms grow to a very large size, their numbers in any industry must be few, and consequently the kind of competitive market often postulated by the economic theorists ceases to exist. The market no longer sets the prices at which firms must sell their output. Each of them is a monopolist, or oligopolist, a 'price-maker' rather than a 'price-taker'. Again these trends have long been a commonplace of economic discussion. Some of the most interesting theoretical work in the 1930s was directed towards the examination of imperfect or monopolistic competition, which was recognised as the normal state over most of manufacturing industry. Indeed, it was asserted that perfect competition, the convenient analytical device of the price theorists, was found only where deliberate efforts had been made by some central authority to establish it, as in the stock exchanges and the organised commodity markets.

Galbraith's criticism of those economists who are obsessed with the merits of a free, competitive market leaves unconsidered the eminent scholars, notably Joseph Schumpeter and J. M. Clark, who have evinced as little respect for the assumption of 'perfect competition' as he himself but who, nevertheless, believe that some kind of competitive pressure is necessary to keep producers up to the mark. I have not seen in any of Galbraith's writings references to Schumpeter's notion of the 'creative destruction' of established positions as a means to progress, or to J. M. Clark's 'workable competition'.

Other economists have shown themselves to be well aware of the defects of the free market as a guide to economic activity. For instance, from the early years of this century the Cambridge economists gave much time to analysing the circumstances in which, under *laissez-faire*, social net product differed from private net product (as when a producer is able to throw on the community as a whole, or persons other than himself, some part of the costs which his operations entail). The divergence, they showed, was a source of inefficiency and they tried to devise means for correcting the distortions. The problem reappears today in the attention given to cost-benefit analysis and in discussions of pollution. It is admitted that liberal economists look kindly on the market, but this does not mean that they are blind to its deficiencies; alternative methods of administering resources seem to them to have even more serious blemishes. Their favour does not rest on religious faith (as Galbraith suggests) but on judgments of expediency. Nor do they think that *all* economic decisions can be taken in the market. To this I shall return.

Galbraith vigorously attacks the orthodox theorist for holding to a belief in consumer sovereignty. Great companies (he declares), in their search for security and growth, cannot leave demand uncontrolled. Production schedules must be drawn up long in advance of marketing. Resources have to be committed many years before some types of goods are ready for sale. The producer of such goods would be at enormous risk unless he took steps to ensure that the product, when ready, would be sold. Hence the use of the arts of persuasion to 'brainwash' the consumer into buying what the firm finds advantage in producing. Galbraith is here following a path marked out long ago by others. Consider this passage in Schumpeter's *Theory of Economic Development* written in 1911:

> Innovations in the economic system do not as a rule take place in such a way that first new wants arise spontaneously in consumers and then the productive apparatus swings round through their pressures ... It is ... the producer who as a rule initiates economic changes and consumers are educated by him ... they are ... taught to want new things, or things which differ in some respect or other from those which they have been in the habit of using.

Another strand in Galbraith's doctrine can be traced directly to Keynes and the Keynesians. 'Full employment' policies were originally proposed and adopted as a means of avoiding the social disasters of the 1930s. But a fully employed economy, with steadily rising incomes, is also necessary for the security and growth of the great firms, for, with their vast fixed investments in high technology, they are vulnerable to recessions. Unlike the small firm, with its labour-intensive processes, they cannot significantly reduce their costs by laying off labour when demand falls. So they become firm allies of the government in the pursuance of a policy aimed at avoiding fluctuations in economic activity. Full employment, however, strengthens inflationary pressures, and these cannot be contained in such conditions without direct controls over prices and incomes. From this necessity there comes about a strange coincidence between the aims of the State and the needs of the great firms. Whereas the entrepreneur-capitalist typical of past times resisted government intervention in the economy as an impediment to progress, the 'technostructure' accepts intervention as essential to its success. This is an unexpected development of Keynesian doctrine. The common interest of the State and the great firms is also displayed in such industries as armaments, aircraft and nuclear energy and in space exploration. Each is necessary to the other, a fact long recognised, especially in war or quasi-war conditions. I recall a remark of Ernest Bevin in 1945: 'When the war came to an end', he said, 'I quite expected to see the directors of Imperial Chemical Industries marching down Whitehall to hand back the British Empire to the Government!'

I call attention to these earlier expressions of Galbraith's ideas, not with the object of denying the importance of his contribution, but simply to suggest that in many respects he has followed a well-worn track. His great merit lies in his having gathered together a miscellany of ideas and produced from the assemblage a coherent doctrine. Greater affluence, the substitution of planning for classical forms of competition in the allocation of resources, the application of science and high technology to industry on a massive scale, the lengthening of the 'lead-in' period, the rise of giant firms with huge, fixed, capital resources, the extension of producer-control over demand, the growth in the economic functions of the State (especially its responsibility for maintaining full employment), all these developments, which have long been a subject for economic discussion, are shown by Galbraith to be organically linked. Here lies his claim to originality which must be readily conceded. Where he lays himself open to adverse criticism is in his failure to recognise the importance of other trends in society and the immoderation with which he insists on his own uncompromising interpretation. Admittedly, in the second edition of *The New Industrial State*, he qualifies some of his more sweeping generalisations. For example, he agrees that what he had originally said about industry applies only to the great firms and that he has not examined the very large sector composed of small and medium-sized undertakings. But obviously he does not think that this qualification in any way disturbs his general conclusions. Moreover, he is apt to brush aside facts that contradict his propositions by arguing that exceptions do not invalidate a rule. Thus he contends that the failure of a particular planned programme—there are some striking examples—does not disprove that *in the main* great firms can plan their production with the assurance that they can persuade consumers to buy their products. His argument is plausible, but it can be countered by pointing out that, in a modern dynamic economy, the existence of a few rebels outside the main citadels of economic power gravely weakens the proposition that everything of significance happens inside.

I must also criticise certain inconsistencies in Galbraith's philosophical position. Like Marx, he comes before us as a determinist. He argues that it is futile to resist the trends he describes so eloquently. Efforts to preserve competition, by legal or administrative devices, must fail in the face of the strong forces that buttress monopoly power and foster concentration. Consumer sovereignty is a thing of the past; why base theories or policies on the assumption that it still exists? State control and intervention have come to stay. Why pretend that the interests of big business and government are not coincident? Why not acknowledge that the vast extension of higher education has occurred chiefly because it serves the technostructure? Yet when Galbraith looks on the sort of society that he seems to think inevitable, he does not like the look of it. The Galbraith of *The Affluent Society* comes to the front, the Galbraith who condemned the modern industrial community in which the quality of life is said to be sacrificed for ever-increasing material benefits and in which public squalor coexists with private opulence. At this point, he abandons his determinism; he ceases to deride those who question his conclusions; he casts about for some means of escape from his nightmare. But since he is precluded from using conventional weapons, he has to look elsewhere for allies and the results of his observation are, to say the least, unimpressive. Loftier standards of value are to be asserted by the intellectual, artistic and academic sections of society. These will confront the battalions of organised business and, with the help of a more enlightened bureaucracy, they will lead our sordidly affluent societies towards nobler destinations. This is a lame conclusion. It is not even logical. Throughout most of his book Galbraith speaks of the academic community as composed of two groups of persons, those who serve the needs of the technostructure and those who inhabit an ivory tower and timidly avert their eyes from the facts of modern life and continue to promulgate obsolete doctrine. Why should he think these are the people to lead a crusade? I do not agree with

Galbraith's unflattering judgments of the academic community as expressed in the earlier part of *The New Industrial State*. At the same time I doubt if that community is equipped to become the spearhead of major social and economic reforms. Intelligently directed good-will is not enough. Great social advances can be accomplished only when the *interests* of powerful groups in society are enlisted on the side of reform. Galbraith has forgotten Alfred Marshall's wise dictum: 'Progress mainly depends on the extent to which the strongest and not merely the highest forces of human nature can be utilised for the social good'.

I now turn to examine Galbraith's main propositions in more detail, and I ask myself: do they provide an adequate interpretation of the outstanding characteristics of modern industrialism? I start with his contemptuous dismissal of the concept of consumer sover-eignty. Such a concept (he declares) was appropriate to times when the economy was able to meet only the most urgent wants; in a rich society the producer, in effect, decides what the consumer shall buy. As I have already said, no-one disputes the influence of the demand-forming activities of the great firms, but Galbraith goes far beyond this. He sees the consumer as an automaton re-sponding quite uncritically to the arts of the advertiser. He also distorts the meaning of consumer sovereignty as the term is used by economists. For by this term they mean simply that the in-dividual exercises choice when he spends his income and that his choice is the major influence on the allocation of resources in the economy. Economists as such do not feel competent to analyse the psychological determinants of choice nor to judge the moral or aesthetic worth of the choices actually made, although this does not mean that they believe that all choices are morally and aestheti-cally equal. They certainly recognise that choices are moulded by a variety of influences, cultural, climatic and social. What people buy has always depended in one sense on what producers can pro-vide and it changes with innovations for which producers are often responsible. The English in the eighteenth century did not begin to substitute tea for other beverages because they felt spontaneously an urge for a drink hitherto unknown to them, but because the East India Company made it available and it pleased them. Of course, the techniques used in marketing today are more elaborate than in the past, but the difference is one of degree. Moreover, at no time does investment in marketing *guarantee* the commercial success of a product. All industries are in competition with one another for the consumer's favour, and the citizen of a rich, modern country is presented by a far wider variety of choice than the peasant of earlier centuries and his choice is far more fickle. The mere fact that firms spend so much effort in market research before they launch a product shows that they do not regard the consumer as a submissive automaton.

So far, I have talked of consumer goods. Galbraith neglects altogether that a high proportion of the products turned out by the giant firms that are the subject of his inquiry are intermediate products and capital goods. These goods are sold to expert buyers whose decisions are reached after a rational examination of prices, specifications and qualities. Steel, aeroplanes, ships, industrial machinery, heavy chemicals, building materials and commercial motor vehicles (all products of great firms) fall into this class. The manufacturers of Concorde and the governments that have sponsored them must by now retain little belief in Galbraith's notion that users can be relied on to buy what it is the advantage of producers to manufacture provided that their efforts are supported by high-pressure salesmanship!

Another target for Galbraith's arrows is the idea that the maximisation of profits is the overriding purpose of business activity. Of course, economists have never imagined that all businessmen are in fact moved solely by that ambition. We know that many businessmen bear little resemblance to the bold entrepreneur alert to every opportunity; some are content with a modest profit and as quiet a life as they can persuade their competitors to allow them. Profit maximisation is merely a rough-and-ready rule to apply in the judgment of rational business conduct; it satisfies the pragmatic test fairly well, or so it has been assumed. Galbraith has no difficulty in showing that the great firms are governed by a variety of motives, among which a search for security and an ambition for growth are outstanding. After all, the members of the techno-structure who decide policy do not depend on profits for most of their income! The concept of profit maximisation is admittedly ambiguous when applied to a giant firm which is obliged to commit huge resources well ahead of sales and must keep its eyes on long-term prospects. Such a firm certainly does not aim at maximising profits in the short period. On the other hand, there is a less serious conflict between the aim of profit maximisation in the long term and that of security and growth than Galbraith concedes. Firms that earn consistently high profits are those that can most readily command security and finance growth. Moreover, officers of a company, in reaching decisions about particular transactions, contracts or investments, when faced with several possible choices, would be considered incompetent if, within the context of the firm's long-run policies, they chose any but the most profitable alternative.

This brings me to the core of Galbraith's argument and, in describing it, I must be excused if I am guilty of some repetition. According to Galbraith, the nature and operations of the contemporary industrial system are determined by a few giant firms in which an increasing part of production is being concentrated. The size of these firms is a function not merely of the economies of large-scale production or the power to dominate markets but also of their capacity *to plan effectively*. By this Galbraith means that they must be large enough, first to prevent interference by rivals who might frustrate their plans, second, to subdue the demand for their output to the requirements of their productive organisation, and finally, to meet contingencies that might damage some part of their business by calling on their vast pool of resources. They have, in effect, become autonomous planning units, immune from the market pressures to which lesser firms must pay obeisance. It is the interests of the technostructure that determine policy and these interests lie in the direction of continuous enlargement. The giant firms are virtually immortal and their capacity to remain profitable is unquestioned.

I think that one of the chief blemishes in this interpretation of modern industrialism is to be found in Galbraith's exaggeration of the power of the giant firms to ensure that the outside world conforms to their plans. There is no doubt about the necessity for forward planning, but that the great firms, because of their size, can free themselves from risk and can oblige consumers or users to take the prospective output in the quantity and at the prices settled in the plans is not in accordance with experience. All estimates and plans are at the mercy of unforeseen changes in technology, fashion, sources of supply and political upheavals. Sir Frank McFadzean, once a managing director of Shell (a giant if ever there was one) has graphically described the impact of uncertainty on his own company. For every one of its vast and complicated operations forecasts have to be made, but few turn out to be correct. And the 'largest errors have usually been in prices', and in the 'assessment of the market returns for some of the products'. 'A few

years ago', he wrote, 'naphtha was a drug on the market and we
had to burn it in the refineries in place of fuel oil. Due to tremen-
dous but unforeseen increases in demand for naphtha both as a
chemical feedstock and as a raw material for the manufacture of
town gas, it is now in short supply and its price is way above fuel
oil'.[3] The international oil companies have now been made well
aware of even greater hazards. Other examples might be taken
from the aircraft industry, which recent experience has shown to
be at the mercy of chance. The most commercially successful
British passenger aircraft, the Viscount, owed its triumph in part
to a series of lucky accidents in timing. The Britannia, on the other
hand, was a fine aircraft which failed commercially because,
through relatively slight technical delays, it had the misfortune to
arrive on the market just as new types of jet aircraft had appeared.
Examples could be multiplied.

To a large extent Galbraith's simplistic view of how great concerns operate is derived from his notion that they enjoy freedom
from competition. Not only so, but he considers that it is futile
to attempt to maintain or restore competition by anti-monopoly
policies. Now, admittedly, whereas policies designed to eliminate
restrictive practices in industries composed of numerous firms have
been fairly successful in several countries, the methods that can
usefully be applied in dealing with single-firm monopolies are not
easy to devise. But this does not mean that competitive pressure is
absent from that sector of the economy or that efforts should not
be made by governments to strengthen the pressure. The real world
does not conform to the model of perfect competition as expounded
in old-fashioned textbooks, but some kind of competitive pressure
makes itself felt throughout every progressive dynamic economy.
In such an economy, where technique and demand are subject to
innovation, established positions are insecure, and firms, however
large, have to make constant adjustments to external forces.
Galbraith emphasises expansionist ambition as the chief motive
governing the strategy of giant firms, but he does not pursue this
idea to its logical conclusion. Expansion is usually accompanied by
diversification, and this often produces conflict because a diversifying giant firm is likely to stray into the provinces hitherto served
by other giant firms. Collisions of this sort may well upset long-
considered plans. The process of 'muscling in' is a source of much
competitive pressure nowadays, Present-day Britain furnishes
many examples. A former specialist giant firm in the tobacco

industry has moved into food manufacture, chemical firms have diversified into textiles, oil companies have taken up the production of chemical fertilisers and general chemicals, a great manufacturer of confectionery and soft drinks has entered the alcoholic drinks trade and the brewers have responded by adding soft drinks to their products. Much the same has happened elsewhere. When a great firm initiates some change in markets or technique it may, in doing so, threaten the apparently assured markets of other great firms. Expansionist ambitions themselves generate competitive pressures.

In other ways Galbraith's model is too crude to help in the understanding of the elaboration and intricacy of modern industrial organisation. He speaks of great firms as dominating their markets. Most of them, in fact, produce a variety of goods and serve markets with different characteristics. They may be monopolists, or near-monopolists, in some markets and may meet with keen competition in others. Imperial Chemical Industries Ltd made this point in its evidence to the Monopolies Commission (United Kingdom), where it described the widely differing price policies it followed in the various types of markets.[4] In a dynamic society, moreover, market conditions are constantly changing and this applies also to the in-dustrial structure. Galbraith draws a sharp distinction between the entrepreneur-capitalist sector (comprised of the smaller firms) and the giant firm sector run by the technostructure. In fact, the dichot-omy is not so sharp. The great firms extend their scope not only by internal **grow**th and by acquiring ownership of new concerns but also by entering into contracts with independent suppliers or by long-term arrangements with subcontractors. In this way some small firms become dependants of the great companies. But the arrangements are not fixed and unalterable. The boundaries of each empire are blurred. Small firms sometimes change their allegiances or are dropped as suppliers if they fail to satisfy the competitive test. In other words, the organisation of an industry, or a typical firm, is much less rigid and fixed over time than is suggested.

Recent statistical investigations both in Britain and the United States show that the position of the great companies is less secure than Galbraith supposes. Thus, of the top hundred companies in the United Kingdom in 1948, only fifty-two remained in that rank in 1968.[5] If the steel companies (which 'died' as a result of nation-alisation) are excluded, the 'death rate' would have been two per cent a year, almost the equivalent of the 'death rate' of comparable American companies. Of course, most of those who lost their rank survived, but (again excluding the steel companies) twenty-seven out or the hundred ceased to exist, usually through being merged with or acquired by others. It is true that the result of this process was to leave some of the biggest companies bigger than ever, and to this extent Galbraith is right. But the investigator concluded his examination of the trends by stating that 'the life of the great firm does not seem to be that of a "quiet life" monopolist; the death rate among the giant firms by take-over and acquisition produces a significant degree of insecurity'.[6] Those who have witnessed in recent years the collapse of one of the largest and most reputable firms in British engineering and have seen how, on several occasions, the State has been called on to rescue great firms from disaster, will be sceptical of Galbraith's claim that such firms can assure themselves a continuously profitable existence. Examples can be found elsewhere, notably in the United States.

The antithetical nature of Galbraith's exposition often leads him to conclusions that are too clearcut for truth. I will give two examples. First, consider the contrast between the firm that was typical of an earlier industrial era and the giant firm of today. The former was often dominated by an individual on whom all authority was concentrated. In the latter, authority is diffused among members of the technostructure; there is a team but no 'boss'. This distinction is true enough as a very broad generalisation, but there are notable cases in which the policies of great companies have been largely decided by a single powerful individual, although of course his decisions have usually been influenced by information and advice supplied by persons lower down the hierarchy. A change for the better in a company's fortunes can often be ascribed to the arrival of an exceptional individual who, though not necessarily occupying the 'top' position, is able to bring his colleagues into conformity with his will. The decisive accents of a leader, even in the greatest concerns, may make themselves heard above the anonymous murmurings of a managerial team.

The same comment can be made on Galbraith's view of the sources of invention and innovation. He is right in affirming that many modern industries depend on teamwork in elaborately equipped research establishments and that development work to bring an investigation to fruition often calls for huge capital. Yet Professor Jewkes and his colleagues have shown convincingly that small firms and individuals have been responsible for an impressive list of innovations in our own day as in the past.[7] Just as at the turn of the century established engineering firms were sceptical of the commercial prospects of the motor car and left its development to a variety of imaginative entrepreneurs outside their ranks, so in the 1930s the large aircraft companies and governments saw little future in the jet engine, with the same result. There are later examples. It may be argued that the chief cases instanced by Professor Jewkes are drawn from a generation ago and that the prospects of a small man who is at odds with the establishment are today very bleak. But this is something we cannot know. Ideas now struggling to be born in the mind of some unregarded inventor or in some insignificant enterprise may contain the seeds of a great, new industry.

One of Galbraith's main contentions is that all advanced industrial societies are subject to the same imperatives which produce broadly identical forms of organisation and social and economic problems. Once a society has decided on a high level of industrialisation it must travel the same road as the others: '. . . the imperatives of organisation, technology and planning operate similarly, and . . . to a broadly similar result, on all societies.' Of course, there are identities, but there are also striking contrasts. Some of the contrasts have recently been brought to light by Professor Dore.[8] His study of the way Japan's industry operates, and especially of her system of industrial relations, goes far towards disproving 'the theory of convergent social evolution' (whether that of Karl Marx or Galbraith). I am inclined to think that Galbraith, like others among his countrymen, is inclined to equate conditions in America with civilisation. Certainly, British experience does not always bear out his confident assertions. For instance, Galbraith thinks that the rise of the giant firms has transformed industrial relations. He declares that the antagonism between the organised workers and the employers, characteristic of an earlier industrialism, has tended to disappear as authority in the firm has shifted to the technostructure and as a high proportion of the employees move into the white-collar group. The class war has no place in the new industrial society. Whatever may be the case in the United States and some other countries, this is certainly not true of Britain. There, in recent years, the most bitter strife has occurred in the great corporations, especially those in the public sector. (Some observers have found the cause in the ennui attendant upon many types of work in the mass-production factories, combined with the remoteness of ultimate authority from the man on the shop floor.) Nor has the increase in the proportion of white-collar workers in the labour force meant a decline in militancy. Of late years, *their* trade unions have taken a far more active part than ever before in the organised labour movement. The bitter conflicts in the public sector in Britain and some other countries can in some measure be attributed to the combination of circumstances which Galbraith regards as inevitable in modern industrial society. He has argued that a full employment policy is likely to subject an economy to intense inflationary pressures which require wage and price controls to moderate. But experience shows that such controls can be brought to bear effectively only on a part of the economy, notably on the part that lies within the public sector. The result is twofold. First, during periods of boom the public corporations have difficulty in maintaining an adequate labour force in the face of competition for workers from the less effectively controlled private sector. Secondly, they often command inadequate capital for efficient production because their prices and profit margins are rigidly restricted. Such has been the fate of several industries in the public sector in Britain. Galbraith, in his condemnation of the excessive growth of industries producing trivialities at a time when public services in many countries are deteriorating, attributes the trouble to the survival of an unwarranted faith in the virtues of a market economy. But it is equally plausible to argue that its roots are to be found in a failure to allow market forces to operate in the public sector, where that is possible.

In his discussion of that sector Galbraith does not seem to me to distinguish clearly between two types of public enterprise which differ widely in their modes of operation. First, there is the publicly run undertaking which sells its goods or services in the market. Such an undertaking may be enjoined to follow the 'commercial principle' in formulating its price and investment policies even though it may receive financial assistance from the Exchequer in obedience to cost-benefit estimates or for some purely political reason. The second type serves a collective demand and must be financed mainly by taxation. I have already touched on the dangers to which the first type is exposed. The problems attending the publicly operated services designed to meet collective demand are more complex. Here the market must be rejected as a guide, and the scale of operations is a matter for political decision. Galbraith holds that a civilised society requires a much greater extension of these collectively provided amenities or services than is reached in an economy where the powerful forces of private industry are arrayed in opposition. But the roots of this problem go very deep. Although we are social beings we remain separate individuals who stubbornly regard collectively provided and financed goods and services in a different light from those which are subject to our own unique decisions. The ordinary citizen does not regard social security benefits or publicly provided amenities as part of his income. Once they have become an established feature of his society, he considers them to be his right and he resents paying the taxes needed to finance them. To him his income is his 'take-home' pay, that is to say, that part of his total income which is his to dispose of at will. My point is, then, that this unbalanced economic development which Galbraith condemns in affluent societies has deep roots in human nature. The problem will not yield easily to rational argument, for even when men are intellectually convinced of the strength of the case, their conduct may still be guided by their instinctive prejudices. Moreover, the general public even when 'State-broken' (to use Schumpeter's term) remains in most countries unconvinced of the disinterested benevolence of the bureaucrats and politicians who thrive on the growth of the public sector in all its forms. My arguments do nothing to disturb Galbraith's contention that development in modern industrial societies has become lopsided, but they do show, I think, that in free democratic countries the application of the right remedy is more difficult than he seems to suppose. There are, therefore, reasons for doubting the truth of Galbraith's proposition, put forward in his latest book,[9] that an improvement in the condition of modern industrial societies is to be sought mainly in a further substantial enlargement of the public sector.

I have said much in criticism of Galbraith's ideas, but I should not wish to conclude without putting this criticism into a proper perspective. As I stated at the outset, Galbraith has undoubtedly made an original and important contribution to the understanding of modern industrial society. But I have shown that, in my view, many of his propositions cannot be accepted without qualification. The industrial system is much more complicated and intricate than it appears in his vision of it. And the solution of the problems created by economic growth and advanced technology cannot be found within the confines of his own ideology. To my mind the greatest issue facing advanced societies is one that Galbraith has not seriously examined, namely the preservation of social unity and order in the face of rapid technical and economic change.

16 Economic Advice for Lloyd George[1]

In this article I propose to recount some personal experiences of a time when I served, briefly, as an economic adviser to Mr Lloyd George and a few of his colleagues. I owed my invitation to act in that capacity to Mr Seebohm Rowntree, which whom I was well acquainted, and I spent part of the summer of 1930 working in close association with him at Lloyd George's headquarters in Old Queen Street. I was then a young man, and the experience left me with vivid memories of events and persons that may today be of some interest. First of all, I must explain the circumstances that led to the economic inquiries in which I participated.

In the early summer of 1930 the Prime Minister, Mr Ramsay MacDonald, moved by the deterioration in Britain's economic condition and the rise in unemployment, proposed a conference of the three political parties on unemployment and agriculture. The Liberal Party gladly accepted this invitation and appointed Mr Lloyd George, Lord Lothian and Mr Seebohm Rowntree as its representatives in the ensuing discussions. The Liberal Party was already well prepared to tender advice, for it had conducted a series of investigations into the country's economic problems. The *Liberal Yellow Book*, published in 1928, had provided a penetrating analysis of Britain's economic ills, and its plans for industrial reorganisation received widespread and close attention. Later, Lloyd George's famous pamphlet, 'We Can Conquer Unemployment', brought to the notice of voters in the general election of 1929 the Party's ambitious and imaginative schemes for solving the country's most intractable economic problem. In addressing themselves to their task, the Liberal triumvirate conceived that their first concern must be to propose measures for meeting the danger of a steep rise in unemployment in the coming winter. They, therefore, began by examining the various emergency schemes already prepared by their experts and, having revised them in the light of current conditions, submitted them to the government. Some of the schemes covered the problems of the depressed areas, the 'regions', as we now say.

This was only a beginning. Lloyd George and his two colleagues assumed that they were also required to tender advice on the general, long-term problems of unemployment and national development. They defined what had to be done under three headings. First, there were the measures needed to restore British industry to prosperity, and among these they gave a high place to a steep reduction in public expenditure. Under the second heading they put forward a policy for reversing the decline in British agriculture by capturing for it a large part of the home market for food. The third group of proposals comprised those directed towards putting to work the mass of unemployed manpower on projects for national development and re-equipment. On the completion of the inquiries, a report on all these matters was sent to the government. Unfortunately, the hopes of all fruitful co-operation between the Liberals and the Labour Government came to nothing because of a quarrel with Lloyd George over agricultural policy, about which he felt deeply. However, a version of the report was published, in October 1930 as a pamphlet entitled 'How to Tackle Unemployment', under the names of Lloyd George, Lord Lothian and Seebohm Rowntree.

Many of the proposals put forward, and the arguments used in support of them, sound quite familiar today despite the difference between the periods with respect to price trends. This is especially true of the schemes for national development which were aimed both at improving the infrastructure and at mopping up unemployment. Some of the proposals have been realised and have long become the accepted policy of British governments, whether Labour or Conservative. Much emphasis was placed, for instance, on the need for constructing an adequate road system, including trunk roads, bypasses, ring-roads round towns, and special schemes for London traffic. Slum clearance was to be tackled more resolutely, and the building of new towns on the lines of Welwyn Garden City and Letchworth was proposed. Other capital investment was advocated for docks and harbours, sewage disposal, water supply and electric power stations. The backwardness of Britain in comparison with other industrial countries in the use of telephones was noted. This was the moment to remedy the deficiency, said the authors, for we now had the resources available to do the work. In connection both with the telephone service and electricity generation, it was declared that progress was being impeded by bureaucratic rules and by the lack of salesmanship among the authorities responsible. The authors drew on the experience of other countries, especially the United States, to show how these hindrances to growth could be overcome.

The proposals, as a whole, were aimed not at combating frictional or cyclical unemployment but at reducing substantially structural unemployment, the 'refractory million', as it was called. The structural unemployment was attributable to the decline in the old staple industries and the failure to find substitutes, a failure resulting from the high level of British industrial costs in relation to those of our competitors. So, one section of the Report was addressed to the improvement of Britain's industrial efficiency. In their analysis of the state of industry the authors found that the root of the trouble lay not in any lack of capital available to finance technological innovations, but in a failure of enterprise. This, in turn, was ascribed in some part to the weight of the dead hand of vested interests and vested prejudices in British society. It showed itself clearly in trade union restrictions detrimental to improvements in methods of production, the preservation in some branches of industry of obsolete forms of organisation, and the failure of the financial system to adapt itself to the conditions of the postwar world. The government had to bear a share of the blame, chiefly because of the heavy burden of taxation on enterprise.

The remedies advocated were various. The deficiencies in the financial system were to be supplied by the establishment of banks modelled on the German Credit Banks. These banks, it was pointed out, were 'properly equipped with staffs of commercial and technical experts capable of investigating both the efficiency of going concerns and the soundness of proposed industrial ventures'. The Report recognised the steps already taken in that direction through the founding of the Securities Management Trust, the Bankers' Industrial Development Company and the Agricultural Mortgage Corporation.[2] But more had to be done. The Big Five should co-operate in founding an Industrial Bank, staffed by commercial and technical experts, with the function of meeting the long-term capital needs of British industry, especially those of the smaller manufacturers. A similar proposal found expression in the Macmillan Report of 1931 and the subject was much debated during the 1930s. The Report went on to suggest that, in a period of depression when the risks of enterprise were enhanced, there was every reason for calling on the State to bear part of the financial burden, particularly in connection with the export trade. This could usefully be done by extending Export Credit Guarantees and by re-enacting the Trade Facilities Act in a modified form. Under that Act the government had guaranteed the payment of three-quarters of the interest for five years on Dominion and Colonial public utility loans spent in the United Kingdom. The proposals formed part of wider and more ambitious schemes for Empire development, although these were not described in detail in the Report.

It was further argued that continuing prosperity would be enjoyed only by those nations that stood in the forefront of innovation. In this process inventions and the commercial exploitation of inventions had a major rôle to play. Some of the advisers had been much impressed with the valuable work done by the Mellon Institute in the United States in the encouraging of research and development. This Institute had been founded and endowed by Mr Mellon, Secretary of the United States Treasury, and his brother, with the object of undertaking industrial and scientific research, for payment, for private firms. It was recommended that the State should take the initiative in establishing a similar institution in this country and that it should maintain a continuing interest in it. The Report also dealt with the rationalisation of industry and with government encouragement of standardisation and simplification, on the lines of the work done by the Department of Commerce of the United States under Mr Hoover. The agricultural proposals were worked out in considerable detail. They included the re-organisation of British farming in such a way as to replace mixed by specialist farms. They also sought to establish a large number of family farms. All this required State intervention and State financial assistance.

In view of the enlarged rôle which the authors' proposals demanded for the government, it is rather surprising to find that a key suggestion was a steep reduction in public expenditure. Today it may seem particularly extraordinary that, in the middle of the Great Depression and with prices still falling, they should look to further deflation as a means to recovery. However, their attitude can be easily explained. For one thing, their eyes were fixed on the long-run weaknesses of Britain's economy, and especially on her chronic industrial ills, and not on the consequences for Britain of the World Depression which was then in its early stages. For another, they were writing six years before the publication of Keynes's *General Theory*, and they were naturally influenced by the then orthodox Treasury view that government expenditure on public works merely diverted savings from one outlet to another and did nothing to increase total activity. The merits of budgeting for a deficit were still hidden from them, and a year later, when the May Committee's highly coloured account of the national finances helped to provoke the financial crisis, they may have felt that events had justified their policy. But there is another point to bear in mind. Their own proposals, as we have seen, involved additional public expenditure for agriculture, industry and the infrastructure. A substantial part of this, they suggested, should be financed by the issue of a great National Development Loan, and other expenditure should be met by economies in administration. In this connection, they noted, anticipating Professor Parkinson, that the decline in the size of the army and navy had been accompanied by a considerable increase in the number of clerks at the Admiralty and War Office! Their proposals for a new 'Geddes Axe', therefore, may be interpreted as aiming not so much at a reduction in the volume of effective demand as at a reallocation of national expenditure. Economies in 'non-productive' forms of public expenditure would permit the easing of fiscal burdens on enterprise, while new financial resources raised by loans would be applied to schemes of national development and industrial rehabilitation.

Such, in brief outline, were the results of the inquiry. However, the main purpose of this article is not to appraise the Report but rather to discuss the light which the inquiries shed upon the state of economics in the early 1930s. My first task, on taking up my duties as adviser, was to acquaint myself with the content of the preliminary proposals then under consideration. My study of them left me deeply pessimistic about their efficacy, both for dealing with the immediate problem of unemployment (the amount of which was approaching 2,200,000) and also for stimulating the development of British industry in the long run. So I decided to seek the advice of some of the most distinguished professional economists of the time. I made the round of the universities and other institutions where economists were to be found and asked, bluntly, not for an analysis of the contemporary economic situation but for practical remedies. It was a disillusioning experience; no doubt, I was inexcusably naïve in supposing that somewhere or other in the world of learned men there was a store of expert, practical wisdom on which statesmen and bureaucrats could draw for the solution of their most pressing problems.

Several of the economists whom I approached were diffident

about their ability to give any practical help, believing, perhaps rightly, that the resources of economics were unequal to the task.[3] The attitude of some was determined not so much by doubts about the capacity of their science to provide remedies as to scepticism about the competence of governments to apply them. In those days neither social scientists nor the general public had become con- ditioned into accepting the pretensions of politicians and civil servants to proficiency in the management of the economy. The triumvirate and their advisers certainly had not, and some of the proposals put to us by others were rejected less because they were unacceptable in principle than because they were judged to be administratively impracticable. At that time politicians and civil servants themselves took a modest view of their qualifications for managing the economy and for putting the world to rights. Their errors were sins of omission rather than of commission. They be- longed to a breed that produced the senior civil servant who expressed his disapproval for unseemly enthusiasm by saying to me: 'If I leave the office on Saturday feeling confident that in the past week I have done no harm, then I am well content'. However, by no means all those to whom I went for practical advice were so deprecating. In particular, some of the economists showed the con- fidence in offering prescriptions for our ills that the world now associates with the practitioners of this science. Some examples will demonstrate the quality of their advice.

Whatever the view taken of the wisdom of Britain's return to the gold standard in 1925, nearly everyone who gave advice assumed that there was no question of abandoning it. In 1930, this assump- tion was more prevalent than was the refusal to contemplate devaluation during the years before 1967. In the latter period, devaluation, though taboo in official circles, was at least a subject for discussion among consenting economists, as a wit has pointed out! In 1930 only two of the economists I consulted, as far as I can remember, considered it a permissible remedy; the rest did not mention the possibility. One of the two (Sir Ralph Hawtrey), how- ever, was a most enthusiastic advocate of Britain's abandoning gold. Within six months of doing so, he asserted, her export trade would have recovered and unemployment, at any rate the 'hard core', would have virtually disappeared. Strangely enough, he was the economist who attributed much of the inflation of the 1950s to the devaluation of 1949 which, in his opinion, left sterling undervalued on the exchanges. A more representative view was expressed by

Professor (later Sir Henry) Henry Clay then economic adviser at the Bank of England. Almost a year later, when sterling was under threat, he delivered a radio address in which he made our flesh creep with his prediction of the dire consequences that would follow the abandonment of the gold standard—a German-like inflation and a collapse of the currency. When, soon afterwards, sterling was devalued without producing the results predicted, his reputation suffered somewhat. If he were alive today, he might say that the fate he prophesied for us had simply been postponed.

I went with high hopes to see Mr Keynes (as he then was) but I was taken aback when he replied, in answer to my question, that the only measure that would do any immediate good was the imposition of a general tariff on imports. He added that he had put this point to Professor Pigou and that Pigou agreed with him. His remedy was not, of course, one likely to commend itself to the Liberal Party, but naturally this objection left him unmoved. In fact, a tariff was a logical, short-term remedy for the imbalance caused by Britain's excessive industrial costs at a time when the abandonment of the gold standard was regarded as out of the question, for it would have greatly improved the competitive position of British producers in the home market. In the circumstances of a World Depression it would also have meant the export of some of our own unemployment, but, as already indicated, the full extent of the worldwide deflation had not yet been realised, and attention was being concentrated on devising remedies for the particular economic ills of Britain. The authors of the Report had no difficulty in finding reasons for rejecting the proposal, and they presented these at some length. Protection, they argued, would raise the costs of manufacturing industry at a time when every effort should be made to reduce them. It would obviously bring no benefit to the exporting industries, the decline of which had been the main cause of Britain's heavy, chronic unemployment. Not long after the Report had been published another attempt was made to enlist the support of leading economists for a tariff. I was told by Lord Stamp that Keynes had promised the Prime Minister that he could obtain from the leading economists a unanimous recommendation in favour of a tariff and that he had arranged a meeting of them to discuss the proposal. The majority acquiesced, but the plan was wrecked by Keynes's failure to persuade the stubborn few. [4] Of course, in the end their resistance was in vain, and by 1932 the era of free trade had passed into history.

Professor Edwin Cannan of the London School of Economics was then living in retirement at Oxford. When I went to consult him I found him in a benign mood. He professed himself to be flattered by my confidence in his power to suggest a solution for unemployment, and declared that it was the second compliment that had been paid him that day. Earlier on, an American lady had stopped him in Cornmarket and asked him if he were Bernard Shaw. 'No, madam,' he replied, 'but I can be just as rude as Bernard Shaw if I want to be.' He then went on to suggest to me that some of our perplexities arose from an even more serious mistake in identity. We had been deceived into thinking that the boom of the late 1920s was a depression; now we were suffering from the real thing. He approached the question of remedies for Britain's troubles rather obliquely. 'Reflect', he said, 'on two points. First, is it a coincidence that unemployment has been so much worse since the Unemployment Insurance Act of 1920? Second, note that a twopenny packet of lettuce seeds now provides enough salad for a family for a whole season. That is typical of what has been happening in agriculture and industry.' He did not positively propose that unemployment insurance should be abolished, but this was the implication. As to the technological unemployment, such as that produced by the improvements in the quality of lettuce seeds, he presumably thought this could be overcome only by restoring flexibility to our costs and prices.

Henry Clay took a different view of technological advances. He and some other economists considered that one of Britain's chief faults, and a cause of the heavy unemployment, lay in her lagging behind her rivals in the application of science to industry. Recovery was to be sought in inventions and the alertness of industrialists in their adoption. He provided examples of new industries recently developed through the exploitation of scientific discoveries; in Britain there were too few of them. The authors of the Report were impressed with Clay's views and, as already stated, they recommended the setting up, on government initiative, of an Institute on the lines of the United States Mellon Institute 'to bridge the gap between science and industry'. To a large extent, Clay's views on these matters coincided with those of Mr L. Urwick, the well-known management consultant. Mr Urwick's career included some years with Rowntree's and Mr Seebohm Rowntree obviously had great respect for his ideas and his judgment. Urwick lamented the slowness of British manufacturers in adopting up-to-date methods of production and in introducing new products. He supported his criticisms by American examples of fruitful innovation. Britain's deficiencies in this respect he ascribed chiefly to her untrained, incompetent management. Mr Rowntree himself held similar views and had taken an active part during the 1920s in launching the Management Research Groups. But the Report itself was silent on this question.

I had a few discussions with H. D. (later Sir Hubert) Henderson at that time working in the Economic Advisory Council which had lately been established by the MacDonald government; this was the precursor of the wartime Economic Section of the Cabinet Office. The Council was engaged on producing a number of reports on the staple industries, including cotton and iron and steel. Henderson's advice was given with the results of those studies in mind. He was sceptical of the usefulness of sweeping, general measures the consequences of which could not be foreseen, and he preferred a policy designed to deal with the special problems of industries in trouble. For example, he favoured the extension of Export Credit Guarantees and the revival of the Trade Facilities Act, since, in his view, the efforts of the government could best be directed towards helping the depressed export trades. In other words, he was inclined to microeconomic rather than macroeconomic solutions, although in those days the world was mercifully ignorant of those terms. I remember that he took the same line in discussions of reconstruction policy (including the full employment policy) towards the end of the Second World War. He thought that specific measures, such as those designed to alleviate the condition of the depressed areas, would be more satisfactory than fiscal or monetary devices to maintain the volume of effective demand throughout the economy.

My inquiries extended to the City, or at any rate to those members of certain merchant banking firms that were known to be well disposed to the Liberals. Their expert advice on the financial proposals that appeared in the Report, was, of course, valuable, but otherwise this field was rather barren. Probably the sample with which I had contact was not representative. Certainly, I came away without any constructive proposals. What I chiefly remember, and recorded, was first the strong support of these bankers for the proposal for a new 'Geddes Axe'; second, their anxiety that nothing should be done that would further endanger sterling; and finally, their disposition to link government intervention in industry and trade, especially if it involved the provision of financial aid, with corruption. For example, the point was made that business probity might well be eroded by a greatly enlarged distribution of public funds to the private sector, whatever the ostensible merits of particular projects. I was slightly surprised to be told at an interview that one of the chief objections to tariffs as a solution for our economic troubles was that they would open the way for corruption both in private industry and among public servants. The triumvirate and their advisers did not give much weight to this argument; at any rate they found other reasons, as we have seen, for their disapproval of protection. The fragility of standards of public honesty, as revealed by recent experiences, may suggest that there was more substance in these arguments than was believed to be the case in 1930.

From time to time, in the course of the inquiries, we were called to Mr Lloyd George's flat on the top floor of 25 Old Queen Street, where we met the great man, still masterful and vigorous, and expounded to him the proposals put to us and our views about them. I remember being slightly shocked at his apparent reluctance to discuss the intrinsic economic merits of the several proposals, with the exception of those relating to agriculture about which he had strong convictions. For the rest of the proposals his concern seemed limited to their political expediency or feasibility. I suppose that my reaction was unjustified. Lloyd George, no doubt, considered that it was for his advisers to judge the economic merits of the proposals. His function was to decide on political possibilities and the appropriateness of the various suggestions to the agreement he had made with the Labour Government. Of course he was not unique among politicians, either before or since his time, in the importance he attached to expediency. If, as it seems, many of the economic problems of the 1930s are still with us, so are the attitudes of politicians towards them. Lloyd George's own attitude was best illustrated by his handling of the proposal that received by far the most widespread support from the economists I consulted—and from many other persons also. The proposal was that the competitive strength of British industry in the world's markets, and ultimately a satisfactory level of employment, could best be restored by a general reduction in wage rates.

In some quarters it was thought that what was required was a reduction in all money incomes, and that this might be brought about by some kind of general consensus which would permit a cut even in contractual incomes. A similar suggestion was made a year later by the Macmillan Committee on Finance and Industry. This

Committee, having considered that a reduction of ten per cent or
more in the level of money costs and income was necessary to
'remedy a position of national disequilibrium', concluded that such
a change could not, in equity, be concentrated on salaries and
wages but must apply to every category of income. It could be
brought about only by general consent, 'a national agreement for
the general and simultaneous adjustment of all money incomes'.
Mr Lloyd George's two colleagues rejected a similar scheme put to
them, on the grounds of administrative difficulties. Indeed, they
regarded it as quite impracticable. But they took seriously the
advocates of wage reduction. Henry Clay pointed out to them the
contrast between the stability of wage rates in the current recession
and the steep decline in rates during the immediate postwar
recession. The reason was that the bargaining strength of the trade
unions had been much increased by the payment of unemployment
benefit. This, of course, had been Edwin Cannan's argument. When
these ideas were brought to Lloyd George's attention they did not
get very far. This was not because of any doubts about whether it
was sensible to reduce demand still further at a time when it was
already insufficient, for, as already indicated, Lloyd George did not
bend his mind to the economic soundness or otherwise of the proposals. His concern was with political expediency. 'If we were
fighting the Labour Government,' he said, 'we could use it. But just
now we are co-operating with them, and it won't do.' So the
question was not raised in the Report.

It was unnecessary for me to seek out the 'unorthodox' economists and the cranks, for they descended on Old Queen Street in
considerable numbers, without any invitation. Among them were
the 'under-consumptionists' who made many representations to us.
The ideas of this group gained a measure of intellectual respecta-
bility after the publication of Keynes's *General Theory*, but in 1930
they were quickly brushed aside. Nevertheless, some of the more
interesting ideas came from persons other than professional
economists. For example, Mr Comyns Carr, a well-known barrister
who wrote extensively on economic affairs, eloquently urged that
the State, instead of paying people to be unemployed, should
subsidise employment in those industries that had become un-
competitive because of their high costs, and he worked out a scheme
for doing this. In principle, the proposal seemed reasonable
enough. It bears a close resemblance to the Regional Employment
Premium of recent years and it would presumably have had the

same effect, since most of the declining exporting industries that
Mr Carr had in mind were situated in the depressed area. In 1930,
however, the practical difficulties appeared to be insurmountable.
Even if the scheme were administratively possible (and about that
there were misgivings), the general view was that it would certainly
be gravely abused and would probably do more harm than good.
So, it did not get far enough to receive an honourable mention in the
Report; I doubt if Mr Lloyd George was even given the opportunity of turning it down. One may perhaps conclude that the
advice tendered by the economists, and quasi-economists, I
consulted exerted about as much effect as it deserved on the
recommendations finally proposed in the Report.

Notes and References

Chapter 1

1. R. E. Caves and Associates, *Britain's Economic Prospects* (Allen and Unwin, 1968).
2. R. E. Caves, 'Second Thoughts on Britain's Economic Prospects', in Sir Alec Cairncross (ed.), *Britain's Economic Prospects Reconsidered* (Allen and Unwin, 1971), p. 212.
3. Cairncross, op. cit., p. 220.
4. S. R. Dennison, *The Location of Industry and the Depressed Areas* (Oxford University Press, 1939), passim.
5. P. M. Hohenberg, *Chemicals in Western Europe, 1850–1914* (Chicago, Rand McNally, 1967) Chapter 3.
6. D. L. Burn, *Economic History of Steel-Making* (Cambridge University Press, 1940), p. 68.
7. Cf. G. C. Allen, *The British Disease* (London, Institute of Economic Affairs, 1976), pp. 37–50.
8. J. A. Schumpeter, *The Theory of Economic Development* (Harvard University Press, 1934). The book was first published in German in 1911.
9. J. A. Schumpeter, *Capitalism, Socialism and Democracy* (Allen and Unwin, 1943), p. 84.
10. W. J. Reader, *Imperial Chemical Industries: A History*, Volume 1 (Oxford University Press, 1970), p. 13.
11. J. A. Schumpeter, *Capitalism*, op. cit., p. 84.

Chapter 2

1. First published in *The Nation and Athenaeum* (26 February 1927) under the title of 'Industrial Changes in the Midlands'.

Chapter 3

1. Read before Section F of the British Association at Glasgow in September 1928 and published in *Economic History* (*Economic Journal Supplement*) (January 1929).
2. A detailed description of these local industries is to be found in S. Timmins, *Birmingham and the Midland Hardware District* (Robert Hardwicke, 1866). The references in this chapter are to books and other publications in the *Birmingham Collection* in the Birmingham Public Reference Library.
3. S. Timmins, *Birmingham and the Midland Hardware District*, pp. 635, 669–70; 'Birmingham Glass Works' in *Household Words* (March 1852); and F. W. Hackwood, *Wednesbury Workshops* (1889), pp. 66–8, 94.
4. S. Griffiths, *Guide to the Iron Trade of Great Britain* (1873), Chapters IV to VIII; and R. G. Hobbs, 'A Midland Tour' in *The Leisure Hour* (1872), pp. 282, 463.
5. Léon Faucher, *Études sur l'Angleterre* (1856), pp. 502–3.
6. E. Burritt, *Walks in the Black Country*, etc. (1868), Chapter X.

7. *Children's Employment Commission* (1862), 3rd Report, p. 53 et seq.
8. R. H. Tawney, *Minimum Rates in the Chain-making Industry*, Chapter I.
9. S. Timmins, op cit., pp. 387–93.
10. Ibid., pp. 271 and 303.
11. Léon Faucher, op. cit., p. 506.
12. *Report of the Factory Inspectors* (30 April 1874), p. 56.
13. *Brass Trade Arbitration Report* (Birmingham Reference Library, 1900), Fifth Day's Proceedings, pp. 33, 47, 60–1.
14. 'Labour and the Poor' in *The Morning Chronicle* (23 December 1850).
15. *Brass Trade Arbitration Report*, First Day's Proceedings, pp. 75–86.
16. 'Labour and the Poor' in *The Morning Chronicle* (16 December 1850).
17. *Brass Trade Arbitration Report*, Third Day's Proceedings, p. 57.
18. Artifex and Opifex, *Cause of Decay in a British Industry* (1907) Chapters I and II.
19. W. H. Jones, *Story of the Japan, Tinplate Working and Galvanising Trades in Wolverhampton* (1900), pp. 134–7.
20. C. J. Woodward, 'Manufacturing Industries' in *The British Association Handbook* (Birmingham Meeting, 1886), pp. 181, 198–9, 202.
21. *Report of Chief Inspector of Factories* (October 1889), pp. 30, 32.

Chapter 4

1. First published in *The Economic Journal* in June 1930 with the title of 'Labour Transference and the Unemployment Problem', and now presented in a slightly amended form.

Chapter 5

1. Delivered as Inaugural Lecture at the University of Liverpool on 4 May 1934, and first published in the *Sociological Review* (July 1934).
2. This disapproval does not extend, of course, to the various methods of monetary management that have been applied. But this exception to the general rule of *laissez-faire* was countenanced even by the classical economists.
3. See *The Listener* (4 October 1933), p. 506.
4. E. Halévy, *The Growth of Philosophic Radicalism* (Faber and Gwyer, 1928), p. 94.
5. That is, broadly speaking. Without qualification this statement would not be true of *all* the classical economists.
6. In this article I am not concerned with attacking or defending the psychology or the political theory of the classical school, but only with explaining why economics was accepted as a guide to policy in the nineteenth century, and why its doctrines are ignored today. Explanations, resembling that which is given here, of the influence exercised by the classical economists have been offered by several writers, notably by Professor W. C. Mitchell in the *Quarterly Journal of Economics* (November 1914), p. 1, and in his contribution to R. G. Tugwell's *The Trend of Economics* (1924). But Professor Mitchell is chiefly concerned with emphasising the weakness of the psychology of the classical economists, and in doing so he seems rather to underestimate the great achievements of that school. The achievements of those economists, indeed, suggest that their psychology and political theory satisfied the pragmatic test and, though no longer acceptable, formed a basis for the

science that was at any rate provisionally useful and valid. And it should be added that as yet a new psychological basis for economics—a basis which should form the starting-point for further fruitful enquiries—is still undiscovered. But it is very significant that an economist with the particular interests of Professor Mitchell should have engaged in this controversy. The late Professor Allyn Young, in discussing the articles mentioned above, expressed surprise that an economist whose own work in the 'applied' field 'fits into and amplifies the general structure of economic knowledge that has been built up . . . during the last century and a half', and whose assumptions and modes of thought are such as are familiar to economists, should criticise so adversely the general structure of theoretical economics 'of which the best of his own work seems to be an integral part'. (see *Economic Problems, New and Old*, pp. 250 et seq.) But surely the economist whose tasks lie mainly in the applied field, who must rely on others to provide the theoretical apparatus necessary for his work, is the very person who is likely to be most conscious of the defects of that 'general structure'. The realistic economist must use whatever apparatus of theory is available; he must seize whatever tool comes to hand; but more than anyone else he is likely to realise its imperfections for dealing, to his own satisfaction, with the facts which his experience and his investigations bring to light.

7. L. Robbins, 'Certain Aspects of the Theory of Costs' in the *Economic Journal* (March 1934), p. 2.
8. *The Wealth of Nations* (ed. Cannan), vol. i, p. 32.
9. L. Robbins, *The Nature and Significance of Economic Science* (Macmillan, 1932), passim.
10. There are, of course, many economic problems for the treatment of which psychological or philosophical considerations are irrelevant.
11. Professor J. M. Clark.
12. M. Dobb, 'The Problem of a Socialist Economy', in the *Economic Journal* (December 1933), p. 390.
13. In this connection the increasing attention which is being given by theorists to conditions of imperfect competition is significant.
14. T. E. Gregory, 'Economic Theory and Human Liberty', in *Economic Essays in Honour of Gustav Cassel*, p. 241.
15. Slightly adapted.
16. J. M. Clark, 'The Socialising of Economics', in R. G. Tugwell, *The Trend of Economics* (New York, 1924), p. 100.

Chapter 6
1. First published in the *Quarterly Review* (October 1937).

Chapter 7
1. First published in the *Economic Journal* (June–September 1945), under the title of 'An Aspect of Industrial Reorganisation'.
2. Other industries which possess highly specific equipment and may well find themselves troubled with a redundancy problem after the war, either because of changes in demand or because of technical innovations, are jute, pottery, tinplate, and certain branches of the hosiery industry.

3. This is seen very clearly to be so in the tinplate industry, where the further development of the continuous-strip method of manufacture involves not merely the removal of much redundant plant of the oldfashioned kind, but a complete financial reorganisation of the trade. It may be expected, more-over, that when during the course of the expansion of an industry firms have become increasingly specialised to a narrow range of products or processes, a subsequent decline in that industry will sometimes require a reversion to a lower degree of specialisation among the constituent firms. This may possibly be true of the cotton industry, where expansion before 1914 was closely associated with the process of vertical disintegration.

4. It may be objected that the experience of the last twenty-five years shows how easily cyclical and secular changes may be confused. Yet by the time of the World Depression the nature of the disease from which many of the industries were suffering had been in many cases correctly diagnosed; the trouble was that the remedies applied were ineffective or harmful. Furthermore, there should surely be less danger of confusing cyclical and secular changes when the former have been abolished by means of the full employment policy of which the success has here been assumed!

5. It has been pointed out to me that where firms are in the hands of owner-managers, compensation for loss of profits alone would hardly be effective in persuading firms to withdraw. This would not be a serious obstacle in an industry in which the proportion of the total production in the hands of reluctant owner-managers was small, since their refusal to accept the scheme would not seriously jeopardise the chances of creating a new, efficient structure for the trade. In the other cases, however, it might be necessary to secure their consent by providing some additional compensation for the loss of managerial income, although the method of doing so should remain unaffected.

6. A method that would be in many ways preferable to the one described would be for the government to provide the cash payment to the closers and to receive from the runners, in exchange, shares in their businesses to the amount judged to be necessary to cover the interest on the capital sum provided. I do not suggest this method in the text, however, as I think that in practice it would encounter two strong objections. The first would come from the government which, I imagine, would be extremely reluctant to become *permanently* an ordinary shareholder in numerous manufacturing businesses and would be embarrassed if this meant, as it probably would, that it would have to appoint representatives on each of the Boards of Directors. The second objection would come from the members of the industry who would feel that the scheme was a precursor of complete government control.

Chapter 8
1. Inaugural Lecture delivered at University College London on 4 March, 1948, under the title of 'Economic Thought and Industrial Policy'.
2. H. S. Foxwell, *Papers on Current Finance*, Paper VII.
3. J. S. Mill, *Principles of Political Economy* (ed. W. J. Ashley) (Longmans, 1920), pp. 947, 950.

4. A. V. Dicey, *Law and Public Opinion in England*, 2nd Edition (Macmillan, 1924), pp. lx, lxxxvi, xc.
5. J. E. Cairnes, *Introductory Lecture* on 'Political Economy and *Laissez-Faire*'.
6. J. H. Chapman, *An Economic History of Modern Britain* (Cambridge University Press, 1938), vol. iii, p. 397.
7. J. M. Keynes, *The End of Laissez-Faire* (Hogarth Press, 1926), p. 50.
8. Committee on Industry and Trade, *Factors in Industrial and Commercial Efficiency* (HMSO 1927), p. 9.
9. D. H. Robertson, *Essays in Monetary Theory* (Staples Press, 1940), p. 111.
10. J. M. Clark, 'The Socialising of Economics' in R. G. Tugwell, *The Trend of Economics* (New York, 1924), p. 100.
11. L. Robbins, *The Economic Problem in Peace and War* (Macmillan, 1947), p. 83.
12. G. Walker, *Road and Rail*, 2nd edition (Allen and Unwin, 1947), pp. 257–8).
13. J. A. Schumpeter, *Capitalism, Socialism and Democracy* (Allen and Unwin, 1943), Chapters XXIII, XIV and passim.
14. Viscount Goschen, '*Laissez -Faire* and Government Interference' in *Essays and Addresses on Economic Questions* (Arnold, 1905), pp. 313–14.
15. Sir Oliver Franks, *Central Planning and Control in War and Peace* (Longmans, 1947), passim.

Chapter 9
1. First published in the *Westminster Bank Review* (August 1948).

Chapter 10
1. First published in the *Westminster Bank Review* (August 1952) under the title of 'The Outlook for British Industry'.

Chapter 11
1. Presidential address delivered to Section F of the British Association for the Advancement of Science. on 1 September 1950 at Birmingham, and published in the *Economic Journal* (September 1950).
2. J. S. Mill, *Principles of Political Economy* (ed. W. J. Ashley) (Longmans, 1920), p. 696.
3. A. C. Pigou, *Wage Statistics and Wage Policy*, Stamp Memorial Lecture, University of London (Oxford University Press, 1949), passim.
4. Lord Beveridge, *Full Employment in a Free Society* (Allen and Unwin, 1944), Appendix C.
5. L. Rostas, *Comparative Productivity in British and American Industry* (Cambridge University Press, 1948), p. 49.
6. W. W. Rostow, *British Economy of the Nineteenth Century* (Oxford University Press, 1948), p. 19.
7. W. S. Jevons, *The Coal Question* (3rd edition, 1906), p. 274.
8. A. C. Pigou (ed.), *Memorials of Alfred Marshall* (Macmillan, 1925), p. 326.
9. Ministry of Fuel and Power, *Report of Technical Advisory Committee on Coal Mining* (HMSO, 1945), p. 29 et seq.
10. Ministry of Works, *Working Party Report on Building Industry* (HMSO, 1950), Chapter 18.
11. Ministry of Labour, *Reports of Cotton Manufacturing Commission* (HMSO, 1948–9), passim.

12. The propositions put forward in this paragraph are also supported by the *Report of the Committee on the Productivity of the National Aircraft Effort* (Ministry of Technology, 1969), especially paragraph 289.

13. Preparatory Asiatic Conference of the International Labour Organisation, *The Economic Background of Social Policy* (1947), pp. 3, 97, 100, 155.

14. A. C. Pigou, op. cit., pp. 331–2.

15. P. W. S. Andrews, *Manufacturing Business* (Macmillan, 1949), p. 284.

16. J. A. Schumpeter, *The Theory of Economic Development* (Harvard University Press, 1934), p. 65.

17. F. H. Knight, *Risk, Uncertainty and Profit* (Reprints of Scarce Tracts, London School of Economics, 1935), pp. 318–19.

18. H. von Beckerath, *Modern Industrial Organisation* (New York, McGraw-Hill, 1933), p. 190.

19. A. C. Pigou, op. cit., pp. 282–3.

20. A. Marshall, *Industry and Trade* (Macmillan, 1921), p. 156.

21. F. H. Knight, op. cit., p. 349.

22. D. H. MacGregor, *Economic Thought and Policy* (Oxford University Press, 1949), pp. 132–3.

23. Board of Trade, *Report of Wool Working Party* (HMSO, 1947), p. 11 and passim.

24. A. C. Pigou, op. cit., p. 284.

25. George Berkeley, *The Querist* (Reprint of Economic Tracts, Johns Hopkins University, 1910), p. 12.

26. F. H. Knight, op. cit., p. XXX.

27. A. Marshall, op. cit., p. 161.

28. Boulton and Watt MSS (Birmingham Public Reference Library), *Cornish Letters*.

Chapter 12

1. First published in the *Economic Journal* in March 1923. The material for this essay was obtained from the Boulton and Watt MSS in the Birmingham Public Reference Library. The letters which Boulton wrote to his partner, while the former was in Cornwall, proved the chief source of information. At the time when the research was undertaken the correspondence was, for the most part, unclassified. A box labelled *Cornish Letters* contained the bulk of the information given here about the Cornish Metal Company, including a valuable account in outline of its activities up to 1787; but there was among the MSS a large amount of material to which it was impossible to refer with any degree of precision. The detailed references to the letters have been omitted from this reprint. Other sources of information were: R. Hunt, *British Mining* (London, 1884) and the *Journal of the Royal Geological Society of Cornwall*.

Chapter 13

1. This chapter has resulted from the conflation of two papers. The first was read at the Conference of the Society of Business Economists at King's College Cambridge in April 1970 and was afterwards published in a volume issued by the Society entitled *Changes in the Industrial Structure of the U.K.* (Unwin Brothers Ltd). The second paper was read before a Seminar on

British Industry and Economic Policy

'Mergers' in London in November 1972, and was afterwards issued in a volume entitled *Mergers, Take-overs and the Structure of Industry* (London, Institute of Economic Affairs, 1973).
2. D. Swann and Others, *Competition in British Industry* (Allen and Unwin, 1974).
3. *Enterprise, Purpose and Profit* (Oxford University Press, 1954), pp. 154 et seq.
4. D. P. O'Brien and D. Swann, *Information Agreements, Competition and Efficiency* (Macmillan, 1968), p. 112.
5. A. Sutherland, *The Monopolies Commission in Action* (Cambridge University Press, 1969), passim.
6. P. Lesley Cook, *Effects of Mergers* (Allen and Unwin, 1958), passim.
7. This note was first published in *Economica* (November 1953).

Chapter 14
1. First published in *British Industry* (8 January 1965), under the title of 'Economic Outlook—A Long Period of "Stop" '.

Chapter 15
1. An address delivered to the Schweizerisches Institut für Auslandsforschung in February 1974 and afterwards published in *Der Streit um die Gesellschaftsordnung* (Schulthess Polygraphicsher Verlag, Zürich, 1975).
2. A. A. Berle and G. C. Means, *The Modern Corporation and Private Property* (Cambridge, Mass., Harcourt Brace, 1932).
3. F. S. McFadzean, *Galbraith and the Planners* (University of Strathclyde, 1968), p. 46.
4. Monopolies Commission, *Report on the Supply of Chemical Fertilisers* (HMSO, 1959), pp. 172, 206.
5. G. Whittington, 'Changes in the Top 100 Quoted Manufacturing Companies in the United Kingdom, 1948–68', in the *Journal of Industrial Economics* (November 1972), pp. 18–22.
6. Ibid., p. 32.
7. J. Jewkes, D. Sawers and S. Stillerman, *The Sources of Invention*, 2nd Edition (Macmillan, 1969).
8. In his book *British Factory—Japanese Factory* (Allen and Unwin, 1973).
9. *Economics and the Public Purpose* (André Deutsch, 1974).

Chapter 16
1. First published in *The Three Banks Review* (June 1975), under the title of 'Advice from Economists—Forty-Five Years Ago'.
2. The first two of these concerns were created by the Bank of England to assist in the financing of industrial rationalisation schemes, such as that which gave rise to the Lancashire Cotton Corporation. The Agricultural Mortgage Corporation was set up by legislation to provide long-term finance for agriculture, its initial capital being supplied by the Bank of England and the joint-stock banks.
3. 'We have no gift to set a statesman right.'
4. This was, I presume, the episode described by Lord Robbins in his autobiography (Macmillan, 1971), pp. 149–55.

Index

215

220 *British Industry and Economic Policy*

'Virtuous circle', 7–8

Wage: drift, 176; systems, 29–31, 131
Wages, public regulation of, 89
Wages rates and unemployment, 56, 205–6
Walsall, 18, 21, 41
War, First World, effects of, 17, 18, 35–6, 37–9, 90–1, 103–4
War, Second World, effects of, 4, 10, 14, 93–4, 113–14, 115ff., 129
Watt, J., *see* Boulton and Watt
Weavers, handloom, 76
Welfare State, 8, 10, 13

Wesley, John, 143
West Midland industry, 4–6, 16–19, 20ff.; diversification of, 39–43; foreign competition with, 33, 36; size of factories in, 21–2, 36; structural changes in, 32–6
Willenhall, 21
Williams, T., 146, 149, 150
Wolverhampton, 21
Wool industry, 25, 141
Wrought iron industry, 17, 21–2, 36, 138

Young, Allyn, 210n.